Management by Responsibility

G. Michael Durst, Ph.D.

Center For The Art Of Living
Evanston, Illinois 60204

This book is available to businesses and organizations
at a special discount when ordered in large-quantities.
For information, contact The Center for the Art of Living,
Special Sales.

Typesetting and paste-up by
Students Publishing Company, Inc.

The Center for the Art of Living
P.O. Box 788, Evanston, Illinois 60204, 312.864.8710

Library of Congress Catalog Card Number

ISBN: 0-9602552-1-4

Contents

Acknowledgements

This book is dedicated...

...To the thousands of graduates of the Management By Responsibility seminar. Through their support and their willingness to share with others, the MBR philosophy was created.

...To the following individuals whose dedication was instrumental in implementing MBR concepts into their organizations:

Dr. Natalie Babcock and Dona McCord, of the State of New Mexico;

Frank Ruck and Employee Transfer Corporation;

Jim Tarling of Johnson and Johnson;

Martha Lawlor of Deltak;

Bill Moye and Stan Urban of Public Service of New Mexico;

Walt Hadley, Vince Vinci and Jim Baumgardner of Standard Oil of Indiana;

Kass Lepore and Bob Gershon of the Federal Reserve Bank of Chicago;

Betty Wishard of Hibernia Bank;

John Hogan, John Bonner and Myron Weintraub of Chicago Transit Authority;

Mary Johnson, Bonnie Morgan and Spencer Smith of Northwest National Insurance;

Stewart Cox, Joe Bouyer and Sally Wakefield of Illinois Central Rail Road;

Tom Overton of Mountain Bell;

Jim Walker of Systems and Programming Resources;

Bob Silzle, Sal Baglieri and Gary Suley of McDonald's Corporation;

Marcia Trelease of International Harvester;

Carl Myers of the City of Farmington, New Mexico;

Marcia Manter of American Hospital Supply;

Jim Fackleman, Erv Baumgart and Pat Hairston of Amity Leather;

Fred Schulman of Baxter Labs;

Ken Paprock of Carle Foundation Hospital;

John Lyons of United Airlines;

Carol House, Karen Schultz and Jan Deiker of Time, Inc.;

Ed Lucasek of Northern Trust Co.;

Ann Harris of Blue Cross/Blue Shield Milwaukee;

Judy Polovich of Exchange National Bank;

Jim Smith of Double Tree Inns;

Gary Coppock of Mead World;

Richard Ermilio of Record Center;

Ron Dilger and John Krome of Osco Drug Co.;

Erin Mathews and Diane Yost of Nieman Marcus; Bill Robinson, John Pullen and Bill Treloar of National College of Education;

Steve Falstad, John Moss and John von Thurn-Taxis of Blue Cross/Blue Shield Chicago;

Cyndy Kaye of Boise Cascade;

Eleanor Miley and Ron Episcopo of Chemical Bank;

Wayne Brown and Burt Morse of Abbott Labs;

Kathleen Cook of Edison Electric Institute;

Hans Roderich, Valerie Hagenback, Kerry Weis and Bob Scherer of Chicago Title and Trust;

Linda Silverstrini, Jerry Burg, Jane Harman and Sue Fisk of Northwestern Mutual Life Insurance;

Jim Elsener and Diane Baxter of Smith, Bucklin & Trade Associate Management;

Barbara Mapplebeck of Trans America Information Services;

Martha Beach of American National Bank.

...Our personal thanks to:
Ron Medved for his marketing and management expertise;

To our distributors:
Ted Kemper of The Canadian Training and Development Group;
Deltak, Inc.;
Daniel V. Swartz of Halebrooke Corp;

...To the individuals who directly worked on this book: Sheena John, Bernie Josefsberg, and Valerie Hagenback. Their patience and perseverance is greatly appreciated.

...To Ken Hanson, Mary Lambert, Dalton McGuire, Pat Moniak, John Partacz, Ginger Rhamey, Lee Smith, Ingrid Wallace, Michael Lee and Chris Isley, for their assistance with the MBR Video production.

...To my sons, Greg, John and David, and to my parents and family for their understanding and support.

...To F. Stephen Barick, Director of Training Systems, Inc., whose inspiration, dedication, encouragement and honesty, has helped to make MBR a reality.

...To those who have waited so patiently for this work, as I formulated and restructured the theoretical basis to make understandable the process of growth in a managerial context.

...and to **you**, the reader, for it was for you this book was written. May you serve others better as a result of reading these words.

INTRODUCTION

Management By Responsibility starts with you.

Indeed, it begins and ends with you. Most management books and seminars teach business theory and the latest management techniques. Their intent is to increase your managerial knowledge assuming that such knowledge will make you a better manager.

Management By Responsibility is different. The purpose of MBR is not to increase your knowledge **about** management. In fact, its purpose is not to increase your knowledge at all. The true purpose of MBR is to expand your wisdom. Once you become aware of what makes life more satisfying and productive, that very wisdom will create a better management style. The more successful you are as a person, the more successful you will become as a manager because your management style directly reflects you.

Theories are excellent and techniques may help your efficiency, yet they may not necessarily make you a better manager.

You make **you** a better manager!

Thousands of managers know the latest buzz words, abbreviations, and theories, and yet continue to be poor managers. However, many individuals who have never taken a management course are exceptional managers. This is not because successful managers are born that way. Rather, our training emphasis has been misplaced. Instead of teaching unrelated concepts and ideas, management training programs should teach participants how to be more successful as individuals, and consequently, how that experience applies to a work environment.

This is what MBR is all about: how life works, and how your job is part of that process.

If you are looking for theory, studies, research, and techniques in this book, you will not find them. If you think this is going to be "soft-minded," "touchy-feely," "groupy" philosophy with no application to the Real

World, you will be mistaken. MBR is based on reality. It begins with who you are as a person and how you became that way.

You are the "missing link" as to whether or not you are successful as a manager. That is why the main focus of this book is on you.

You may discover by reading this book a related benefit involving your relationships with others. Some relationships are productive, some are non-productive, and some are down-right destructive. You will learn how to have productive relationships—those that produce results. Some of these results are tangible, such as sales volume; results such as an increase in staff morale are intangible and subjective.

Sometimes managers are so myopic they forget the major purpose for being in a management position is to produce results. These results must be in line with major corporate objectives.

To insure that one's individual goals are in sync with corporate goals, MBR relates individual and interpersonal experiences to the organizational environment. What you will discover, of course, is that it all comes back to you. The means to produce satisfaction and success in your personal life are exactly those used in your professional life.

The Purpose of this Book

The purpose of this book is to assist you in becoming aware of your ability to experience success and satisfaction in your life and on your job.

From this perspective its purpose is ongoing: to point you in the right direction. The purpose is not finished after you have read this book. The purpose actually begins once you have completed reading these words.

The very nature of a purpose is that it is never-ending. There will always be more success and more satisfaction for you to experience. You may have several goals along the way, and yet, the achievement of goals does not complete your purpose. The achievement of goals only directs you toward your purpose.

If your purpose is job satisfaction, you will have countless goals along the way. Each goal will provide satisfaction, and yet there will always be more satisfaction available.

The MBR process **starts** on the day you begin to implement the philosophy presented here. It starts with your life. The book simply provides "station identification." The real program starts with you.

What you gain from this material is your choice. Words have no meaning until one applies them to experience. Therefore, the process of reading this should be an active one. You will need to apply the material to your own life experience.

The kind of information contained within these pages is not complex or abstract. When you incorporate the information from your own perspective, it will seem much easier, and far more simple. When you share this information with others, you will receive even greater benefit.

The information presented is essentially philosophic because MBR applies to everyone in all professions and jobs. Even if you are not in a management position, you can profit greatly by learning to manage yourself.

It is important not to simply "understand" these words. To gain maximum value it is important to **experience** what the words mean. For instance, if you have never tasted mustard, I could help you "understand" what mustard tastes like, and yet the instant you taste, (that is, experience) mustard, you will know exactly how mustard tastes and you will never forget it. Once you start taking total responsibility for your life and assisting others to do the same, you will be experiencing what MBR is all about—to understand the process will not make it happen. (Wisdom is inherent within you. However, once you have read and incorporated what follows, you will know that you know, and that's when change occurs.)

The Theme of this Book

The major theme of this book is that you are 100% responsible for your own experience. Taking responsibility assists you in becoming a better person and manager so that you can "get on with" producing results and satisfaction.

If you are like most people, you play from a position of "no responsibility" if you do not like what is happening. Management By Responsibility assumes that you are 100% responsible for everything that you experience, whether you like it or not.

Once you implement the MBR process you will realize the countless opportunities that the work place presents to help in the actualization process. It is one of the most exciting, absorbing, and rewarding experiences you can have. Your experience of life may never be the same . . .

And that's the challenge and the excitement of the MBR system!

Responsibility is a unique concept.
It can only reside and inhere in a single individual. You may share it with others, but your portion is not diminished. You may delegate it, but it is still with you. You may disclaim it, but you cannot divest yourself of it.

—Admiral Hyman Rickover

For mankind to actualize his true potential, we need the kind of people

"who don't need to staticize the world, who don't need to freeze it and to make it stable . . . who are able confidently to face tomorrow, not knowing what's going to come, with confidence enough . . . to improvise in that situation which has never existed before.

This means a new type of human being . . . the process person, the creative person, the improvising person, the self-trusting, courageous person, the autonomous person. The society which can turn out such people will survive; the societies that cannot turn out such people will die."[1]

—Abraham Maslow

Chapter One

MANAGEMENT'S ROLE IN HUMAN DEVELOPMENT

The emerging manager in the last quarter of the twentieth century is unable to rely upon a strong, socially sanctioned work ethic. The "new" manager can no longer "force" employees to be productive or to be loyal to the organization. Union resentment, declining productivity, and worker apathy are symptomatic of a system that has become anachronistic and whose ills require appropriately new approaches.

Early management theory, reflective of the mindset of the Industrial Revolution, viewed workers as machines. To the extent that the resulting techniques are still current, this mechanistic view of human beings has created a "no-win" situation for all corporate members. Management attempts to maximize employee output while paying them as little as possible. Correspondingly, employees expect as much pay as possible, though expending the least amount of energy. Such a situation creates inherent resentment on both sides—a resentment traceable to a fundamental misconception about people and their labor:

People are not machines and cannot be treated as such.

To be truly successful in today's world, the manager must fulfill a contemporary role—that of a human development specialist. As social scientists have demonstrated, people are productive, creative, and internally motivated to the extent that they have matured. Thus, dedicated employees do not have to be "forced" to do a good job; they "want" to do a good job. To assist employees to grow into responsible, mature beings is the ultimate, on-going purpose of management. And yet, many ask, "Why management?" Aren't these the functions performed by educational institutions? Isn't the creation of an enlightened citizenry a government task? Though the obvious answers are in the affirmative, management will still need to be the **primary** motivator in the process.

The facts are simple. Educational institutions, for the most part, stress subject matter at the expense of personal growth. Thus, as John W. Gardner writes in No Easy Victories, "Much of education today is monumentally ineffective. All too often we are giving people cut flowers when we should be teaching them to grow their own plants."[2] By emphasizing retention of meaningless facts, and de-emphasizing creativity and growth, educational institutions present the business community with a work force that not only resents the learning process, but distrusts authority on all levels. Despite Kierkegaard's admonishment that, "What is really important in education is not that the person learns this and that, but that the mind is matured, that energy is aroused,"[3] discouragingly little seems to be changing in education to reverse the emphasis upon retention of facts and conformity. Such an emphasis can be so detrimental to a free society whose well-being depends upon fostering responsible growth and creativity.

What ends up being an unfortunate misdirection for education, becomes an indictment of government. Like most large bureaucratic institutions, only more so, the U.S. government promotes a non-thinking conformist mentality by being unconcerned with actualizing the growth potential of its citizens. Though this country was initially conceived by and for an enlightened, informed, and independent group of individuals, our governmental system not only seeks to stifle disagreements, but seeks to shortcut even the process of questioning itself. The fact remains that it is easier for a government to control a nation of people who do what it tells them to do, who think as it wants them to think, and who quietly pay their taxes without so much as a glimmer of the staunch independence and courage that created the foundation for America in the first place.

Responsible people resist unthinking conformity. As Abraham Maslow discovered in his research, "Perceptively healthy human beings do not like to be controlled. They prefer to feel free, and to be free."[4] As might be expected, a responsible, thinking citizenry will resent a government that sets up extensive controls and limits personal choice.

Thus, the role of management in human development becomes one of necessity and opportunity. Since the educational system is not emphasizing human development, and since a controlling government will not become involved for fear of losing that control, management **must** become involved. Who else can?

Yet, more than ever, American business needs to realize the advantages of becoming involved with the development of people. As the Management by Responsibility process is implemented, more and more managers realize that responsible people make better employees. The most direct benefit of the growth process accrues to the institution of business, and, by extension, to the entire free enterprise system.

This does not mean that corporations need to become social institutions, riddled with "self-help" programs. The very nature of work, in and of itself, can and should assist people in transforming the quality of their lives. The Management by Responsibility process promotes independence, creativity, emotional stability, organization, and discipline, as well as physical and spiritual well-being. The lack of such qualities is displayed in ineffective, apathetic, self-destructive behavior on the job. Thus, MBR is based on a "win-win" situation: the more the employees grow, the more the organization itself, benefits.

The Process of Human Development

To effectively transform the work place into a context for human growth and development, managers need to understand the levels of human growth. This understanding can only stem from self-awareness and the willingness on the part of managers to grow and change themselves. In his article, "The Power to See Ourselves," Paul Brouwer describes such a process as "manager" development as opposed to "management" development. According to Brouwer,

> ...the growing manager changes because he wants to and because he has to in response to new insights and understandings that he gains on the job.
>
> The point is clear that the growing person examines himself; and, as he does so, he emerges with new depths of motivation, a sharper sense of direction, and a more vital awareness of how he wants to live on the job...And such growth...is at the heart of a real manager development effort.
>
> In short, the more realistic one's view of himself, the more guaranteed is personal effectiveness.[5]

Philosophers, religious leaders and social scientists have all described human behavior, providing people with a rich source of insight into their own nature. From Aristotle, Plato, Freud, Allport, Sullivan, Rogers, and Berne, descriptions of human behavior have been plentiful. Yet in all of the writings on human behavior, each individual describes and identifies only a certain spectrum of the whole. As in the old adage of the three blind men describing an elephant, Management by Responsibility attempts to describe the totality of human growth from immaturity to maturity, from rigidity to adaptability, from sickness to wellness. Only through the total "Gestalt" of human experience can we see ourselves and others clearly, with a sense of understanding and compassion.

As human beings we need to see things in perspective, in a context. As Nathaniel Branden writes, "As a being who possesses the power of self-consciousness—the power of contemplating his own life and activity—man experiences a profound need for a conceptual frame of reference from which to view himself..."[6] To provide such a context, we may differentiate the elements of growth among various levels of maturity. Researchers such as Loevinger and Wessler, Gladstone, Maslow, Sullivan and Allport have all provided models for understanding stages of growth.[7] For the purpose of this book, the following levels have been established.

Levels of Growth

Each of five different levels of growth will be described in great detail in the following chapters. These levels are not necessarily sequential, nor are they specifically age-related. Since the behavior of any adult is neither wholly consistent nor uniform, aspects of these levels may be evident at any given moment. No single level, by itself, fully describes the totality of our being.

Perhaps the easiest analogy to describe these levels is that of a ladder. As one matures one spends more and more time on the upper rungs of the ladder. That does not mean, as suggested above, that one cannot, at any given moment, revert to the lower levels.

Even though individuals operating at the higher levels experience more success and satisfaction in their lives, it is not more "right" to be at the top levels than the lower levels. To use an analogy, it is not "better" to be a senior in high school than to be a fifth grader. One has to go through the fifth grade to become a senior. However, seniors sometimes act like fifth graders and vice-versa. In addition, both levels provide their own unique problems. Since no level of maturity is problem-free or without opportunity for further growth, no phase is right or wrong, good or bad. One needs to accept one's level of maturity to realize that any level may be necessary to experience as part of our development. At the lower levels, abounding in negative feelings and situations, one must become aware that it may be **exactly** those situations and feelings that will provide the most growth potential for increased maturity. With acceptance of the situation as it is, as "perfect," growth takes place exactly as it should.

The Five Levels

Figure One shows the ladder of growth. The five "rungs" on the ladder each represent a level of growth: (1) The Unconscious Level, (2) The Self-Protective Level, (3) The Conformist Level, (4) The Achievement Level, and (5) The Responsible Level. Of course, the ladder represents a continuum, rather than distinctly different stages in development. The following is a brief description of each level.

The Ladder of Growth

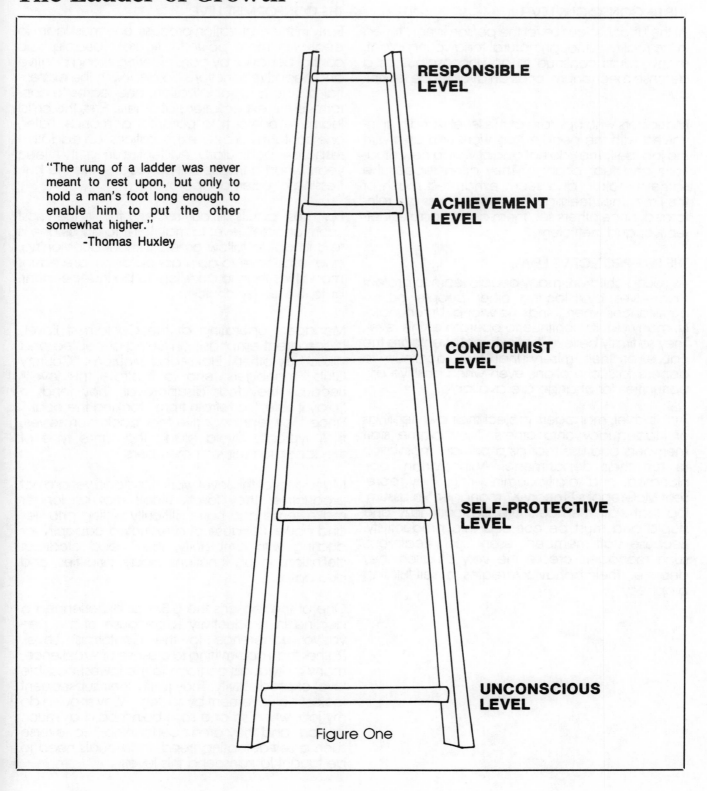

"The rung of a ladder was never meant to rest upon, but only to hold a man's foot long enough to enable him to put the other somewhat higher."

-Thomas Huxley

RESPONSIBLE LEVEL

ACHIEVEMENT LEVEL

CONFORMIST LEVEL

SELF-PROTECTIVE LEVEL

UNCONSCIOUS LEVEL

Figure One

THE UNCONSCIOUS LEVEL

At the Unconscious Level the person is not "tuned in" to reality. Although natural for a young infant, many adults continue to go unconscious as a defense mechanism, or as an avoidance technique.

Managers who operate at this level remain uninvolved with the people they work with and with the job itself. They do not adapt well to new situations and fear change. They often repeat the same mistakes, and seem exhausted much of the time. Their feelings of powerlessness are reinforced, since others see them as incapable, ineffective, and inefficient.

THE SELF-PROTECTIVE LEVEL

As young children, many people learn to protect themselves by blaming other people or circumstances when things go wrong. Unfortunately, many adults continue to operate at this level. They so firmly believe that external events are the cause of their misery that they continue to adhere to such notions even when positive opportunities for change are available.

At this level, managers project their own feelings of inadequacy onto others. They blame staff members and use fear as a primary motivation to run their departments. Authoritarian, opinionated, and totally domineering, they represent McGregor's "Theory X" manager,[8] in assuming that staff members are basically lazy and stupid and must be coerced into productivity. Because staff members resent such treatment, such managers create the very situation they deplore. Their behavior creates a self-fulfilling prophecy.

THE CONFORMIST LEVEL

Early in the maturation process, one must learn to deal with more powerful figures—people who control behavior by administering strong positive and negative sanctions. To deal with the existential problem of socialization, one learns to conform to the expectations of others. First, the child learns to conform to parental demands. Later, one conforms to peer expectations, an adaptive response particularly evident during the teen years when a fragile self-concept seeks the buttressing of external approval.

For most adults in our society, this is the most "comfortable" level to maintain. To do as one is told to do, to follow orders without questioning, and to behave to gain acceptance, are easier modalities than to question, to be independent, or to live life by choice.

Managers operating at the Conformist Level, place great emphasis on being accepted and "liked" by others. Blake and Mouton's "Country Club" managers tend to illustrate this level.[9] Because they fear disapproval, they tend to "play it safe," to refrain from "rocking the boat." Since they fear negative feedback themselves, they typically avoid giving the same type of feedback to their staff members.

Managers at this level work hard and yet are not productive. They follow rituals that no longer make sense and have difficulty setting priorities and goals. Because of a restricted capacity for dealing with ambiguity, they need clear-cut definitions in job functions, goals, priorities, and due dates.

One of the reasons the U.S. has experienced a decline in productivity is because of the pervasive adherence to the Conformist Level. Rather than committing to a sense of excellence, many individuals conform to the lowest possible level of productivity. They justify their subsequent lack of achievement by saying, "Why should I do my job, when so and so is being paid as much as I am and they aren't performing." To reverse such a self-defeating trend, individuals need to be taught to transcend this level.

THE ACHIEVEMENT LEVEL

In addition to following external dictates to gain acceptance, one may strive to achieve in order to get approval. At the Achievement Level, individuals look to achievements in order to establish a sense of self-worth.

Unlike the Conformist Level, managers at the Achievement Level are productive, goal-directed, and typically meet deadlines. They question rituals and have a sense of independence.

The major problem at the Achievement Level is that managers seem hassled and under a great deal of pressure. Because everything seems to be an "emergency," these managers often "manage by crisis." Ironically, since Achievement Level managers often do not take the time to plan ahead or to anticipate possible problems, they end up creating the very crisis situations they are attempting to control and to quell.

Physical problems resulting from continued crisis situations often manifest themselves in a great deal of stress, "executive burn-out," and, in many cases, coronary disease.

THE RESPONSIBLE LEVEL

The individual operating at the Responsible Level has been described by Abraham Maslow as a "Self-Actualized Person," by Carl Rogers as "The Fully Functioning Person," by Carl Jung as an "Individuated Person," by Erich Fromm as the "Autonomous Person," and by Eric Berne, as a "Winner." People at this level of functioning evidence a high level of adaptability and creativity. The ultimate goal in any organization is to have as many people operating at this level as possible.

Managers are effective at this level without the undue stress evident at the Achievement Level. They are able to make decisions and lead effectively. They provide effective feedback to staff members, by acknowledging positive performance and providing constructive feedback for negative performance.

Rather than blaming others or circumstances when they experience failure, they assume responsibility and, therefore, are much more resilient. Their activities are directed and they exhibit far more energy than any other level in the accomplishment of their activities.

Since managers at the Responsible Level can communicate very well, they tend to have very positive relationships with staff members as well as with their own supervisors. This ability also manifests itself in their personal lives where they maintain a very healthy balance with work, love, and play. In short, managers at this level have a strong sense of who they are, what they need to do, and why they are doing it.

The Dimensions of Life

Each of the previously discussed five levels of growth can be observed across the seven dimensions of one's life: (1) Emotional Reaction, (2) Intellectual Functioning, (3) Activity Involvement, (4) Self-Discipline, (5) Relationships, (6) Physical State, and (7) the Spiritual Dimension.[10]

Each of these seven dimensions are affected by the five levels of growth. Although each is relatively independent, interaction among the various dimensions is quite common. Changes, both positive and negative, in one dimension will affect changes in another dimension. For example, when one is ill, (low physical state), one is often more irritable, (low emotional reaction) and unable to think effectively, (low intellectual functioning). Conversely, if one starts jogging and eating properly (high physical state), it may affect one's ability to think more clearly (high intellectual functioning), as well as produce more energy to get more activities accomplished (high activity involvement).

One can operate at any one level in any dimension of one's life. However, just because one's emotional reaction is at the Conformist Level most of the time, does not mean that the person is a "Conformist." However, if one consistently operates at the Conformist Level in almost all dimensions of life, then that individual can be said to be typically a Conformist.

Figure Two is a grid system that will be used in the next five chapters to describe each level of growth for each of the seven dimensions. Refer to it in order to become familiar with how the five levels affect each of life's seven dimensions.

The following is a description of each of the dimensions.

The Grid

	Emotional Response	Intellectual Functioning	Activity Involvement	Self-Discipline	Relationships	Physical State	Spiritual Dimension
RESPONSIBLE							
ACHIEVEMENT							
CONFORMIST							
SELF-PROTECTIVE							
UNCONSCIOUS							

Figure Two

DIMENSION ONE: EMOTIONAL REACTION

Emotional Reaction refers to **how** one reacts to situations, as well as **how long** the reaction continues. For example, at the lower levels one may become angry and stay angry for hours, or even days after the event has occurred. So the reaction refers to the type of emotional response, to the extent of the response, and to the duration of the particular response.

At the higher levels, individuals are emotionally stable, and, if negative emotions are experienced they are appropriate responses to legitimate causes and are typically of short duration. At lower levels, emotions fluctuate dramatically, are long-lasting, and are often without apparent cause or reason.

DIMENSION TWO: INTELLECTUAL FUNCTIONING

Intellectual Functioning refers to one's ability to problem-solve, to be intellectually creative, to be logical, as well as to one's cognitive preoccupations, i.e., the type of thoughts that typically occupy one's mind.

At the higher levels, managers are able to problem-solve creatively, and to reason to logical conclusions. Additionally, they are able to control and direct their thoughts to produce positive results.

At lower levels, managers appear intellectually confused. Because they are unable to input, process, and output information effectively, they cannot make valid decisions, or they avoid making any decisions. Intellectually, individuals at the lower levels are characterized by extreme cognitive rigidity.

DIMENSION THREE: ACTIVITY INVOLVEMENT

Activity Involvement refers to the activities with which one becomes involved. These include both personal and professional activities.

At higher levels, individuals are interested in a wide variety of activities and perform well in them. They are not afraid of failure, since they are resilient and learn from mistakes. Furthermore, they are competent in a wide range of activities.

At lower levels, people are not involved in their activities, and feel little sense of accomplishment or competence. Their activities are often ritualistic and compulsive. Individuals at lower levels can operate at two extremes: either they are hyperactive in their activities without a sense of direction, thereby producing limited results, or they are so lethargic and rigid that nothing happens.

DIMENSION FOUR: SELF-DISCIPLINE

Self-Discipline refers to more than mere discipline—it refers to one's ability to effectively plan and to implement ideas. This dimension is crucial for success, both in one's personal and professional life.

At the higher levels, managers are "self-starters" and can complete tasks without feeling harried or frustrated. They are able to plan strategically and then act with confidence. They are self-motivated and so do not need prodding or encouragement from others.

At the lower levels, people are motivated externally. They either need constant encouragement or threats to continue performing. Since they do not plan how to implement their ideas, they feel frustrated.

DIMENSION FIVE: RELATIONSHIPS

Relationships refer to one's ability to respond effectively with others, as well as to the stability of the relationship itself.

At the higher levels, managers have the ability to maintain close, open relationships with others. Since they do not manipulate others and are not dependent upon others for feelings of self-worth, they have long-term, stable relationships.

At the lower levels, relationships are characterized by instability and negative projections onto others. Thus, "drama," in which the roles of persecutor, rescuer, and victim are dominant, becomes the typical modus operandi in their relationships. In addition, destructive patterns evident in psychological game playing are common, along with harboring grudges for retaliatory use. Lower level relationships tend to be ephemeral and volatile, as opposed to the stable, close relationships seen at the higher levels.

DIMENSION SIX: PHYSICAL STATE

Physical State refers to one's physical sense of well-being, as well as to certain physical symptoms affecting one's health.

At the higher levels, individuals typically feel well, take responsibility for their health, have a high energy level, and are active physically.

At lower levels, individuals experience fluctuations in weight and sleeping patterns, skin problems, headaches, and gastro-intestinal problems. They are often prone to alcohol and/or drug abuse. Such chronic conditions often dramatically affect other dimensions of life.

DIMENSION SEVEN: SPIRITUAL DIMENSION

Spiritual Dimension refers to one's concern for ethical and moral factors, and to sources beyond that of mankind, commonly called God, the Almighty, the Supreme Being.

At the higher levels of consciousness, individuals often report intense spiritual experiences. Called "peak experiences" by Abraham Maslow, these experiences are powerful, mind-expanding, and "cosmic." Individuals operating at the Responsible Level have a high sense of moral and ethical standards, refusing to become involved in activities that are unethical.

At the lower levels, individuals personalize spiritual and religious factors. The God figure is seen as an extension of the parental role, with the individual often playing the role of victim. At these levels, one avoids unethical behavior for fear of getting caught or for fear of disapproval from others. Such a modality qualitatively differs from positive moral behavior.

Summary

As might be evident, Management by Responsibility is an holistic approach to management. Factors that affect one's personal life can and will affect one's professional life and vice-versa. For example, if managers are having domestic problems, they may be adversely affected on the job because they are going unconscious, are not able to concentrate on the task at hand, or may be suffering from physical tension. Likewise, if job situations are very dissatisfying, managers may be irritable with their family members and may feel generally frustrated and anxious at home.

Thus, the MBR process of growth **should** affect one personally as well as professionally. Growth in one area will have positive effects in others as well. As human development specialists, managers cannot ignore factors that occur outside the job, but rather should utilize them in the growth process.

The following chapters will focus extensively on each level of maturity. Though many managers will be operating at the higher levels, the lower levels will be discussed in detail as well, so that managers can recognize lower level functioning in themselves and others, and thus ground their perceptions in a realistic and mature perspective. As Carl Jung stated in <u>Psychological Reflections</u>:

> Unfortunately, we are inclined to talk of man as it would be desirable for him to be rather than as he really is. . . True education can only proceed from naked reality, not from any ideal illusion about man, however attractive.[11]

Thus, Management by Responsibility assists in the journey of understanding ourselves and others. Only in this way can we assist others in their development as effective and happy employees. The true purpose of MBR is to assist people in becoming more responsible in all dimensions of their lives—for their own success and satisfaction and for the success of the organization. To. meet the demands and challenges that lie ahead, the manager of today must remain true to this purpose.

"If a man understands he is asleep and if he wishes to awaken, then everything that helps him to awaken will be good and everything that hinders him, everything that prolongs his sleep, will be evil.

You will then see that you can think, feel, act, speak, work without being conscious of it. And if you learn to see in yourselves the moments of consciousness and the long periods of mechanicalness, you will as infallibly see in other people when they are conscious of what they are doing and when they are not."[1]

—Georges Gurdjieff

"The condition of alienation, of being asleep, of being unconsciousness, of being out of one's mind, is the condition of normal man."[2]

—R.D. Laing

Chapter Two

THE UNCONSCIOUS MANAGER

The first step in becoming a responsible, mature manager is to become more conscious. Consciousness is the ability to BE HERE NOW. By its very nature it assumes total responsibility and total choice. As Nathaniel Branden pointed out:

> Consciousness is man's tool for perceiving and identifying the fact of reality. It is an organ of integration. To focus is to set the integration process in purposeful motion—by setting the appropriate goal: awareness. Non-focus is non-integration. Evasion is willful disintegration, the act of subverting the proper function of consciousness, of setting the cognitive function in reverse and reducing the contents of one's mind to disconnected, unintegrated fragments that are forbidden to confront one another.
>
> Man's life and well-being depend upon his maintaining a proper cognitive contact with reality—this requires a full mental focus, maintained as a way of life. The more consistently and conscientiously a man maintains a policy of being in full mental focus, of thinking and judging facts of reality that confront him, of knowing what he is doing and why, the easier and more "natural" the process becomes. The steadily increasing knowledge he requires as a result of his policy, the growing sense of control over his existence, the growing self-confidence—the conviction of living in a universe that is open to him—all serve to put every emotional incentive on the side of his continuing to think . . . It is too clear to him that reality is not and never can be his enemy—that he has nothing to gain for self-inflicted blindness, and everything to lose.[3]

One of the major problems at the Unconscious Level is its pervasiveness: many people seem to be unconscious much of the time. Philosophers, religious leaders, playwrights, and authors have noted that most people are "sleepwalking" through life:

Wakefulness is the way of life.
The fool sleeps
As if he were already dead,
But the master is awake
As he lives forever.
He watches.
He is clear.
How happy he is!
For he sees that wakefulness is life.
How happy he is
Following the path of the awakened.[4]

　　　　　　　　　—Buddha

Everyone is familiar with the phenomenon of feeling more or less alive on different days...Compared with what we ought to be, we are only half-wake.[5]

　　　　　　　　　—William James

People would rather sleep their way through life than stay awake for it.[6]

　　　　　　　　　—Edward Albee

How to become conscious?...It means that you will suffer still more—that's the first thing to realize. But you won't be dead, you won't be indifferent...you will want to understand everything, even the disagreeable things. You will want to accept more and more—even what seems hostile, evil, threatening.[7]

　　　　　　　　　—Henry Miller

People "died" all the time in their lives. Parts of them died when they made the wrong kinds of decisions—decisions against life. Sometimes they died bit by bit until finally they were just living corpses walking around. If you were perceptive, you could see it in their eyes; the fire had gone out ..But you always knew when you made a decision against life. When you denied life you were warned. The cock crowed, always, somewhere inside of you. The door clicked and you were safe inside—safe and dead.[8]

　　　　　　　　　—Anne Morrow Lindbergh

Unconsciousness seems to be part of the human condition, and yet, transcending the unconscious state defines the essence of "enlightenment," "actualization," and management development.

The Ability to "Be Here Now"

THE ABILITY TO "BE HERE NOW"

At the lower levels of maturity, much of a person's time is spent feeling resentful or guilty about the past, or by worrying about the future. Not only can people go unconscious by going to a different place, they can also go to a different time zone.

To be an effective manager, one needs to "BE HERE NOW." Now has been called the eternal instant. Now is all that is ever experienced. Negating the experience of "Now" can greatly lower productivity, as people spend time agonizing over the past, complaining about what is happening now, and worrying about the future. In some work environments, one wonders if anyone is doing anything else!

Living in the past or worrying about the future is not only non-productive, it robs people of satisfaction. For centuries, successful individuals have realized the importance of "Being Here Now" in order to live to the fullest:

> If we haven't learned to live now, we'll always be living on the hope that perhaps the future will be somehow better. Now is the future we were thinking about last year. And if you don't make it into tomorrow—will you have enjoyed, and been aware of today?[9]
>
> —Earl Nightingale

> Live all you can; it's a mistake not to. It doesn't so much matter what you do in particular so long as you've had your life. If you haven't had that what have you had? What one loses, one loses, make no mistake about that. The right time is any time that one is still so lucky as to have. LIVE.[10]
>
> —Henry James

> It may be that a good working guide to conduct might be framed on this ideal — living to the fullest here and now . . .[11]
>
> —Stephen MacKenna

Unfortunately, many people surrender self-fulfillment, because they live in the past. Yet, the past does not exist—not NOW. It cannot exist, because it is past. The past **did** exist, and is stored as memory. The mind makes tape recordings of what one experiences and then conveniently stores the tapes. The past does not exist in any other form but the tape recordings of "Now" moments that occurred in the past. Therein lies the problem. One can only record from his or her individual perspective. Each person records selectively. People hear what they want to hear; they see what they want to see. The mind can block certain tapes; it can also censor them partially or totally.

Just as the past does not exist, neither does the future. The future will not exist until it becomes a moment of NOW. The future, like the past, only exists in the mind. The future is the mind's anticipation.

At the lower levels of maturity, one ineffectively lives in a time that does not actually exist. Many managers have trouble staying in the here and now. For them, it is much easier to blame past circumstances for their plight, or to project themselves into a future that does not exist. For example, there are still people living in the Depression. It never ended for them. They continue to live and respond as though it still existed or they have blamed it for so long that it has become an intimate defense against the reality of their situation. Since they avoid responsibility by blaming, and since blaming causes people to go even more unconscious, a self-fulfilling cycle is created.

Of course, there are times when certain forms of unconsciousness can be very productive. A creative job may demand the ability to let the mind free-associate. At other times being unconscious may be an appropriate response in a situation. The problem is that most people are unconscious of their own unconsciousness. Some workers would be great candidates for the "Unc-Unc" award:

We would like to acknowledge Sam Brown for not missing a single day of

work in fifteen years . . . and for not being there mentally for any of them!

Unconsciousness is not an unnatural process. It is necessary for survival. Real problems occur however, when the mechanism goes "out of control," and takes over. At the Responsible Level, managers have learned to control their minds, by only going unconscious when it is appropriate to do so.

Discomfort often causes unconsciousness. When people dislike what is going on in their lives, they can always escape by going unconscious. If staff members dislike their jobs, they will go unconscious much of the time. If managers dislike what someone is telling them, they will go unconscious. This process is particularly noticeable during interviews and performance appraisals.

The constant escape from reality creates many distinct problems. The following are just a few.

The Split

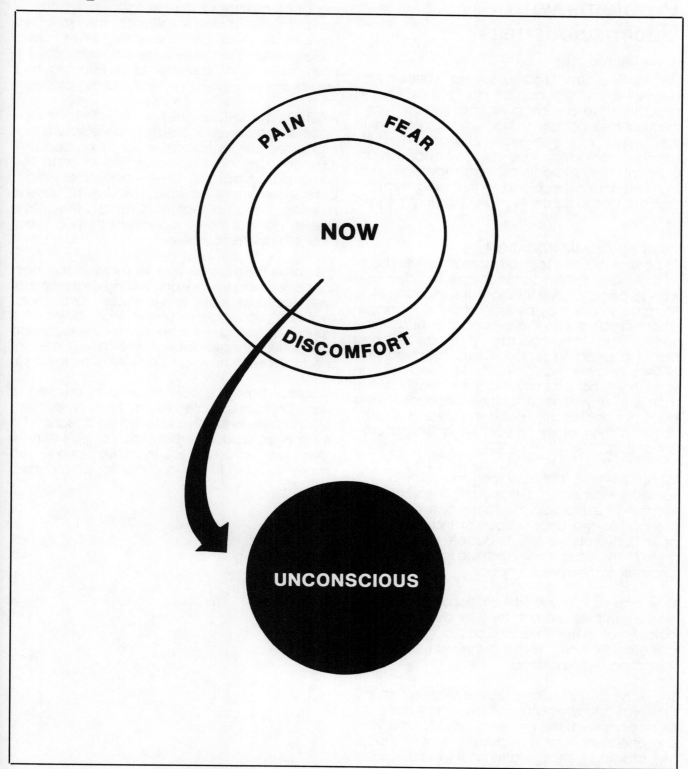

Problems with Unconsciousness

PHYSICAL DANGER
Unconsciousness creates several distinct problems. First of all, it can be dangerous. People typically drive automobiles unconsciously as if they put their bodies on "automatic pilot" while their minds are elsewhere. Similarly, most industrial accidents take place because individuals are asked to perform repetitious acts that become boring, and so the mind "leaves" and the body becomes injured during the process.

IMPAIRED COMMUNICATION
To communicate successfully, both parties have to "be there" for the communication. Often, one talks to people while thinking of something else. A staff member may be talking to the manager about problems on the second shift and at the same time, the manager may be thinking about a pending report. One's mind can be anywhere other than "there" with the other person. The mind can split from the reality of the moment any time it wants. Unconciousness does not necessarily mean the person is comatose; it may simply mean he or she is daydreaming.

When there is difficulty communicating with someone—whether a boss, a co-worker or a vendor—it is typically because one or both of the parties are unconscious at that time. How often do we converse with people who are "not there?" Yet, people will continue to talk "at" one another, sometimes for hours.

One can usually tell when people are "there" and when they are not. They tend to get a very distant look in their eyes. It is as though they took a mental "break," making the conversation a frustrating waste of time.

The ways to go unconscious at work are many. One way is to attend a staff meeting! If there are eight people at the meeting, usually only three are checked in at any given moment! Doodling, tapping pencils, staring out windows, thinking of other things and going to sleep are all ways to avoid the reality of the situation. Likewise, one can go unconscious while talking on the telephone. Since there is no eye contact, both parties can "pretend" to be listening, and yet no communication is really taking place.

WASTED TIME AND ENERGY
Another problem with being unconscious is that producing results becomes very time consuming. Consider how long it takes to read the same paragraph 14 times—as typically happens when one is not interested in what one is reading. Reading technical reports that have little to do with one's job may cause a great deal of unconsciousness.

The same things holds true for many of the functions one performs at work. Writing a memo that one does not want to write can take hours. Avoiding work takes longer than doing the work. Compiling information for reports can take hours longer than necessary if the individual resents having to take the time to do so.

Because being unconscious can create so many problems related to productivity, efficiency, and effectiveness, the following descriptions of the Unconscious Level in each of life's dimensions are offered to increase one's self awareness and to aid in understanding others.

Dimensions of the Unconscious Level

Emotional Response

EMOTIONS UNRELATED TO REALITY
Since the fantasies created by Unconscious people become their "reality," their emotional response is typically detached from external reality. Thus, such individuals often delude themselves. They may distort reality to relieve the stress that they experience, or they may hallucinate, i.e., hear or see things unheard or unseen by anyone else—to cope with reality. To handle the high level of stress, people at this level look to "magical" or "miracle" solutions to their problems, and then become depressed when they fail.

EXTREME EMOTIONAL SHIFTS
Individuals at the Unconscious Level often experience extreme emotional shifts. From feelings of euphoria and hyperactivity to depression and inactivity these shifts seem to have no real basis in reality. Such shifts may prompt delusionary behavior, in some cases involving "paranoia"—feelings of persecution or victimization. These feelings can eventually lead to severe depression or acute anxiety. Yet, delusions can also lead to a sense of euphoria. In this regard, people can feel elated because they convince themselves that their "ship will come in," that they will win the sweepstakes, or that some high official will recognize their value. In other words, they count on magical intervention to remake their lives.

These emotional shifts not only interfere with an individual's ability to work; in extreme cases they could lead to suicide or even homicide.

GREAT STRESS AND ANXIETY EVIDENT
Nothing seems to relieve the tension, anxiety, and high level of stress experienced at the Unconscious Level, except perhaps heavy doses of medication or drugs. Yet, because people at this level use medication or drugs to evade reality, underlying problems remain unresolved. The very act of avoiding an unpleasant situation by going unconscious initiates a chain of self-destructive consequences which ultimately incapacitates. As a result, the Unconscious Level creates a circular response to reality. Because the tensions caused by being unconscious are only relieved by heavy drug usage, and because the drugs prompt even more unconsciousness, a self-defeating cycle is created.

Dimensions of the Unconscious Level

Intellectual Functioning

DIFFICULTY IN INTELLECTUAL PROCESSING

Operating at the Unconscious Level creates difficulty in thinking. To input and process information requires that one's mind "be there" for the process. The more a person evades reality the more difficult thinking becomes. As Nathaniel Branden points out:

> . . .the more a man maintains a policy of focusing as little as possible, and of evading any facts he finds painful to consider—the more he sabotages himself psychologically and the more difficult the task of thinking becomes for him. The inevitable consequences of his policy of non-thinking are feelings of helplessness, of inefficacy, or anxiety—the sense of living in an unknowable and inimical universe.
>
> Since the habitual evader has spent his time, not on improving the efficacy of his mind, but on sabotaging it, he suffers the consequences in terms of mental strain, slowness, and internal chaos, when he does decide to think. If he perseveres, he can redeem and raise the efficacy of this thinking.[12]

The ease of going unconscious leads many individuals to stop using their mental capabilities to face problems. As a consequence, the mind ceases to operate efficiently, like a muscle that has atrophied.

OBSESSIVE THOUGHTS LEADING TO FUNCTIONAL IMPAIRMENT

The Unconscious Level is marked by obsessive thoughts that continue to occur even though they are clearly inappropriate. Focusing on them to the point where he is "unable to get them out of his mind", the individual becomes obsessed with certain ideas and desires. These desires are typically either impossible to achieve or are so unrealistic that to pursue them would be totally non-productive. Although periodic obsessive thoughts occur at higher levels of development, obsessions at the Un-

conscious Level are so intense that these thoughts can block other information or reality itself.

GROSS PERCEPTUAL DISTORTIONS

For Unconscious individuals, reality becomes a fantasy world. Since all of their wishes are fulfilled in fantasy, anything that threatens to rob them of their dream world—such as the intrusions of reality—becomes a threat. As William Gladstone writes,

> To deal with this conflict between their perceptions of the world with their eyes, ears, and other senses and the idealized world of thoughts and fantasies they carry within, they begin to resort to distortions. They no longer see what they don't want to see. They destroy images so that they will agree with their private vision of how the world ought to be . . . [13]

Activity Level

RITUALISTIC AND COMPULSIVE BEHAVIOR
Unconscious individuals repeat the same behavior over and over, even though it is ineffective, inefficient, and inappropriate. Although ritualistic behavior can be a problem at higher levels of maturity as well, at this level it becomes extreme. Rituals become an end in and of themselves: they are not used to reduce tension or to facilitate work.

DIFFICULTY IN CHANGING INEFFECTIVE PATTERNS
Activities and behavioral patterns are extremely difficult to change at the Unconscious Level. Since definite, virtually obsessive routines safeguard a fragile sense of security, the mere threat of change and consequent disruption often provokes a hostile response. Change is viewed as extremely threatening and is avoided at all cost.

EXTREME FEAR OF ATTEMPTING ANYTHING NEW
The Unconscious Level represents the lowest level of flexibility. New activities are constantly avoided. New situations, new people, and new jobs are seen as threats. New opportunities for growth or development are declined without further consideration.

Self-Discipline

LITTLE SELF-CONTROL OR MOTIVATION
At this level of maturity, people show little control over their life circumstances. Like ships adrift in the sea of life, they allow themselves to be carried to wherever fortune wills. Because they feel that life is out of their control, Unconscious individuals exhibit little, if any, self-motivation. Employees at this level seldom initiate any projects or activities on their own volition.

WORK CONTINGENT UPON EXTERNAL CONDITIONS
At the Unconscious Level, external conditions have to be "perfect" if any work is to be accomplished. For effective functioning to occur, everything has to be exactly right: the weather, the other people, the environment—in short, everything. Even the individual's moods have to be correct. Thus, if such individuals do not feel in the mood to work, they simply do not work. Since people at this level are often feeling "down" and depressed, the right conditions for effective work are seldom present.

IMPULSIVE BEHAVIOR INTERFERES WITH PRODUCTIVITY
At this level, people are like young children in their impulsiveness. Basically, they feel: "I want what I want when I want it." Though such impulsiveness is evident at higher levels—and may even lead to spontaneity at the Responsible Level—at the Unconscious Level such impulsiveness is often disruptive and sometimes destructive. People will only work on a project "when they feel like it," which may be seldom. As might be expected, this impulsiveness severely restricts their capacity to relate to other workers as well.

Dimensions of the Unconscious Level

Relationships

UNCONSCIOUSNESS IN THE PRESENCE OF OTHERS
Since one has to be conscious in order to participate with others in a meaningful relationship, people at the Unconscious Level have severe problems relating to other people. Individuals at this level are unconscious around others, and so, they do not listen or respond to others effectively. In extreme cases, they can become "autistic,"—totally unable to respond to external reality.

TOTAL COMMUNICATION BREAKDOWN
Because they do not listen or respond appropriately, Unconscious people are unable to communicate with others. Often they talk only of what is of interest to them or about their fantasies, to the extent that others find them one-dimensional or strange and thus avoid them. As a consequence, growth-promoting interactions are curtailed, further inhibiting their communication skills.

NO CONCERN FOR OTHERS
Since people at the Unconscious Level may be responding to others not as they are, but as they imagine them to be, they sometimes become sociopathic. According to Gladstone,

> Such behavior is characteristic of individuals who will stop at nothing to satisfy their needs and desires. They show no concern for others or for conventional morality and do not experience guilt feelings even after blatantly and ruthlessly hurting relatives or friends. As a consequence, they seldom maintain friendships for long and are often loners.[14]

These individuals seem to take on a life position described by Dr. Thomas Harris as "I'm Not-OK-You're Not-OK."[15] Since they feel so "Not-OK" about themselves, their low self-esteem seems to be constantly reflected in others. Their negative behavior is, therefore, consistently reinforced.

LITTLE CHANGE FROM NEGATIVE FEEDBACK
At this level, individuals resist change at all costs. Negative feedback is not comprehended, and so provides little impetus for change. Negative feedback may be provided by friends and business associates, or it may involve dismissal, legal action, or even criminal indictment. Unconscious individuals hold tenaciously to their behavior patterns, hoping to avoid even greater internal psychological stress which such change might require.

26

Physical State

CONSTANT BLANK STARES

One of the most common symptoms of the Unconscious Level is a constant blank staring—a characteristic for anyone functioning at this level, whether severely unconscious or simply day-dreaming. When one is talking to someone whose mind has "split," it is fairly easy to determine unconsciousness through eye contact.

SEVERE PHYSICAL PROBLEMS

Individuals at the Unconscious Level experience serious physical problems—many of which can destroy their lives. Because they are more involved in fantasy than reality, they are accident-prone. They will walk into oncoming traffic, fall over objects, or dismember themselves with industrial machinery. They are also apt to make errors that could endanger others as well as themselves.

Moreover, the time needed to recover from these accidents and illnesses is extremely long. In fact, just when they seem to be recovering from one physical problem, another one occurs. Because of concurrent and intense anxiety and stress, their bodies seem to function as receptive hosts for a variety of diseases. Unwilling or unable to take responsibility for their own health, Unconscious people do not eat, sleep, or live in a healthy manner. When ill, they often fail to follow their physician's orders, or even worse, they will avoid medical assistance until the disease has progressed too far. In many cases, behavior at the Unconscious Level seems to be a pre-programmed, slow form of suicide.

ADDICTIVE DEPENDENCIES ON DRUGS AND MEDICATION

People at the Unconscious Level often become addicted to alcohol, tranquilizers, heroin, even aspirin—indeed any substance that can create initial relief from the anxiety experienced. Later, of course, the individuals feel they are unable to live without such substances. In some cases, the addiction is physical as well. At this point, the individual often needs total medical assistance to break the addictive patterns.

Dimensions of the Unconscious Level

Spiritual Dimension

ETHICALLY OR MORALLY UNCONCERNED
At the Unconscious Level, the spiritual dimension seems to be almost dormant. Since fantasy is the dominant experience, questions of morality and ethical considerations seldom occur.

FANATICAL BEHAVIOR
If Unconscious individuals have fantasies that include religious forms—such as God, the angels, the devil, and other forms of good and evil—they may "hear" voices or start operating on directions from God or the devil. In this respect, such behavior, based on delusions and hallucinations, does not involve true spiritual concerns. If severe, the fanatical, frenzied, and emotionally manic-depressive person often requires medical assistance.

Summary

The first stage of growth is the Unconscious Level. Although natural and common at infancy, this state can impede one's progress and can thwart one's attempts to become happy. By becoming aware of this level in themselves, managers can become more effective. They need to be aware of the Unconscious Level in others so they can assist them to effectively become more efficient and productive and to avoid accidents and illness. Billions of dollars are lost each year because people are "not there" for their jobs. It behooves management to find ways to help people gain greater control of their lives. The following chapters will aid that process.

The Five Levels

	EMOTIONAL RESPONSE	INTELLECTUAL FUNCTIONING	ACTIVITY INVOLVEMENT
UNCONSCIOUS	Unrelated to reality. Extreme shifts. Great stress and anxiety evident.	Difficulty in processing information. Obsessive thoughts. Gross perceptual distortion. Cognitive preoccupation: survival.	Ritualistic and compulsive behavior. Difficulty in changing. Extreme fear of attempting anything new.

SELF-DISCIPLINE	RELATIONSHIPS	PHYSICAL STATE	SPIRITUAL DIMENSION
Little self-control or motivation. Work contingent upon external conditions. Impulsive.	Unconsciousness in presence of others. Total communication breakdown. No concern for others. Little change from negative feedback.	Blank staring. Severe physical problems. Addictions.	Ethically or morally unconcerned. Fanatical behavior.

"The individual is responsible for what happens in the future, no matter what has happened in the past. . .and as long as people are bound by the past, they are not free to respond to the needs and aspirations of others in the present."[1]

—Thomas Harris
I'm OK-You're OK

"When at last we understand how we do it to ourselves and create the world we experience, we can live an awakening life."[2]

—Kenneth Keyes
Handbook to Higher Consciousness

Chapter Three

THE SELF-PROTECTIVE MANAGER

At the lower levels of maturity, especially at the Self-Protective Level, one recurring theme dominates: people blame others or external factors for their negative experiences. And yet, this very process of blaming keeps people functioning at low levels. Assuming an "effect" position, ("They did it to me"), only masks the symptoms of the underlying and unresolved problem. Specifically, many people are unwilling to take responsibility for their own experience. Eliminating one symptom of the problem simply allows another to emerge. Until the core issue of responsibility is addressed, this self-defeating process of evasion will continue unabated.

When individuals are pleased with what is happening in their lives—(i.e., their proposal was accepted, they received a promotion, the project was completed)—they take 100% responsibility. They did it! Yet when they are dissatisfied—(their proposal was rejected, they lost an account, they did not receive the raise they deserved)—they take no responsibility. Other people or circumstances "did it to them;" the boss did it to them; the secretarial pool failed to follow through; the economy was poor, and so forth.

People at the Self-Protective Level take very little responsibility for their lives. When they do not like what is happening, they shout "I'm **not** responsible, I had no choice." Yet when they like it, they are willing to take 100% of the responsibility: "I'm the one who worked overtime, I'm the one who talked to the customer!" "I chose to go the extra mile."

Not taking responsibility for acknowledging one's choice is called being the "effect" of one's experience. Usually people at the Self-Protective Level experience life from an "effect" state. Unknowingly, most corporations support the "effect" position by asking for excuses, rather than action plans to correct the situation.

The fact that the corporate world actually promotes an effect position does not make it desirable. Being the effect of one's experience keeps individuals from being satisfied and productive. Conceptually, Management By

Responsibility assumes people are the "cause" of their experience whether they like it or not. One cannot be a responsible manager and continue to assume an "effect" position.

The Management By Responsibility philosophy assumes that people are totally, 100% responsible for everything in their experience. No one and nothing is "doing it to them," unless they consciously or unconsciously create such a circumstance.

In reality, all people determine the satisfaction they experience on the job. Waiting for positive events to happen **for** them is totally non-productive because they may be waiting a long time. As an ancient Chinese proverb says: "Starving man wait long time for roast duck to fly into mouth."

Initial exposure to such a concept often triggers ingrained evasive habits in the form of a typical question such as, "Yeah, but why do I have to take responsibility if I get a new boss or there is a downturn in the economy, or a vendor strike, or one of my key staff members moves to a new city?" The reason becomes obvious once people recognize that they are the source of their own experience.

For Self-Protective individuals, the assumption that they are responsible for everything in their experience may be difficult to accept. They have been avoiding responsibility for what they dislike for a long time. If they ask someone to "prove" that they are responsible, there is no one who can do so. Even if they could, the Self-Protective mind would probably reject the proof anyway. There are no verifiable statements to prove responsibility—just the facts of reality.

Responsibility is not the same as "fault" and "blame." Such concepts are linked to "right" and "wrong." The question, "Is it my fault when the computer goes down and I can't meet the deadline?" is in reality, "Am I wrong?". The answer is "no." Computer programmers may not be "at fault" or "to blame." Yet, they are totally responsible both for their reaction to the event and for having put themselves in a position to experience that event in the first place.

Figure One explains the two phases associated with taking total responsibility. The first phase requires taking 100% responsibility for the reaction to each life event. This is contrary to the way Self-Protective people view reality. Yet to grow and to increase one's level of maturity, people must realize that "Response-Ability" enables them to choose their reactions. If the computer goes down, a programmer can become so angry that he or she can be non-productive for a day or even a week. But also possible is the simple acknowledgement that the computer is down, providing an opportunity to do something else productive in the meantime. What good does it do for the programmer to stay angry and upset?

In each situation, one has a myriad of choices. One can choose any emotion. Because of certain patterns, the individual may be predisposed to use one particular reaction. And yet, the ultimate choice belongs with the individual.

Recognizing that one has options is initially disconcerting. But later, as one grows to higher levels of maturity, one appreciates the freedom that responsibility and choice bring.

The second phase—taking total responsibility for the events themselves—may be even more difficult to accept. One must ask, "Who put me here?" At certain choice-points, there are always decisions to be made. In fact, every moment of "Now" provides options which lead to new experiences of "Now." When one recognizes that there was a choice, one can also recognize certain patterns. Awareness of negative patterns allows one to effectively address and dissipate them.

Response-Ability

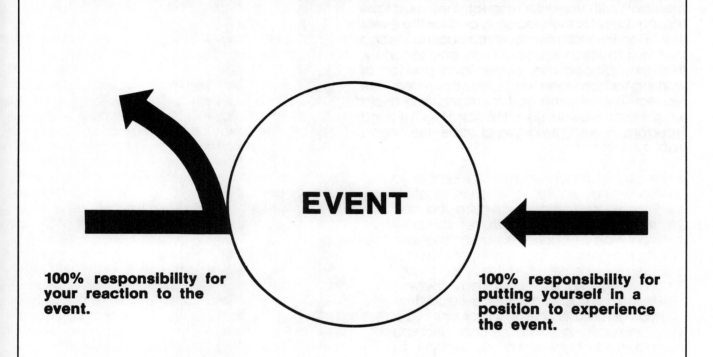

EVENT

100% responsibility for your reaction to the event.

100% responsibility for putting yourself in a position to experience the event.

PERHAPS IT'S REALLY RESPONSE-ABILITY!

You are totally responsible for your reaction to each event.
After each event reflect upon it:

- Has that event or a similar event ever occurred before?
- Is there a pattern?
- What do the patterns have to do with your belief systems?
- What might you be doing to set up the situation?
- What can you do to avoid negative events in the future?
- Whose responsibility is it to react in a positive manner, learn from the experience and change negative patterns?

Notice it all comes back to you.

Figure One

In other words, if a manager treats staff members with very little respect, they must take responsibility for their reaction and for the event itself. First, the staff members must acknowledge that their reaction is their choice, and secondly, that they placed themselves in a position of working for someone who gives them very little respect. This way the staff members can avoid what Harry Browne, in his book How I Found Freedom In An Unfree World, calls the "rights trap":

> If you've made yourself vulnerable to someone whose self-interest conflicts with yours, remember you're the one who put yourself in the vulnerable position. You've chosen to associate with those who cause your problems—whether they be your family, business associates, employees, friends. If you're not being treated as you want to be treated, it's your vulnerability that must be changed. You could spend the rest of your life trying to educate the others to change their natures and values, to get them to respect your rights, but you probably wouldn't succeed.[3]

To grow beyond the Self-Protective Level, people should ask themselves what they are getting out of troubling life situations and whether they are willing to do everything necessary to change them. If not, they should not complain or blame others for their experience.

Those who remain at the Self-Protective Level, do so for the following reasons.

Causes of Staying at the Self-Protective Level

BLAMING RATHER THAN LEARNING FROM THE PAST

People at the Self-Protective Level make something or someone else responsible for their experience of NOW. They say, "I could have been successful if it had not been for. . .!" Something or someone else did it to them! They have become the "effect" of their past experience. When people blame something else for their experience, they often remain in the past.

All one can say about the past is that it was exactly the way it was. It does not matter whether the individual "liked" the experience or not. The past was the way it was and, whether or not we enjoyed it, it was "perfect" for everyone. In this context, each individual's past was totally unique and complete for that individual; thus, it was "perfect." People could not be who they are now and have had a different past. To transcend the Self-Protective Level, one needs to ask, "How can I learn from my past experiences?" By resisting the past, feeling badly about it, or somehow making the past wrong, one does not gain from the experience itself.

Responsible managers mentally tape record past experiences, review them and learn from them. Reviewing a mistake or some kind of failure enables such individuals to alter themselves or their circumstances to be more successful in the future. As Alexander Pope stated, "A man should never be ashamed to say he has been wrong, which is but saying, in other words, that he is wiser today than he was yesterday."[4] Henry Ford had realized the importance of learning from the past when he said, "One who fears, limits his activities. Failure is only the opportunity to more intelligently begin again."[5]

Unfortunately, most Self-Protective managers do not learn from their past mistakes. When they fail, they spend most of their time justifying their behavior by blaming other people, other departments, or external circumstances. Since they assign cause elsewhere, they never ask what they need to do to become more successful in the future. Their Self-Protective stance roots their ineffectiveness. As Figure Two shows, Responsible managers learn from their past and plan for the future. Self-Protective managers do neither.

Figure 2

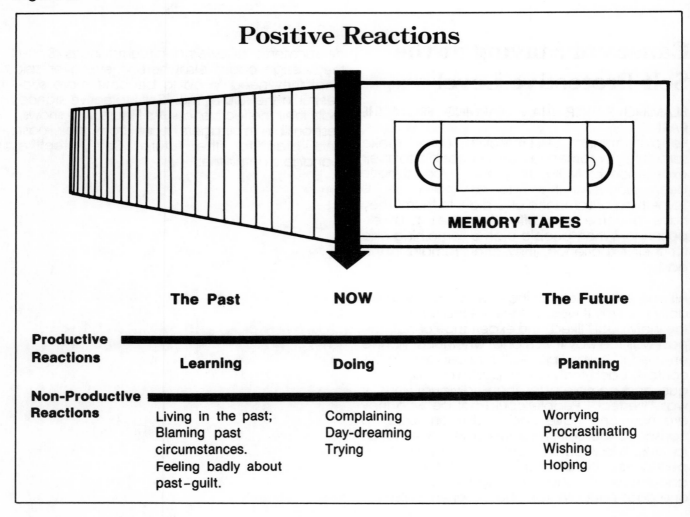

Positive Reactions

MEMORY TAPES

	The Past	NOW	The Future
Productive Reactions	Learning	Doing	Planning
Non-Productive Reactions	Living in the past; Blaming past circumstances. Feeling badly about past–guilt.	Complaining Day-dreaming Trying	Worrying Procrastinating Wishing Hoping

WORRYING ABOUT THE FUTURE RATHER THAN PLANNING FOR IT.

Effective managers plan for their futures—now. They realize that worrying about the future is as ineffective as feeling guilty about the past. Worrying is an excuse for doing nothing; planning promotes an effective future. Worrying simply takes away from the consciousness of NOW.

Worry's off shoot, procrastination, is one of the deadly corporate sins. "I'll do it tomorrow . . . I'll do it when I get around to it," are costly examples of time and energy misuse. Now is the time to produce results. If one needs to create a change, now is the time to make it happen. Change is a function of accepting the situation the way it is and then assuming total responsibility for producing the necessary changes.

COMPLAINING ABOUT THE PRESENT RATHER THAN DOING SOMETHING ABOUT IT.

Change means giving up ineffectual complaining in favor of effective effort. One way to remain at the Self-Protective Level is to complain about negative situations rather than doing something about them. Constant complaining without taking action, is not only non-productive, but self-destructive. An estimate of the number of corporate hours and the amount of corporate energy spent complaining about the way things are is equivalent to an estimate of **wasted** corporate time and energy. Needless to say, corporate America pays a high cost for squandering such resources.

LYING AND WITHHOLDING RATHER THAN ACTING ETHICALLY

Not only do people stay at the Self-Protective Level because of ineffective time usage, they also remain there by acting unethically—particularly when they lie to themselves and to others. Since people are ethical beings, whenever they lie, they compensate in a number of ways, one of which is by going unconscious. That is why honesty is such an important attribute of being at the Responsible Level.

When people tell themselves that they will do something they have no intention of doing, they are lying to themselves. "I'm going to finish that report by Friday"; "I'm going to lose ten pounds next month"; "I'm going to sit down and talk to Joe about coming in late," are all examples of this type of lie. Constant focus on the incomplete event creates a kind of mental overload and the mind goes unconscious as a result.

There are two ways to rid oneself of these kinds of lies: either, **just do it—or tell the truth about it.** Life is more satisfying for those who live it from the truth.

At the Self-Protective Level people not only lie to themselves, they lie to others. People sometimes feel that it is permissible to lie from a position of authority, especially to those who have little authority. Parents lie to their children; teachers lie to their students; the government lies to the people; managers lie to staff members. Yet, when those in authority are themselves the recipient of lies, they become very upset. Staff members sometimes lose their jobs when their supervisors find they have been lied to. An environment in which staff members lie to each other or the manager lies to employees inevitably incubates rampant job-dissatisfaction.

Most people typically think of lies as acts of commission; yet, there is another type of lie: a lie by omission, or "withholds." These are the ones in which people fail to communicate the real truth. Withholds are the "what they don't know, won't hurt them," type.

Withholds come in both negative and positive forms. Negative withholds occur when a staff member knows the project will not be completed for another two months, and he or she also knows that the manager assumes it will be completed in three weeks. The staff member then "forgets" to mention it. A positive withhold is when someone on the staff is doing a good job and the manager neglects to say anything. Many managers at the Self-Protective Level have adopted a belief that if people are doing a good job "that's what they're being paid for!" Yet, when the same staff member makes a mistake, the manager is very ready to give negative feedback.

Positive withholds can create extreme dissatisfaction. One of the real reasons people leave their jobs is because they do not feel appreciated. An administrative assistant, who was leaving her job "for more money" was acknowledged by her boss in superlatives at her going-away party. He said, "It's going to take three people to replace you. You've been the best assistant I've ever had." After he left, she turned and said, "Why didn't he tell me that while I was here. Maybe I wouldn't be leaving!" Do managers have to wait until people quit or retire before they tell them they are doing a great job?

Positive withholds can create dissatisfaction, while negative withholds can create stress. Often negative withholds can keep staff members from growing. Fortunately, interpersonal stress begins to dissipate the more honest one becomes.

Many managers have learned to accept lies as part of business: "That's just the way it is in the real world." Possibly, yet one needs to ask if lies really produce the satisfaction one wants in the work environment. To become more effective at work, to increase the level of job satisfaction, and to transcend the Self-Protective Level, one may need to make some changes. Techniques will not do it. Individuals can only do it for themselves.

The following suggestions are guidelines for personal growth:

1. **Live your life based on truth.**
   Give up the lies and withholds that keep you distant from others. and cause you to remain at an immature level of functioning.
2. **Take responsibility for your experience of Now.**
   Recognize that you are the only one who set it up that way. Your reaction to any event is your choice.
3. **Ask introspective questions of yourself.**
   (a) What am I getting out of what I'm going through right now?
   (b) Who gets to be right?
   (c) What are the patterns or decisions involved?

   Typically, you need to acknowledge your payoff—positive or negative—in any given situation. If the payoff is negative, you may be experiencing frustration and disappointment.

   The second question is a very direct one. Your mind always strives to be "right" when you do not like what is happening. Managers who always have to be "right" create non-productive work environments.

   Finally, look for the patterns and decisions. Are you always disappointed with your staff members? Do you typically have expectations higher than they could ever reach? Have you made decisions such as "You just can't trust anyone to do what they are supposed to do anymore," or "If you want something done right, you have to do it yourself!" Recognize your patterns and decisions so you can start doing something about them.

4. **Disclose the truth of the situation directly to the people involved.**
   Disclosure should be direct. Saying, "Bill, please tell Shirley I didn't mean anything by my comment at the staff meeting," is not direct. You need to communicate directly to the person involved.
5. **Change what needs to be changed.**
   Do what you have to do and learn from the past. Develop a specific action plan and then follow it. It is frustrating for people to hear the words and not see the results. Don't just talk about it, **do** something NOW.
6. **Stay fully conscious when others communicate with you.**
   Constantly practice staying conscious with others by listening to what they are saying. Become more conscious of what they are saying, non-verbally as well as verbally.
7. **Accept yourself and others as they are.**
   Acceptance allows people to be more conscious together. Often when people feel they are being judged, they go unconscious.
8. **Associate with responsible, alive, and successful people.**
   Model your behavior after those who exist now, as you would like to be in the future. The managerial "mentor" system is a valid means of becoming more effective in your job. Assess your friends, associates and staff members. What do they tell you about yourself?

Dimensions of the Self-Protective Level

Emotional Response

EMOTIONAL CAUSATION AFFIXED TO EXTERNAL CIRCUMSTANCES. BLAME PLACED ON OTHERS, CIRCUMSTANCES AND EVENTS.

Individuals operating at the Self-Protective Level spend much of their time blaming other people, circumstances, and events for their experience. They actively seek and support an effect position. Though ancient and current wisdom suggests that human beings are inherently the cause of their experience, Self-Protective individuals feel that life is out of their control—that their experience is determined by external forces. According to Nathaniel Branden, such a deterministic perspective

> . . .denies the existence of an element of freedom or volition in man's consciousness. It holds that, in relation to his actions, decisions, values, and conclusions, man is ultimately and essentially passive: that man is merely a reactor to internal and external pressures; that those pressures determine the course of his actions and the content of his convictions. . .that man has no actual power of choice, no actual freedom and self-responsibility.[6]

To the Self-Protective, emotions are caused by external events. Other people or external circumstances make them angry, upset, frustrated, or happy. Yet successful people have been telling others for centuries to take responsibility for events in their lives and to assume a "cause" position:

"The causes I am inclined to think are there all along, and the events which we see, and which look like freaks of chance, are only the last steps in long lines of causation."[7]

—Alfred North Whitehead

". . .in the moment of death many people undergo the curious sensation not only of accepting, but having willed everything that has happened to them. This is not willing in the imperious sense; it is the unexpected discovery of an identity between the willed and the inevitable."[8]

—Alan Watts

"We have already had to re-think so many of our conceptions of motion, we will also gradually learn to realize that that which we call destiny goes forth from within people, not from without into them."[9]

—Rainier Maria Rilke
Letters to a Young Poet

"To be a man is precisely, to be responsible."[10]

—Antoine de Sainte-Exupery
Airman's Odyssey

"We know, we affirm, I know and I affirm that at the very core of our being, of my being, there is the fact of responsibility."[11]

—Eric Gill
Modern Christian Revolutionaries

"We choose our joys and sorrows long before we experience them."[12]

—Kahlil Gibran

"Whatever you blame, that you have done yourself."[13]

—George Groddeck
The Unquiet Grows

Dimensions of the Self-Protective Level

Though an easier approach in some respects, blaming others destroys one's ability to be effective and happy. Rather than using time productively to correct mistakes, Self-Protective individuals attempt to cover up errors or complain that others created the difficulties. Both factors compound the problems ensuing from the initial error.

This process, of course, makes working with people who are operating at this level extremely frustrating. Not only do they needlessly consume valuable time, they do so in ways which demoralize fellow staff members. A disproportionate amount of energy is spent by managers with Self-Protective staff. As A.G. Sertillanges said, "The one who complains the loudest is generally he who contributes the least."[14]

One of the primary functions of management is to help people realize that they are responsible for their reactions to events and for their emotional states. Not to do so, only allows the Self-Protective state to continue to create more problems.

EMOTIONAL SHIFTS
People operating at the Self-Protective Level often experience complete emotional shifts. They become very excited about projects and new ideas and they get others involved with their ideas and plans. Their enthusiasm makes them feel invincible. Then, suddenly, because they do not follow through or otherwise complete the project, Self-Protective individuals fall into depression. They negate their original enthusiatic fervor and feel even less worthy and competent.

This feeling of depression continues until the next wave of excitement hits when the entire process repeats itself. Thus, Self-Protective people can be very impressionable, changing fundamental beliefs from one week to the next. Because of their inevitable disenchantment, the process then starts all over again.[15]

HYSTERICAL BEHAVIOR
At this stage of maturity, individuals often experience hysterical outbursts and temper tantrums. These tantrums typically last far beyond any "normal" range and may be explosive in nature.

During such an "uproar" these same people can become very destructive—of property, of others, or of themselves. Suicidal and homicidal tendencies are not uncommon at this level.

DOMINANT EMOTION: FEAR
Fear is the dominant emotion at the Self-Protective Level. Individuals are unable to enjoy themselves or be productive because of their fears. To the Self-Protective person past failures and mistakes seem destined to repeat themselves. Since individuals at this level find it difficult to learn from failure, such fears are well founded. As Emerson said, "What we are, that only can we see."[16] Therefore the Self-Protective only sees repeated failure. Moreover, they even insure failure by putting themselves in situations that are beyond their capability to cope or function.

Intellectual Functioning

BLIND TO FACTUAL INPUT

Individuals operating at the Self-Protective Level are blind to factual data. They only accept data that supports their biases, rather than remaining open to new ideas and information. As Alfred North Whitehead suggested, "[We] can catch [ourselves] entertaining habitually certain types of ideas and setting others aside; and that I think, is where our personal destinies are largely decided."[17]

Because of this blind adherence to prior beliefs, people functioning at this level experience mental blocks that inhibit creative-problem solving. Managers at this level simply do not "see" solutions to problems that are before them. Even when the obvious is pointed out, the Self-Protective person seems unable to retain the facts or to utilize them effectively.[18]

> Our ability to sabotage solutions creates a strange paradox: Man is the only living species able to reject, sabotage, and betray his own means of survival, his mind. He is the only living species who must make himself competent to live—by the proper exercise of his rational faculty. It is his primary responsibility . . . How man chooses to deal with this issue is, psychologically, the most significant fact about him—because it lies at the very core of his being . . .[19]

Managers at this level need to be taught to open their minds for the input of new data. Otherwise, they can make decisions that actually undermine organizational productivity and success.

DIFFICULTY IN PROCESSING INFORMATION AND MAKING DECISIONS

Because Self-Protective managers repeatedly review the same facts without effectively analyzing the data for pertinent information, they have difficulty focusing on relevant problems and issues. Furthermore, their thinking and processing is circular—seldom advancing to a logical conclusion.

Even when managers at this level process information effectively and reach a valid decision, they often fail to act on their decision, or they attempt still other alternatives. Plagued by doubt, these managers become sidetracked by searching for "better" solutions. So they continue to gather data. Finally, even though their research has produced stacks of information, they often act impulsively. Later, of course, they regret their choice and blame others or circumstances for not adhering to their original plan.

CHRONIC DISTORTION OF REALITY

Just as Self-Protective managers make gross generalizations and so act ineffectively, they also tend to distort reality to conform with their beliefs. They often misinterpret events and overpersonalize insignificant occurrences.

For example, if a major client does not return a call, a salesperson operating at this level takes it as a personal affront or as an indication that the client may be considering cancelling a large order. If a supervisor fails to respond to a greeting while quickly passing in the hallway, the Self-Protective employee may distort the incident, thinking it is an indication that he or she is about to be fired. Conversely, an enthusiastic greeting becomes a signal that a promotion is imminent.

COGNITIVE PREOCCUPATION WITH BODILY FUNCTIONS: SEX AND AGGRESSION

At this level, individuals are preoccupied with sexual and aggressive fantasies to the extent that such thoughts often disrupt work and relationships. Instead of listening at a staff meeting, individuals may be totally preoccupied with their aggressive fantasies against individuals who do not support their position. Though these fantasies may not be acted upon, they, nonetheless, render the individual ineffective and incapable of efficient activity.

Dimensions of the Self-Protective Level

Activity Involvement

AVOIDANCE OF NEW OR CHALLENGING ACTIVITIES
Managers at the Self-Protective Level tend to avoid new activities as much as they possibly can. Since they feel overburdened just coping with their present level of activity they attempt to insulate themselves from new challenges or changes of any type.

LITTLE SELF-CONFIDENCE
Because of consistent negative reinforcement, Self-Protective managers display little confidence in their abilities. They constantly state they "can't" perform their activities. Yet, they make no attempt to successfully complete the tasks at hand.

Paralyzed by the fear of error managers at this level reinforce feelings of unworthiness. Attempts to build self-confidence are often met with resistance and sometimes sabotage, as when the Self-Protective person exclaims, "See, I knew I couldn't do it!" To counteract such behavior, managers need to clearly define simple tasks that Self-Protective employees can perform without anxiety. They then need to consistently reinforce successful behaviors while providing new challenges to each project.

WORK AS ANXIETY-AVOIDANCE RATHER THAN A SOURCE OF SATISFACTION
Unlike higher levels of maturity in which work provides a sense of satisfaction and accomplishment, work at the Self-Protective Level is only performed to alleviate anxiety. Even when Self-Protective managers are successful, they do not feel a sense of satisfaction. Success is simply a sign that they are still able to cope.

At this level, people are primarily motivated externally by fear. They feel they "have to" work and they've "got to" do a good job—or else! In short, fear of negative consequences motivates such employees. Unfortunately, until they start operating at higher levels, this may, by necessity, be the most effective—although not the most efficient—management style.

Consistent with their reluctance to work except by being threatened, Self-Protective employees have an impending sense of doom or punishment. Emotionally, they act somewhat like a child who knows that he is about to be spanked. Consequently, they attempt to avoid management involvement and interaction, typically preferring solitary activities which they perform with a sense of foreboding.

Self-Discipline

OBSESSIVE RITUALS NECESSARY TO FUNCTION

At the Self-Protective Level, ritualistic behavior is performed compulsively to enhance feelings of security. For example, always sharpening all of one's pencils prior to writing memos, or always drinking a sip of water before speaking at a staff meeting, become ends in themselves rather than preliminaries to productive functioning.

ROBOT-LIKE BEHAVIOR

At this level, individuals behave almost mechanically at times. Saying certain things or behaving in certain ways can "push their buttons" and cause them to respond in characteristic ways. Many arguments begin with such "button-pushing," for example:

Manager: "Have you seen the Carter, Inc., file?"

Secretary: "No, but if you'd put things back, it wouldn't be missing!"

Manager: "Well, maybe if you'd do more filing and less talking about TV shows, I could count on things being filed properly!"

Secretary: "Is that so! You think playing golf on company time is working up to capacity! Maybe you should just look around and . . . (etc. etc. etc.)

Such arguments at times even have the same verbiage repeated word for word. In such cases people are functioning on "automatic pilot."

Ironically, according to William Gladstone, these same individuals even envy machines: At this level

> . . . you would like to be able to treat yourself like a machine, to be totally certain of always making the same response and doing the same action. You envy the routine and total structure in which a machine operates—you know exactly what is expected of you and you don't have to cope with any human factors or uncertainties; you do not have to set your own pace or create your own work procedures; at least this is how you imagine your ideal work situation.[20]

Thus, individuals at this level resent a "participative" management style. They do not want to be asked to re-define their jobs or to act creatively. They tend to prefer repetitive, tedious, non-thinking jobs.

Because they want the security of knowing what to do, Self-Protective managers are radically upset by unexpected events. Delays are accompanied by emotional outbursts. Minor deviations from expected norms destroy the Self-Protectives' ability to implement their ideas or to formulate plans. These unexpected events can and often do create work stoppage.

Since they are virtually intolerant of any deviation in their plans, managers at this level often attempt to organize a system that will take every detail into account. To insure that no mistake is made, such managers engage in obsessive and ritualistic behavior which, although it provides a sense of security, bears little resemblance to effective functioning.

Dimensions of the Self-Protective Level
The Wurlitzer

IMPULSIVE BEHAVIOR

Although driven by a methodical, ritualistic approach to detail, Self-Protective managers paradoxically also tend to behave impulsively—a tendency which only fuels their need for compulsive ritual. By intensifying frustration and anxiety, impulsive action is not only disruptive, but self-destructive as well. For example, an unanticipated detail in the operation of a new system will prompt the now distraught Self-Protective manager to abandon the system even though he may have spent months devising it. Later, he resolves to avoid a repeat of the situation by becoming overly ritualistic and concerned with minutia.

OPPORTUNISTIC

Since their only major fear is that they "might get caught," Self-Protective individuals tend to be opportunistic when they feel they can "get away" with unethical behavior. Recent examples of "white collar" crime are indicative of this phenomenon.

DIFFICULTY IN LEARNING FROM EXPERIENCE

At the Self-Protective Level, individuals repeat the same mistakes—a consequence of their focus on blaming external causes. They fail to realize the wisdom of a Bulgarian proverb that states, "Your own calamity is more useful to you than another's triumph."[21] At this level, managers may fail to correct the inadequate procedures or take responsibility to do something to insure subsequent success.

As Helen Merrill Lynd suggests in her book, On Shame and The Search of Identity,

> . . . we could live less painfully with the almost overwhelming conflicts of the present, and find more of ourselves in the midst of them, if instead of protecting ourselves from them, we allow ourselves to realize more fully their immense difficulty.[22]

At the Self-Protective Level, people are afraid to look at the "immensity" because they worry about what they may find out about themselves. Fearing a breakdown under such scrutiny, they can only reduce their ever-present anxiety by restricting their cognitive field and no longer being objective. At this level managers tend to exaggerate their strengths and to underestimate their weaknesses, thereby avoiding change—even if it is change for the better.[23]

Dimensions of the Self-Protective Level

Relationships

EXTREME WITHDRAWAL, DEPENDENCY OR HOSTILITY

At the Self-Protective Level, managers typically avoid involvement with others. They withdraw from social events, and isolate themselves at work. They tend to be "loners," avoiding social contacts or acting with such extreme hostility that others avoid them.

Yet, people at this level may rely so heavily emotionally upon a few people with whom they form dependency bonds, that eventually the relationship can be destroyed. In this respect, they may feel that their total existence depends upon these few "significant others." Because people are seen as a source of supply, Self-Protective people are primarily concerned with manipulation and domination. Either they allow themselves to be totally dominated by these significant others, or they themselves dominate the relationship. Such a dependent and exploitive nature in their relationships usually means short-term and often dramatic alliances with others. The concern for retaliation and their penchant for extreme grudges almost always insures interpersonal disaster.

UNCONCERNED WITH AGREEMENT, COMMITMENTS, OR RULES

At this level, individuals worry most about "getting caught" in breaking the rules. Thus, breaking agreements is as common as is lying, cheating, and "withholds." At work, deviating from basic standards of conduct by lying, cheating, stealing, and breaking commitments are fairly common behaviors for Self-Protective individuals. Yet, these same people often delude themselves into thinking that they are not actually lying or cheating; they are wholly capable of rationalizing and justifying such behavior. As R.D. Laing says in The Politics of Experience, "Human beings seem to have an almost unlimited capacity to deceive themselves, and to deceive themselves into taking their own lies for truths."[24]

Managers at the Self-Protective Level tend to be exploitive of others and the organization as a whole by trying to "get away with" as much as possible. If caught, they will attempt to lie their way out of problem areas. They will protect themselves by blaming others or by bringing up their transgressions, often whining, "Why does everyone always point the finger at me?"

Because they never forget when others have not supported them, they will use grudges as excuses for later retaliation. Some individuals at this level are actually psychopathic. According to Maslow, these people

> . . .can be described briefly as having no conscience, no guilt, no shame, no love for other people, no inhibitions, and few controls, so that they pretty well do what they want to. . .These people, because of their own lacks, are generally unable to understand in others, the pangs of conscience, regret, unselfishness, love, compassion, pity, guilt, shame and embarrassment.[25]

Physical State

PSYCHOSOMATIC ILLNESS WITH NO APPARENT CAUSE

At this level, individuals can experience extreme physical problems without the antecedent physical causes. Such problems as—ulcers, colitis, the absence of menses in women, and severe migraine headaches are typically related to prolonged stress reactions. Even minor symptoms in these areas should be viewed as possible indications of low level behavior in other dimensions.

Extreme thinness or obesity may also be indicative of functioning at the Self-Protective Level. When one does not eat in response to stress, the loss of appetite can lead to other problems such as anemia or malnutrition.

In addition, individuals at this level often experience chronic insomnia and muscular stiffness and pains. In some cases, they display an extreme haggard look or a slow gait, walking stiffly and slowly.

A major problem at this level is that individuals refuse to take responsibility for their health. They almost seem to be determined to "self-destruct" by not eating well, not exercising, or avoiding taking medication for illness. They also tend to abuse the drugs they take to help them cope. Then, they can blame the drugs for their behavior. Alcoholism and extreme drug abuse are common at the Self-Protective Level. They are not jovial, social drinkers; usually they are alone when drinking or using drugs.

Spiritual Dimension

SPIRITUAL DIMENSION

At the Self-Protective Level, there is little intellectual concept of God or a spiritual force. Since fear of retaliation is the primary motivator at this level, God is typically viewed as the extreme punisher. Such a fear suggests an underlying emphasis on avoiding being "caught" with one's sins and transgressions. Individuals may also become totally dependent upon God to rescue them from the problems of "this life."

The Self-Protective's spiritual dimension contributes to and helps perpetuate the distortions common to this Level. It is not—as it could be—a source of positive action. Though the environment may confirm the Self-Protective's limited view of one's spiritual nature, it does not negate one's fundamental responsibility to change. As Nathaniel Branden states:

> If a man is pounded from childhood with the doctrine of original sin, if he is taught that he is corrupt by nature and must spend his life in penance, if he is taught that this earth is a place of misery, frustration, and calamity, if he is taught that the pursuit of enjoyment is evil, he does not have to believe it: he is free to think, to question and to judge the nature of a moral code that damns man and damns existence and places its standard of the good outside of both.[26]

49

The Five Levels

	EMOTIONAL RESPONSE	INTELLECTUAL FUNCTIONING	ACTIVITY INVOLVEMENT
SELF-PROTECTIVE	External causation. Emotional shifts. Hysterical behavior. Fear dominant emotion.	Blind to factual data. Difficulty with decision-making. Chronic distortion of reality. Cognitive preoccupation: sex and aggression.	Avoidance of challenging activities. Little self-confidence. Work as anxiety-avoidance not a source of satisfaction.
UNCONSCIOUS	Unrelated to reality. Extreme shifts. Great stress and anxiety evident.	Difficulty in processing information. Obsessive thoughts. Gross perceptual distortion. Cognitive preoccupation: survival.	Ritualistic and compulsive behavior. Difficulty in changing. Extreme fear of attempting anything new.

SELF-DISCIPLINE	RELATIONSHIPS	PHYSICAL STATE	SPIRITUAL DIMENSION
Obsessively ritualistic. Robot-like behavior. Opportunistic. Difficulty in learning.	Withdrawal, dependency, hostility. Unconcerned with agreements, commitments or rules.	Psychosomatic illness. No appetite/muscular soreness. Chronic drug abuse.	Non-ethical. Moral level: "Don't get caught".
Little self-control of motivation. Work contingent upon external conditions. Impulsive.	Unconsciousness in presence of others. Total communication breakdown. No concern for others. Little change from negative feedback.	Blank staring. Severe physical problems. Addictions.	Ethically or morally unconcerned. Fanatical behavior.

These are the persons
who cannot bear to be alone,
who cannot live without sleeping pills;
who drink too much to calm a nervousness that
    comes too often;
who jump at every unexpected sound;
who feel a constant pressing need to be amusing
    and to entertain;
who go to too many movies they have no desire to
    see and to too many gatherings they have no
    desire to attend;
who sacrifice any vestige of independent self-
    confidence for an obsessive concern with
    what others think of them;
who long to be emotionally dependent or to be
    depended upon;
who succumb to periodic spells of unaccountable
    depression;
who submerge their existence in the passivity of un-
    chosen routines and unchallenged duties,
    and, as they watch their years slip by, wonder,
    in occasional spurts of frustrated anguish, what
    has robbed them of their chance to live,
who run from one meaningless sexual affair to
    another,
who seek membership in the kind of collective
    movements that dissolve personal responsib-
    ility.

—a vast, anonymous assemblage of men and women who have accepted fear as a built-in-not-to-be-wondered-about fixture of their soul, dreading even to identify that what they feel is fear, or to inquire into the nature of that which they seek to escape.[1]

                              —Nathaniel Branden

Chapter Four

THE CONFORMIST MANAGER

People at the Conformist Level may constitute the greatest single threat to the ongoing function of the American business community, free enterprise, and indeed, to democracy itself. At the two previous levels, something is obviously "wrong" with the individuals who spend most of their time unconscious or protecting themselves. However, since a majority of the population functions at the Conformist Level most of the time, people at this Level are considered quite "normal."

This "vast, anonymous, assemblage" of people constitute the bulk of employees and managers in any organization. They are the scores of organization people—the "yes" men—marching lock-step to what they perceive to be the music of the corporate body.

Yet, because these people fear disapproval, they often conform to negative standards of behavior. A major function in declining American productivity is the insistence to conform to the lowest possible level of performance. "Why should I do my work, when Joe doesn't do his," is an all-too-familiar refrain. By conforming to the lowest possible level, not only does the organization and the nation suffer, so does the individual who thereby diminishes his self-respect. As Maslow points out, the ". . . evasion of one's own growth, setting low levels of aspiration, the fear of doing what one is capable of doing, voluntary self-crippling, pseudo-stupidity, mock humility are, in fact, defenses."[2] These very defenses keep people from maximizing their potential and, as a consequence, limit their productivity.

Conformists fear success and job satisfaction because they do not want to appear "different." Yet, the ability to see clearly and to disagree with the majority opinion needs to be encouraged within any organization unit. As David Grayson stated, "Commandment No. 1 of any truly civilized society is this: Let people be different."[3] By demanding an adherence to "group-think" and by lowering one's expectations and aspirations to what will be "approved" by others, the peer group acts as a dehumanizing agent—an agency that creates real problems for a nation committed to independence and to a democratic system. As Carl Jung warned, "Collective man is threatening to suffocate the individual who is absolutely indispensible—for it is on his sense of responsibility that every human achievement is ultimately founded."[4]

American management needs to recognize and support individualism rather than blind adherence to "policy" and to the corporate model. It needs to encourage people to suggest new ways of solving old problems, to teach people how to interrelate productively and satisfactorily, and, most importantly, to promote flexibility and adaptability.

This realization comes at a time when the evident demise of individualism is producing concomittant frustration over its absence. People who are truly themselves, seem more difficult to find in an age in which world-wide telecommunication systems provide archetypal behavioral models to the interglobal village. At some level of consciousness, workers are becoming cognizant of a growing fear that they, too, are being standardized like machines.

To counteract the effect of mass communication and the conformist nature of our society, educational experiences that cherish and promote individuality need to be pursued. According to Carl Rogers,

> If we value independence, if we are disturbed by the growing conformity of knowledge, of values, of attitudes, which our present system induces, then we may wish to set up conditions of learning which make for uniqueness, for self-direction, and for self-initiated learning.[5]

It is exactly to those ends that this chapter is devoted. Before individuals can cherish the choice they have, they have to become aware of the forces that are keeping them from actualizing. The following descriptions of the dimensions of the Conformist Level are designed to create that awareness.

Dimensions of the Conformist Level

Emotional Response

STRESS AND TENSION WITHOUT APPARENT CAUSE

At the Conformist Level, managers act perpetually as though they are responding to an emergency situation, although none exists. They feel constantly pressured without real cause, apparently as a response to a more generalized fear. As Nathaniel Branden states:

> There is no object of fear more terrifying than that for which he knows no object. Yet, to live with such fear as a haunting constant of their existence is the fate of countless millions of men and women. . . .Psychological anxiety is a state of dread experienced in the absence of any actual or impending objectively perceived threat.[6]

Whereas it is "normal" to experience anxiety in response to occasional problem situations, the Conformist experiences this type of generalized anxiety on a day-to-day basis. It is not that individuals at the Conformist Level never relax; they simply do not relax very often. The "anxiety attacks" that individuals at this level experience often interrupt work and may be a primary cause of absenteeism of the job.

PERVASIVE SENSE OF FEAR, GUILT, SHAME AND INADEQUACY

At the Conformist Level, managers often behave in negative and defensive ways. They are motivated not to produce end results, but to defend themselves against a sense of inadequacy, guilt, doubt and anxiety. A person at the Conformist Level often experiences:

> . . .a profound sense of helplessness, of impotence. He feels a sense of shapeless, but impending disaster. And often he feels a unique, nameless wrong, wrong as a person, wrong in some fundamental way that is wider than any particular fault or defect he can identify.[7]

Often, these feelings are rooted in family background. Conformists may have received strong negative messages from their parents. These messages were later converted into a pervasive feeling of inadequacy. At the Conformist Level, all the "shoulds," "oughts," "musts," and negative messages are internalized to the disadvantage of the individual's productive functioning.

Later, the same individuals may project the negative images onto others. As Maslow observed:

> This internal drama of fear and defense is within one man's skin, but it tends by this man to be generalized, projected outward in the whole world, and he is apt to see the whole world in this fashion. What he's really fighting off are dangers within himself, but then anything that reminds him of or resembles these dangers within himself, he fights in the external world whenever he sees them.
>
> He fights against his own impulses to disorderliness by becoming extra-orderly. And he will be threatened by disorderliness in the world because it reminds him and threatens him with this revolution from the suppressed, from within. Anything that endangers the control; anything that strengthens within the dangerous hidden impulses or else weakens the defensive walls, will frighten and threaten this kind of person.[8]

Dimensions of the Conformist Level

Thus, the Conformist experiences the crippling emotions of fear, guilt, shame and inadequacy, and then projects them outward as well. Consequently, Conformists typically fluctuate between being "nice" and being critical of others, thereby compounding relationship difficulties. When their anger is directed toward themselves, the resulting self-inflicted anxiety often creates fears and phobias. Interestingly, some Conformists form "counter phobias"—denying their fears and acting in contrary fashion. Hence, if one has an extreme fear of criticism, he may become highly critical of others.

EMOTIONS REQUIRE LONG RECOVERY TIME

Conformists are often psychologically attached to their negative experiences. Just as Self-Protective people collect grudges to rationalize a tendency to retaliate, Conformists collect negative experiences to justify their sense of inadequacy, though these emotions could be alleviated almost ·immediately. By taking responsibility for the reaction to the event, one can discount much of the negative impact of the emotion. Still, at the Conformist Level, people often cling to their emotions. If a manager is depressed because of office politics, even receiving notice that he has been promoted does not lift the depression. A long emotional recovery time characterizes response at the Conformist Level.

INTERMITTENT, HYSTERICAL BEHAVIOR

According to Gladstone, other strong indications of the Conformist identity are the intermittent hysterics,

> . . . such as irrational behavior, temper tantrums, crying fits or strong denial of one's problems and weaknesses. Hysterical behavior is that which, as seen by outsiders, is clearly an attempt to release tension by denying reality. You are not aware of what you are saying; you jump from feeling totally depressed to feeling suddenly elated for no apparent reason. You read into acts of others motives which are not there. If someone compliments you, you think that he (or she) is in love with you or is going to offer you a promotion. If someone is abrupt with you, you think they hate you.[9]

Thus, the Conformist often experiences mood shifts, related to aspects in their environment that actually do not call for such strong responses.

HOSTILE WIT

Another way for an individual to deal with a sense of self-rejection is through a hostile wit. Individuals at the Conformist Level often use sarcastic humor to belittle others. This type of humor is often displayed on television and is typical in situation comedies, especially those showing a work environment.

A hostile wit is a learned response to deal with inner dissatisfaction and anger. By projecting negatives on to others in a seemingly socially acceptable manner, one attempts to quell inner hostility.

BLOCKED EMOTION/PROBLEM DENIAL

At this level, individuals often block strong emotions for fear that they might "go crazy." Even their ability to describe emotional states is often quite banal and undifferentiated, making use of the most global terms such as "happy-sad," "love-hate," or "mad-sad."[10] By keeping their emotions under control, such individuals hope to maintain their stability. Maslow graphically describes such individuals:

> These are rigid and tight people who can't play very well. These are people who try to control their emotions and so look rather cold and frozen in the extreme case. They are tense; they are constricted. And these are the people who in a normal state . . . generally tend to be very neat and very punctual and very systematic and very controlled . . . This is the only way in which such a person can achieve safety, order, lack of threat, lack of anxiety, that is via orderliness, predictability, control, and mastery. The "new" is threatening to such a person, but nothing new can happen to him if he can order it to his past experience, or he can freeze the world in flux, that is, if he can make believe nothing is changing. If he can proceed into the future on the basis of "well-tried" laws and rules, habits, modes of adjustment which have worked in the past, and which he will insist on using in the future, then he feels safe and he doesn't feel anxious.[11]

In today's fast-moving, ever-changing society, to attempt to avoid anxiety that results from change is fruitless. Nothing seems to be the same from one day to the next. Hence, Conformists often resort to psychological denial. If no change is preceived, no feelings of anxiety will be triggered. If a business associate becomes concerned when responses seem inappropriate, the Conformist will typically protest that "Things couldn't be better" and "Don't worry, everything is fine."

Intellectual Functioning

The intellectual functioning at the Conformist Level, although more effective than the two previous levels, is nonetheless quite restricted. Negative emotional responses, limit the cognitive field of Conformist Level individuals.

Just as with the Unconscious and Self-Protective Level, fear is the major restrictive emotion while also the primary motivator at this Level. According to Nathaniel Branden, just as fear rules the Conformist by

> . . . undercutting the clarity of his perception, distorting his judgments, restricting his cognitive ambition and driving him to ever wider evasions—so fear rules him motivationally, subverting his normal value development, sabotaging his proper growth, leading him toward goals that promise to support his pretense at efficacy, driving him to passive conformity or hostile aggressiveness or autistic withdrawal, to any path that will protect his pseudo-self-esteem against reality.[12]

The following manifestations demonstrate how such fear restricts intellectual functioning:

Dimensions of the Conformist Level

GREAT COGNITIVE SIMPLICITY; RIGHT-WRONG/MALE-FEMALE/GOOD-BAD

Cognitive simplicity is one of the hallmarks of the Conformist Level. There is a right way and a wrong way to think and to behave. Behavior is governed by rules that are set by the group or by authoritarian role models such as parents, teachers, managers, or group leaders. In their study of ego development, Wessler and Loevinger characterize Conformist cognition in these terms:

> Formulas for what does happen or what ought to happen tend to be stated in absolute terms, without contingencies or exceptions. A particular category is applied to all within the group, rather than to just certain ones of them.[12]

The Conformist is preoccupied with the Right/Wrong dichotomy. Often they will go to any lengths to prove their "rightness" to the point of risking their jobs, their valued relationships and even their lives. Any data that conflicts with their viewpoint is disregarded or distorted to fit their beliefs. They tend either to generalize their beliefs, to distort reality to fit their beliefs or to deny the conflicting information.

The following dialogue between Carlos Castaneda and don Juan, his sorcerer teacher, illustrates this point:

don Juan: "You held that thought and naturally you had to find ways to make the world conform to that thought."

Carlos: "But I was not thinking at all, don Juan."

don Juan: "Let's not call it thinking then. It is rather the habit of having the world always conform to our thoughts; when it doesn't, we simply make it conform."

...we involved ourselves in a long discussion about the reflexive nature of our world. The world, according to don Juan, had to conform to its description; that is, the description reflected itself."[13]

To the Conformist, the world conforms to the beliefs held to be true and accepted by the group to which he adheres. At this level, prejudice and stereotyped roles are tenaciously maintained. Such stereotypic roles are most common in terms of sex-role identification. Conformists feel that men and women have certain functions, duties, and behaviors inherent to their sex. As such, Conformist males are often locked into controversy and conflict with proponents of the women's movement. They approve of such traditional-female roles as raising children and "being a good wife," and if she "must" work, certainly it should only be in those sanctioned service roles of teacher, nurse or secretary. Women at the Achievement Level, of course, are questioning such a view, by demanding equal pay for equal work and a place in the executive suite, thereby creating stress for chauvinistic co-workers.

The major problem at this level is that Conformists are blinded by their own prejudice. They see what they want to see, and hear what they want to hear. As George Bernard Shaw wrote: "The moment we want to believe something, we suddenly see all the arguments for it and become blind to the arguments against it."[14] Options that are available at higher levels of maturity do not appear to Conformists, thereby restricting their creativity and intellectual function. According to John W. Gardner,

> Creativity, requires the freedom to consider 'unthinkable' alternatives, to doubt the worth of cherished practices. Every organization, every society is under the spell of assumptions so familiar that they are never questioned—least of all by the most intimately involved.[15]

The Conformist often resorts to ritualistic thinking and activity, because it is "safe" to do so. The statement, "But we've always done it that way around here!" is a typical refrain. These are the individuals who are quick to point out company policy and procedure with a certainty and a sense of "rightness." As Branden points out, the Conformist does not question:

> This is the person who accepts the world and its prevailing values, ready-made. His is not to reason why. What is true? What others say is true. What is right? What others say is right. How should one live? As others live. Why does one work for a living? Because one is supposed to. . . .[16]

INTELLECTUALIZES AND ANALYZES FEELING, RATHER THAN EXPERIENCES EMOTIONAL STATES

Though at times Conformists may exhibit hysterical reactions, some managers at this level intellectualize their emotional states. Ironically, even though their cognitive field is restricted, they sometimes want to become totally "rational." This appears to be especially true for males who were given messages to "act like a man," by not displaying emotions, and by always being "logical" and "rational." Such a compulsively rational person is

> . . .one who can't live in the world of emotion at all; who doesn't know whether he's falling in love or not, because love is illogical; who can't even permit himself to laugh very frequently because laughing isn't logical and rational and sensible. . .[This type of] person not only loses much of the pleasure of living, but also becomes cognitively blind to much of himself, much in other people, and even in nature.[17]

The "rational" Conformists are able to analyze their relationships, yet they seldom **experience** emotions of love, closeness, or anger. They know analytically that they must love others and yet they remain out of touch with their emotions. When emotional reactions do appear, they often divert the conversation, leave the room, or deny their feelings. At times, managers operating at this level even question their ability to experience any strong emotional states. Their emotions have been so strongly suppressed and are so threatening to ongoing functioning, that the mind simply denies their existence.[18]

Dimensions of the Conformist Level

CIRCULAR WORRYING

At the Conformist Level, many individuals engage in circular worrying—worrying that serves no constructive purpose. Conformists constantly consider, "What if. . ." situations and yet take no action to counter the feared negative situation. At the Conformist Level such worrying is frequent. They often:

> . . .hypothesize possible malfunctions and problems, many of which are unlikely to occur. . .Most important, they don't do anything to prevent those possible occurrences (often because they're the kind of thing you can't prevent). . .Circular worrying is more than ordinary concern which is non-productive in dealing with external factors which actually influence events. It is more akin to fantasizing and daydreaming than rational planning.[19]

Managers who engage in such circular worrying often think that they are contingency planning. Yet, because of their inability or unwillingness to take action to prevent the possible negative occurrence, they are non-productive and thus frustrate their colleagues.

PERFECTIONIST-MIND MODEL

Conformists operate on a model of the way reality "ought" to be. Since at this stage of development there is little cognitive differentiation between the way people "are" and the way they "ought" to be, frustration is the inevitable consequence.

To the Conformist, one's boss "ought" to act in a certain way; the company "ought" to treat employees better; one's spouse and children "ought" to live in a particular type of home, drive a particular type of car, and have particular types of friends. When reality does not live up to this perfectionist model, the Conformists feel a great deal of frustration and anxiety.

Because of such perfectionist models, Conformists often think stereotypically and speak in clichés. They can also be quite severe to others who do not fulfill their model of "shoulds" and "oughts."

COGNITIVE PREOCCUPATIONS: SOCIAL ACCEPTANCE AND BELONGING, APPEARANCE, MATERIAL OBJECTS, REPUTATION

At this level of development social disapproval is used as a very potent sanction. Therefore, staff members are taught to take great strides to avoid any form of embarrassment or to resist going outside the accepted norm.

At the Conformist Level, managers are strongly preoccupied with anything affecting their social acceptance within their reference group. In their study of women subjects operating at this level, Wessler and Loevinger found that they

> . . .value a pleasing, friendly, personality and like to be part of the group. They depend on popularity and expression of social approval. Belonging makes them feel secure. They often disapprove of hostility and aggression. . .even when they admit to anger or temper. They may even ignore hostile provocations.[20]

Many males also value the same characteristics. Wanting to be accepted and liked, Conformist managers become like Blake's "Country-Club" managers, with a high concern for acceptance and a low concern for productivity.

Such a concern for physical appearance and material objects is a matter of degree and purpose. Though existing at higher levels of maturity, it is expressed differently. At the Conformist Level, individuals may become totally preoccupied with concerns about their appearance, so that others will accept them. They will at times go to any extreme to gain the acceptance of the group to which they aspire. They can spend hours primping and shopping for clothes and material possessions that others will admire. This is not to say, however, that people depicted in "slick" advertisements are the only type of Conformists. Indeed, the lack of good grooming and the absence of material possessions constituted conformity's marching beat in the "hippy" generation. Whatever its manifestation, the controlling concern at the Conformist Level is the fear of rejection.

In a work environment such cognitive preoccupations can waste hours, as individuals talk of the latest styles, acquisitions, or the "right" activities. They can be so swept away by the "importance" of such talk that departmental goals become secondary, as they become "forgetful" of important deadlines and tasks.

Dimensions of the Conformist Level

Activity Level

FRENZIED, POINTLESS ACTIVITY

At the Conformist Level, activity is not calm, steady, or goal-directed. People at this level alternate between periods of high energy and total inertia. Yet, much of their frenzied activity is pointless. Involved in a myriad of activities at the same time, they seldom finish anything or do well the first time. As such, they personify Gracian's dictum: "Many people who pretend to be very busy have the least to do."[21]

Conformist managers often have difficulty completing the projects they start or in initiating new projects. Typically, they want to make up for weeks of little activity in a sudden burst of energy, leaving co-workers and staff members exhausted and frustrated. Even so, Conformists can and do complete some projects and can work well if conditions are nearly ideal. However, emergencies and interruptions can often be totally disorienting for the Conformist.

INDECISION AND REDUCED RISK-TAKING

At the Conformist Level, people find it difficult to make decisions. So fearful that they might be "wrong," or might incur the disapproval of others, they find themselves consequently plagued by inertia. However, as noted by psychologist William James, "When you have to make a choice and don't make it, that is in itself a choice."[22] At a managerial level avoiding decisions can be demoralizing for staff members as well as totally ineffective.

The Conformist strives for certainty even though such a condition is seldom possible. As John Dewey observed: "Love of certainty is a demand for guarantees in advance of actions."[23] Unfortunately, such certainty is seldom possible. Mark Rutherford in his treatise, "Principles," offers good advice for the Conformist:

> The demand for certainty is a sign of weakness, and if we persist in it, induces paralysis. The successful man is he who when he sees that no further certainty is attainable, promptly decides on the most probable side, as if he were completely sure it was right.[24]

The Conformist continually waits for more information, for some "sign" as to which direction to take, and thus remains mired.

Because of their lack of self-confidence and their fear of disapproval, Conformist managers often avoid risk-taking. Because they are unsure of their ability to adapt to new people or new challenges, Conformist managers resist change and avoid new situations. Thus, they adhere to practices and to methods of operation that worked previously to insure a sense of security.

NEED FOR PRAISE

For Conformist managers to work consistently and well, they need positive reinforcement from their supervisors and co-workers. Without encouragement or a positive working environment, they have problems staying involved in their work. They need to be reminded that their work is important and necessary, and that their efforts are appreciated.

Moreover, they have trouble working independently. Because Conformist managers try to please everyone, confusion often sets in. Since ambiguity is difficulty for them, they need explicit directions and clearly defined goals to operate efficiently. By breaking the work/task into smaller steps, and providing positive reinforcement, one can assist the Conformist to reach higher levels of maturity.

Supervisors need to recognize this need for positive recognition, without failing to provide constructive negative feedback as well. Regular, consistently scheduled feedback sessions are required in working with employees that are generally operating at this level of activity.

Dimensions of the Conformist Level

Self-Discipline

LACK OF FLEXIBILITY

For Conformist managers everything has to be "just right" for ongoing functioning. They display little flexibility or adaptability to changing circumstances. Unexpected delays, interruptions, or changes in plans are frustrating and anxiety-producing. Woodrow Wilson must have had the Conformist Level in mind when he said, "If you want to make enemies try to change something. You know why it is: to do things exactly the way you did them yesterday saves thinking."[25]

Yet, the world does change and new ways of responding and directing activities constantly are required. Rigidity may restrict personal opportunity and effectiveness as well as organizational succcess. Gladstone describes clearly the Conformist dilemma:

> Because of this need for regularity in organizing your life, it is almost impossible to achieve. Given the fluidness and unpredictability of most of life, you often find yourself over-extended, doing work which is not up to your sense of your potential. Because rigid organization requires planning for events which infrequently occur, much effort is wasted and you take longer to get your work done. You often demonstrate perfectionist behavior, spending too much time with details which aren't really very important procedures or taking shortcuts which reduce the quality of your work.[26]

Organizations need to provide training for people at this level to increase their flexibility, thereby reducing rigidity in thinking and action. Despite what many believe, such rigidity is not inherently restricted to older employees or managers. As Robertson Davies humorously stated:

> The whole world is burdened with young fogies. Old men with ossified minds are easily dealt with. But men who look young, act young, and everlasting harp on the fact that they are young, but who nevertheless think and act with a degree of caution that would be excessive in their grandfathers, are the curses of the world.[27]

NEED FOR CLEARLY-DEFINED FUNCTIONS, GOALS AND PRIORITIES

Because of their fear of ambiguity and of making mistakes, Conformists have an excessive need for clearly defined situations, to know exactly what is expected of them—what the priorities, goals and objectives are, as well as standards of performance. Vague departmental goals and directions are not enough; the Conformist requires specifics as an ongoing functional need.

Not to provide such clarity on management's part is to function irresponsibly. Unless procedures are clearly defined, the Conformist will often resort to ritualistic activity or impulsive behavior, more indicative of the Self-Protective Level. Ritualistic behavior does provide Conformists a sense of tension release and a feeling of accomplishment, even though such activities may be counter-productive to the goals of the department or the organization. Conformists without clearly designated tasks and functions can spend more time cleaning their desks in preparation for a task than the task itself would take. They typically develop a series of steps that are unnecessary for accomplishing the task. Their behavior becomes almost mechanical, treating all problems as though they were identical. Conversely, they often act impulsively, taking long lunches or coffee breaks, "to clear their heads." Or, they will take the afternoon off to go to the beach, or spend an inordinate amount of time chatting with co-workers about insignificant items. Such impulsive acts, like ritualistic behaviors, are non-productive and further evidence for providing clear and precise guidelines.

RESTRICTED CAPACITY FOR INTERNAL MOTIVATION AND CHANGE

Individuals at the Conformist Level will typically wait for something or someone else to motivate them. Still, they do make some effort to do something about situations that occur in their lives. At the higher levels, most motivation comes from "within." At the Conformist level, internalized motivation is just starting to develop.

William Gladstone sums up some of the major problems with self-discipline at the Conformist Level. At this level,

> You have difficulty learning from experience. Because you try to force everything and everyone into set patterns, you are unable to change and to grow. Your rigid responses are incapable of perceiving individual differences. You react to problems rather than acting on them. You are afraid to experiment with new strategies or to stray from tried solutions. You are cautious about changing behavior patterns and seek situations with which you are comfortable and which pose few threats. You do not experiment or modify your plans or your behavior. You do not generate changes but passively react to your environment. You are more often acted upon rather than being the actor. You have difficulty in directing and defining yourself and your life. You get by, sometimes very satisfactorily, but your success and happiness depends more on the actions of others than on any self-realizing behavior. You feel that your life is not as full as it might be and that you are not reaching your potential.[28]

Dimensions of the Conformist Level

Relationships

Conformist behavior characteristically emerges within relationships. Because people at this level react to others based upon what they learned as children, many relationships serve to re-enact childhood positions or as an opportunity to project onto others roles that are not part of reality. According to Abraham Maslow, this carry over from childhood can create major problems in the adult experience:

> . . . the greatest cause of our alienation from our real selves is our neurotic involvements with other people, the historical hangovers from childhood, the irrational transferences, in which past and present are confused, and in which the adult acts like a child . . . This means dropping our efforts to influence, to impress, to please, to be loveable, to win applause.[29]

RELATIONSHIPS BASED ON DRAMA

Stephen Karpmann in an article, "Fairy Tales and Script Drama Analysis," relates a concept called the "Drama Triangle."[30] According to Kartmann, every dramatic character can take one of three positions: the Persecutor, the Rescuer or the Victim.

For example, the traditional role of the boss is that of the Persecutor. Such a manager may begin an admonishment with, "If you don't start coming in on time, I'll have to write you up!" He may then switch to a Rescuer positon by explaining to the employee, "I'm only trying to help you." Finally, the same manager may feel victimized by the whole incident by saying, "Why doesn't anyone ever listen to me!"

Because they crave universal acceptance, Conformists often love to play Rescuer. They try to "help" others by doing their jobs for them. By so doing, Rescuers hope to gain recognition and induce others to depend upon them, thereby insuring constant interaction and a feeling of importance. Rescuer managers have an "open-door" policy and explicitly state that all problems should be brought to their attention. They then attempt to solve those problems **for** their staff members, (the Victims). Since these managers value friendliness, they hate making unpopular decisions and constantly try to please staff members even at the expense of the organization and the effectiveness of the department.

Unfortunately, playing the Rescuer is not effective. Typically, one becomes victimized by the people rescued. For example, a staff member may play the Victim by presenting a Rescuer boss with a problem, hoping for a solution. The Victim can then switch roles and persecute the Rescuer by evaluating the solution negatively or by saying to other staff members, "I gave my boss a problem two weeks ago, and he hasn't even solved it yet!"

Of course, the way out of the Drama is to take total responsibility. Instead of the manager attempting to solve problems **for** staff members, he or she needs to insist that they solve their problems, or recommend alternative solutions.

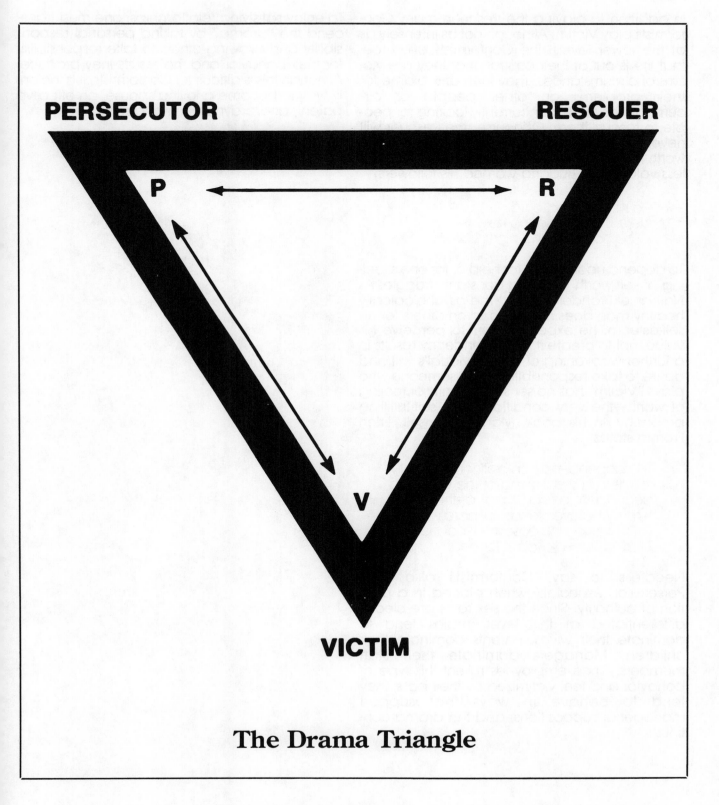

The Drama Triangle

Dimensions of the Conformist Level

In addition to playing the Rescuer, many Conformists play Victim. Although not as intensely as at the lower levels, the Conformists often feel that life is out of their control; that they are victims of circumstances. They then affix blame for their problems on other people or circumstances, while concurrently looking for people to rescue them. Of course, the Rescuer will never be able to provide a lasting sense of worth to the Victim, and so the Victim feels even less valued. As Buddha warned his followers:

> Do not depend on others;
> there is no grace, no help
> to be had from the other side.[31]

To depend upon others for help or for one's feeling of self-worth insures a constant struggle. As Nathaniel Branden states, "The psychologically healthy man does not depend on others for his self-esteem, he expects others to **perceive** his value, not to **create** it."[32] Dependency results in a further weakening of the individual's will and desire to take responsibility. Thus, someone who plays "Victim" has no sense of dignity or feeling of worth—the very conditions of a self-fulfilling prophecy. In his book, Man for Himself, Erich Fromm states:

> The dependence on irrational authority
> results in a weakening of the will in the
> dependent person, and, at the same
> time, whatever tends to paralyze the
> will fosters an increase in dependence.
> Thus, a vicious cycle is formed.[33]

Needless to say, Conformists also play Persecutor, especially when placed in a position of authority. Since the sex roles are clearly differentiated at this level, males tend to dominate their wives. Parents dominate their children. Managers dominate their staff members. Since employees resent this type of behavior and feel victimized by their boss, they tend to behave in ways that support managerial suppositions, and the drama continues.

To enjoy satisfying relationships, one must transcend the "Drama" by taking personal responsibility and allowing others to take responsibility for their behavior and the results they produce. Although this is diffcult for Conformists, it is the only way to become a loving spouse, an effective parent, and a dynamic manager.

RETENTION OF NEGATIVE EXPERIENCES: "STAMP COLLECTING"

Typical of the Conformist Level is the tendency to collect feelings of resentment, anger, jealousy, hurt, envy, and other negative emotions. After "enough" feelings are collected, the individual justifies negative behavior by recycling all the negative experiences.

Eric Berne referred to such a process as "stamp collecting." Comparing Conformist behavior to trading stamps, such as S&H Green Stamps, Berne described how Conformists often collect stamps whenever anything goes wrong. "Brown Stamps" refer to times when individuals say, "Oh Shit!" If they lose a major account they collect Brown Stamps. If their boss is angry or fails to notice when they've done a good job, they collect more Brown Stamps. At the "redemption center," one may select from "guilt-free" items such as a day off from work, an argument, a transfer, or a quit. Conformists save enough stamps to justify all kinds of behaviors from stealing from the company to sabotaging the production line. Typically they will exclaim "I've had it up to here!" or "That's the last straw!" before they go to the redemption center to "cash in" their stamps.

Other colors of stamps include "Red Stamps" for angry feelings. Red Stamp collectors can feel angry again just talking about whatever incident prompted their anger. At lower levels of maturity, individuals having collected enough Red Stamps can even justify homicide.

Conformists also collect "Blue Stamps" every time they feel hurt. Blue Stamp collectors often use such stamps for "guilt-free depressions." They will not stop feeling depressed until they close their Blue Stamp Book.

As observed earlier, Conformists constantly seek "Gold Stamps," or "good feeling" stamps which may be given as compliments or as acknowledgements for a task well-performed. Unfortunately, Conformists seldom give themselves Gold Stamps since they are so other-directed. Such is the plight of the typical "Organization Man":

. . .the person for whom reality "is" the world interpreted by the "significant others" of his social environment—the person whose sense of identity and personal worth is explicitly a function of his ability to satisfy the values, terms and expectations, of those omniscient and omnipresent "others." I am "as you desire me," such is the formula of his existence, such is the "genetic code," controlling his soul's development.[34]

Since most organizations cannot possibly satisfy their unquenchable desire for positive recognition, Conformists turn a lack of positive feedback into Brown Stamps.

To make matters even worse, Conformists often reject positive recognition when it is offered because they do not feel "worthy" of the recognition. They will "discount" or lower the value of the acknowledgement, or they will deny the Gold Stamp by giving it to others. For example, Conformists might respond in the following ways:

Manager: "Sue, you did a great job on that report."

Sue: "Well, anyone could have done it."

or

Manager: "Bob, the system you installed is really operating beautifully."

Bob: "Well, it was Fred's design."

Thus, one can see the Conformists' "dilemma": wanting recognition constantly and yet, not feeling worthy of the recognition.

Dimensions of the Conformist Level

Stamp Collecting

PLAYS PSYCHOLOGICAL GAMES

Because their behavior is predictable, Conformists play what Eric Berne referred to as psychological games.[35] Each person enacts a series of "moves" with a final outcome. These games become the scenes in the Drama and are the sources of the stamps.

Games in business cost billions of dollars. Their primary purpose is to play life from effect and to avoid responsibility. Games are used to avoid authenticity, to structure time, to fulfill negative life positions and to ensure the maintenance of the life script. The following are classifications of games, using a description of business applications.

Berne's Games People Play is a complete description of the maneuvers and consequences of such behaviors. People generally are unconscious of the games they play and are often unaware that they are involved in a game until it is over and they are left with bad feelings. Although played at all levels, except at the Responsible Level, games are more serious at the lowest levels. People at the Unconscious Level and the Self-Protective Level can lose their lives through such game playing.

At the Conformist Level games are played frequently, but with a "pay-off" of bad feelings and drama. Since most people spend most of their time at the Conformist Level, games are frequently played at work. Games allow participants to avoid responsibility and to create "scenes" that add drama and interest—at the expense of personal and professional satisfaction and productivity.

Dimensions of the Conformist Level

Psychological Games to Prove "You're Not OK"

Blaming Others

If it weren't for you.................. "I could get some work done, etc., etc."

Now see what you made me do......... "It's your fault, not mine!"

Uproar.......................... A shouting, accusing game, extolling "It's your fault."

Look how hard I've tried............. "Are you so blind that you can't see how valuable I am?"

Look what you're doing to me.......... "See the bags under my eyes; my recent divorce, etc."

You got me into this................ "I didn't want that transfer, new position, etc."

Saving Others

I'm only trying to help you........... "Are you so dumb that you won't follow my advice?"

What would you do without me?........ "I'm so valuable—you'd probably just shrivel up and die without me."

Why don't you—Yes, but............ "Why didn't you plan ahead?" "Yes, but I couldn't because Joe . . ." "Why didn't you ask Joe to . . ." "I could have, but then I would have had to . . . so that wouldn't have worked either." "Did you try?" "Yes, but . . . etc. etc."

Finding Fault

Mine's better..................... My idea, my house, my car, my spouse, my kids, my job, etc.

Blemish......................... "Your report was fine, Bill, but you missed a comma on page 16."
Or, "You're 82¢ off on your budget calculations."

Getting Even

"N.I.G.Y.S.O.B."................. The original "Got-Cha" game.

I'll show them.................... Ha. Ha.

Let's make the boss sorry............ He didn't listen to your suggestions.

Let's you and him fight.............. "Well, John said that you said that . . ."

Psychological Games to Prove "I'm Not OK"

Provoking Put-Downs

Kick me.............................."You didn't say the report was due on Friday, you said..."(After you stated three times that it was due).

Stupid.............................."Oh, Mr. Smith, you know that urgent letter that you needed mailed last Friday: I just found it right here in my desk!"

Cops and Robbers....................Extortions, embezzlement, petty thievery, very risky behavior.

Debtor.............................."I know my third payment is past due but..."

Drop me.............................From the committee, staff, or group...

Schlemiel, schlemiel................"Oh, Mr. Kozek, I'm sorry I spilled coffee all over your final report. I really am. I just can't do anything right. I'm really sorry. I am, really."

Copping Out

Harried.............................Volunteering for more assignments than one could possibly handle.

How do I get out of here?...........Transfer to another department, division, or company.

Enjoying Misery

Poor me............................."I've got so much work to do and no one to help and now my car broke down and my kids are giving me fits and..."

Wooden leg.........................."If only I didn't have this wooden leg, then I could be successful."

You'll have to take me as I am......"I don't like me either, but we're all stuck with me this way!"

Lush..............................."I'm so depressed, I need a drink and I'm so hung-over, I just can't be effective. So I get depressed..."

Why does this always happen to me?......One gets to be right, over and over again.

Martyr..............................Playing the Victim and being the "effect" of one's negative experiences.

73

Dimensions of the Conformist Level

Physical State

At the Conformist Level individuals experience many physical ailments because they do not live particularly healthy lives. They often exhibit poor eating, sleeping, and exercise habits, and so are often prime candidates for infectious diseases. In addition, they generally feel tired and exhausted much of the time. Psychological game playing and going through "Drama" are serious energy drains. Much of the Conformist's life is spent trying to keep things "under control." As Maslow noted:

> It is a desperate effort at control. A good deal of his energy is taken up with it and so he is apt to get tired just simply controlling himself. It is a source of fatigue. But he can manage and get along by protecting himself against...his real self, which he has been taught to regard as dangerous.[36]

Whenever the "real self" is exposed, the Conformist feels anxiety. According to many theories and research, anxiety and stress seem to be the real culprits behind the physical problems. The ailments, according to Nathaniel Branden, are:

> ...direct physical consequences of anxiety, such as headaches, choking sensations, heart palpitations, intestinal ailments, dizziness, tremblings, nausea, excessive perspiration, insomnia, painful bodily tensions, and chronic fatigue. Sometimes they represent defenses against anxiety, such as hysterical paralysis, obsessions, compulsions, and passive depression.[37]

TYPICALLY EITHER OBESE OR THIN

A typical symptom of Conformity is over-eating to avoid tension rather than to reduce hunger. Because Conformists show such a compulsion to eat and because they do not exhibit much self-discipline, the vicious circle is complete. Even worse, because of the resulting excess weight, Conformists seldom exercise enough. Since social approval is so important to them, Conformists often feel too "embarrassed" to jog or swim. The opposite effect of anxiety for some people is not to eat because of a lack of appetite, indicative of withdrawal and self-punishment. Though there may be physical reasons for weight problems, these are typically indications of inner stress and functioning at lower levels of maturity.

The main point is the individual's refusal —however, subtle and justifiable—to do anything to ameliorate such self-abusive conditions.

SLEEP DISTURBANCES

Similarly, opposite extremes of sleep disturbances can be symptoms of Conformist functioning. Some Conformists use sleep to escape rather than to face problems. By doing nothing about the cause of their anxiety, they can experience mild depression and chronic oversleeping.

Others enact just the opposite condition. They have insomnia or wake up in the middle of the night and have difficulty going back to sleep. Typically, this allows the people to go through circular worrying and to punish themselves for not doing certain things or for going against parental or social injunctions.

GASTRO-INTESTINAL PROBLEMS

Individuals at this level often experience **chronic** problems with upset stomachs, gas, and diarrhea or constipation. Such chronic problems can lead to serious diseases if the anxiety is not alleviated.

FREQUENT, SEVERE HEADACHES

Americans use literally tons of aspirin each year to rid themselves of the symptoms of the anxiety they experience. Rather than asking themselves **why** they may be experiencing the headaches, Conformists look for ways to alleviate the symptoms, rather than the problem.

SKIN PROBLEMS

Skin rashes, hives and eczema seem to be indicative of the stress at this level. Severe acne following emotional outbursts or feelings of unworthiness is typical.

PHYSICAL TICS/STUTTERING

Although physical conditions are often related to tics and stuttering, both conditions are exaggerated by nervousness. In the case of tics, the individual is often unaware of a twitching eye or the movement of a wrist until someone else points it out. Tics, like stuttering, are related to the stress experienced at this level.

MEDICAL ASSISTANCE TO FEEL BETTER

Most physicians spend most of their time with individuals at the Conformist Level who depend and rely on medical assistance to "feel better." Yet, when they do not take their prescriptions or follow their doctors advice to quit smoking, lose weight, or exercise more, they typically blame their doctor for their feelings of ill health and attempt to find another one. Mild cases of hypochondria are typically found at this stage of development.

EPISODIC DRUG ABUSE

At the Conformist Level individuals come to rely on drugs to help them cope. Rather than take drugs for specific problems, they do so to relieve general tension. Gradually, they become dependent upon sleeping pills, tranquilizers, stimulants, and aspirin to feel better.

In addition, marijuana and alcohol are used in excess to alleviate signs of stress. As Gladstone reports,

> In both cases, you know you have problems when you can no longer control your intake of these substances. It is this dependence and overindulgence that indicates underlying mental problems, not the substance, per se.[38]

75

Dimensions of the Conformist Level

Spiritual Dimension

In his life-long search for a description of how mentally healthy individuals function, Abraham Maslow finally concluded that much of what was considered to be neurotic behavior, was more related to spiritual disorders than anything else. The roots of such behavior may be attributed

> . . . to loss of meaning, to doubts about the goals of life, to grief and anger over a lost love, to seeing life a different way, to loss of courage or of hope, to despair over the future, to dislike of one's self, to recognition that one's life is being wasted, or that there is no possibility of joy or love.[39]

Conformists experience just such a state of spiritual disorder. They think that religion and church-going will fill the void, and yet continue to experience a sense of something missing. The following are typical manifestations of the Conformists' spiritual dimension.

RITUALISTIC BEHAVIOR DETACHED FROM SPIRITUAL UNDERSTANDING

Conformists tend to prefer rituals in religion. They do not see any need to ask **why** the rituals were created in the first place or why they are important now. Because they like specifically defined tasks, they tend to look for a "policy manual" for getting to heaven.

Going to church for them is often more of a social event than a religious experience. There, the emphasis is on appearance, being nice to others, and a sense of belonging. Since they lack flexibility, changes in church rituals can be extremely difficult for Conformists. They cling to tradition for its own sake.

Ironically, though Conformists usually are staunchly in favor of religious values, they often behave quite differently. Since they can compartmentalize their lives, what is said and agreed upon on Sunday morning seems to have little bearing during the other six days of the week.

TYRANNY OF "SHOULDS" "OUGHTS" AND "MUSTS" ACCOMPANIED BY A CONSTANTLY PUNISHING CONSCIENCE

Spiritual concerns at the Conformist Level center upon one's behavior. Because they accepted and internalize their parents' demands and values, they transfer the same approach to the spiritual dimension.

This emphasis is manifested intellectually by a punishing conscience. Rather than emphasizing positive action, the internal dialogue concentrates on what one should **not** do, say or think. Considerable time is spent avoiding potentially sinful places and people, without concern for positive action. Because they are more concerned with what others think of them, the greatest sin for the Conformists is to be talked about or even thought about negatively by others. For this reason, "What will people think?" is a primary concern for the Conformist.

SELF-VIEWED AS "VICTIM"

Because the Conformist relationships are marked by Drama, the same dramatic scenes are projected outward, even to one's spiritual values. At this level, the God-figure is typically seen as either the Persecutor (punisher) or the Rescuer (Savior) with the individual assuming a Victim position.

Feelings of helplessness and of unworthiness are indicative of this level. Ironically, such feelings are also used to justify negative behavior as well. At the Conformist Level one often feels existentially helpless in the face of more potent forces.

At this level, communication with the greater being typically takes the form of asking forgiveness—as one would do with a punishing parent; or of praying for some special prize: the health of a loved one, a raise, a lover, or the recovery of something lost. Yet, when life does not go as planned, the Conformist is quick to chide God, "Why did you not come to my rescue?" or "Why did you do this to me?"

Some religious leaders also act out roles in the Drama—either assuming a "hell, fire, and brimstone," threatening, accusing, punishing persecutor role, or a kind, gentle, "shepherd" rescuing role. At this level little thought is given to implementing the concepts of love of fellow man or to what spiritual life truly means.

TENDENCY TO FOLLOW THE RULES, WITHOUT REGARD TO EVALUATION OF CIRCUMSTANCES

To the Conformists, rules are made to be followed, not questioned. Thus, "let your conscience be your guide" is very disturbing advice for the Conformist. People at this level want to be told what to do, under what circumstances and with whom. They do not want to think about spiritual questions. They blindly accept their leader's words and follow, almost sheeplike, without challenging the authority. The Jonestown incident, in which over 500 people took their own lives, is a frightening aspect of such a non-thinking, rulebound Conformist view. Religious wars have been fought and are still being fought with no awareness that the actions being taken are a direct antithesis of the religion to which they ascribe their values.

Since the emotions of fear, guilt, shame and inadequacy are frequently experienced by Conformists, they are easily manipulated by leaders who can trigger such emotions. Because Conformists follow perfectionist mind models, they establish impossible models for themselves. Then whenever they fall short, they experience the same sense of being unworthy in the eyes of God that they often especially feel in the eyes of others.

The Five Levels

	EMOTIONAL RESPONSE	INTELLECTUAL FUNCTIONING	ACTIVITY INVOLVEMENT
CONFORMIST	Stress and tension without cause. Fear, guilt, shame and inadequacy. Long recovery time. Intermittent hysterics.	Cognitive simplicity—"right/wrong". Intellectualizes rather than experiences. Circular worrying. Perfectionistic. Cognitive preoccupation: acceptance, appearance.	Pointless activities. Reduced risk taking. Need for praise.
SELF-PROTECTIVE	External causation. Emotional shifts. Hysterical behavior. Fear dominant emotion.	Blind to factual data. Difficulty with decision making. Chronic distortion of reality. Cognitive preoccupation: sex and aggression.	Avoidance of challenging activities. Little self-confidence. Work as anxiety-avoidance not a source of satisfaction.
UNCONSCIOUS	Unrelated to reality. Extreme shifts. Great stress and anxiety evident.	Difficulty in processing information. Obsessive thoughts. Gross perceptual distortion. Cognitive preoccupation: survival.	Ritualistic and compulsive behavior. Difficulty in changing. Extreme fear of attempting anything new.

SELF-DISCIPLINE	RELATIONSHIPS	PHYSICAL STATE	SPIRITUAL DIMENSION
Lack of flexibility. Need for clear definitions. Restricted internal motivation.	Drama roles. Retention of negative experiences. Psychological games.	Obese or thin. Sleep disturbances. Gastro-intestinal problems. Headaches. Skin problems. Physical tics/stuttering. Medical assistance necessary. Episodic drug abuse.	Ritualistic emphasis. Tyranny of "shoulds," "oughts," and "musts." Self-view as victim. Rules followed not questioned.
Obsessively ritualistic. Robot-like behavior. Opportunistic. Difficulty in learning.	Withdrawal, dependency, hostility. Unconcerned with agreements, commitments or rules.	Psychosomatic illness. No appetite/muscular soreness. Chronic drug abuse.	Non-ethical. Moral level: "Don't get caught".
Little self-control of motivation. Work contingent upon external conditions. Impulsive.	Unconsciousness in presence of others. Total communication breakdown. No concern for others. Little change from negative feedback.	Blank staring. Severe physical problems. Addictions.	Ethically or morally unconcerned. Fanatical behavior.

"You can never get enough of what you don't need to make you happy."[1]

—Eric Hoffer

"If there is one prime principle that should never be forgotten, it is this: the thrust of creative energy is always weakened by repetitive urgency."[2]

—Dr. Freidman and Dr. Rosenman
Type A Behavior and Your Heart

"The fool is his own enemy.
Seeking wealth, he destroys himself.
Honor the man who is without passion.
   hatred, illusion, and design,
What you give him
   will be given back to you
   and more."[3]

—Buddha

Chapter Five

THE ACHIEVEMENT MANAGER

At the Achievement Level, managers are in a state of perpetual striving and frenzied activity. The notion of "Management By Crisis" seems to have been coined with them in mind. Yet, because their energies are focused on achievements and meeting deadlines, most corporations and organizations have reinforced Achievement Level behavior. Indeed, not to do so, would seem almost anti-business, not to mention un-American.

The Achievement Level appears to be the result of what such men as De Tocqueville, Thoreau, Henry Adams, and Sir William Osler[4] warned us about in their writings. These men of vision saw the increasing pace of life that seemed to affect all urban people, especially in America. The frenzied pace, coupled with an industrial society's emphasis on acquiring more and more wealth, is characteristic of the Achievement Level.

Americans did not just learn to accept the hurried pace; indeed, in many respects, we have made it an ideal. Until recently, the Achievement Level has been considered a very desirable way of thinking and living, and an end toward which the American system of education and free enterprise has striven.

Historically, America's rapid pace and emphasis on acquisitions, coupled with a "classless' society, has produced a large number of individuals at the Achievement Level:

> America's own economy means that while opportunity is at least theoretically available to all, the absolute need to compete is also universal. In our century, the struggle has become stronger with each succeeding decade. Today, with the ownership of almost all large corporations in the hands of shareholders and foundations, management jobs go to the able. It is the performance, not pedigree, that achieves high economic status.[5]

Therein lies the crux of the problem for American management. Because growth and financial success are based on achievement and because managers, themselves, have come to use achievement as a measure of stature, how can organizations promote achievement without promoting the sense of frenzy that can kill people?

Recent medical research points to the conclusion that emotional stress can inflict physical illness and deterioration, even to the point of death. Studies noted by Drs. Friedman and Rosenman in their book, Type A Behavior and Your Heart, reinforce the causal relationship between Achievement Level behavior and coronary disease.

In this respect, organizations need to ask whether "executive burnout" and early death or disability are not expensive prices to pay for short-term gains. Such pragmatic reasoning has led many organizations to promote health programs, jogging marathons, and stress seminars.

Apart from the human considerations, organizations are beginning to realize that managers at the Achievement Level are not as effective or as efficient as those who have learned to plan and to delegate effectively. Paradoxically, Achievement Level managers do not actually achieve as much as their less frenzied peers at the Responsible Level.

By "slowing down" and becoming more reflective and psychologically secure, managers become much more effective, creative, and skilled in working with others. Thus, organizations need to become increasingly concerned with helping managers grow so they can transcend the Achievement Level.

To grow beyond the Achievement Level one has to attain internal security by relinquishing behavior patterns which only deflect the individual from that goal. The Achiever associates satisfaction with successful competition and acquisition. Because of a never-ending search for new challenges and competition, not only is the satisfaction short-lived, it is never quite "good enough."

Since their happiness is primarily dependent upon external events, managers at this level seldom achieve a sense of internal security. Eventually, many Achievers reach ". . .a stage in which the habits developed to achieve this goal break lose to take command over the person's whole life. They emerge to harass their possessor even when there is no longer any real need for him to hurry or to fight."[6]

The following description of the various dimensions at this level are offered to assist managers to transcend this level. By becoming truly successful and finally finding the sense of internal security which they have been trying so hard to create externally in the past, managers can begin to operate at the Responsible Level.

Dimensions of the Achievement Level

Emotional Response

The emotional response at the Achievement Level is the primary cause of coronary disease. Such responses are tantamount to a state of emergency. Because of their sense of urgency and impatience, managers at this level often create "emergencies" of time constraint where none would have to exist. In addition they often underestimate the time it takes to accomplish tasks. So the self-inflicted emergency coping cycle is constantly being reinforced.

The following emotions are indicative of Achievement Level:

SENSE OF FUTILITY

Many of today's managers ask, "What's it all about?" They somewhat desperately, though often quietly, insist that there is more to life than achievement and the fast pace. As Erich Fromm observed in Man for Himself:

> There is an increasing number of people to whom everything they are doing seems futile. They are still under the spell of the slogans which preach faith in the secular paradise of success and glamor. But doubt, the fertile condition of all progress, has begun to beset them and has made them ready to ask what their real self-interest as human beings is.[7]

Many managers caught in the Achievement syndrome are beginning to ask, "When is enough. . .enough?" Thousands of others complain of feeling "empty" and "unfulfilled," without knowing why. They function as though their mental computers were programmed to "try harder," while never being satisfied in the process or by the outcome.

Dimensions of the Achievement Level

HARRIED AND AGGRESSIVE

The most indicative emotion of the Achievement Level is a feeling of being harried, rushed, or otherwise frenzied. Yet according to Friedman and Rosenman, the Achievement syndrome

> . . . is not a psychosis or a complex of worries or fears or phobias or obsessions, but a socially acceptable—indeed, often praised form of conflict. Persons possessing this pattern also are quite prone to exhibit a free-floating, but extraordinarily well-rationalized hostility.

> But, excess aggression and certainly hostility are not always easily detected. . .if only because they so often keep such feelings and impulses under deep cover. Very few are even aware of their excess aggression and almost none is aware of his hostility.[8]

Such hostility may be an unconscious reaction against one's parents who may have placed conditions for their love as in "If you do such and such, then we'll love you." Parents may also have rejected any achievement as not quite good enough. Despite these conditions, Achievers learned to strive for parental love and acceptance, thereby establishing their characteristic pattern while also creating the resentment they still feel, but rarely acknowledge. Because the resulting hostility was against strong, powerful parental figures and could not be openly displayed, it became free-floating. Thus, the Achievers sometimes display hostile reactions against time, other people, objects and even themselves.

INSECURITY

Though most individuals at the Achievement Level appear very self-confident and quite secure, they suffer from an insecurity that others will not give them their rightfully-earned status or esteem. Such a problem stems from the fact that Achievers measure their own sense of self-worth by their achievements that are perceived by others who are deemed to have status in the Achiever's world.

For this reason, Achievers often react quite negatively when they are contradicted or when others blatantly disagree with them. The classic example of the Achiever boss, surrounded by a group of Conformist "yes men" is indicative of their insecurity. Achievement Level managers and executives need to heed Francois de Fenelon's advice:

> Trust only those who have the courage to contradict you with respect, and who value your character more than favor.[9]

HYPEREMOTIONAL STATES

One of the common signs of the Achievement Level is overly demonstrative displays of emotions. Achievers sometimes laugh too loudly at jokes or shout when things are not working according to plan. Individuals at this level are responding to actual events and situations. Yet, the intensity of their response is in excess of what is appropriate. Because of this tendency, Achievers may show disproportionate concern or affection for people with whom they are not close, and yet have trouble establishing intimacy with family members.

Intellectual Functioning

SELECTIVELY UNCONSCIOUS

Individuals at the previous levels of development are often not aware that they are unconscious. At the Achievement Level, individuals realize that they have the capacity to "tune out" information that they do not want to hear or see. Indeed, they have developed this capacity so well that they can appear to be listening when they are thinking of other things.

Rather than risk potential frustration, Achievers can ignore situations or people that upset them by simply going unconscious. Because of this ability, Achievers create a corollary problem—that of keeping their attention focused on a particular task or problem. According to Friedman and Rosenman, people at this level:

> . . .do not experience free-flowing, constructive thinking. Problem-solving is not effortless, but demands concentrated thinking which is intense and immediate. They cannot allow thoughts to wander, for fear of not being able to return to the problem at hand.[10]

RIGID SOLUTIONS UTILIZED FOR EXPEDIENCY

When time constraints become intolerable, Achievers sometimes resort to stereotypic thinking and rigid solutions to accomplish the given task as quickly as possible. In short, the Achievement-oriented often sacrifice creativity for speed. According to Friedman and Rosenman,

> If sometimes he still seems to display brilliance, it is usually due to those original and creative concepts which he may have formulated in his younger years—before he became totally enslaved to this [Achievement Level]. But this earlier collected cache of concepts can serve him well as long as the milieu and its demand remain relatively unchanged.

> Desperately he tries to run faster in his old ways to overcome a problem whose solution cannot be achieved by stereotyped and hasty thinking, but only by creative, time-free contemplation and deliberation. The ranks of corporate middle management contain more than just a few thousand such condemned hangers-on.[11]

Dimensions of the Achievement Level

CONCEPTUAL COMPLEXITY

Unlike previous levels, managers at the Achievement Level are capable of true conceptual complexity. They are able to perceive multiple possibilities for solutions to problems and are aware of the many choices available in any given situation.

In addition, people at the Achievement Level recognize and acknowledge psychological causation for events in their experience.

POLYPHASIC THOUGHT PATTERNS

Achievement Level managers often attempt to think along several lines at once. Because they release stress through a rich fantasy life, they can become ineffective. For example, while at a staff meeting they may imagine aggressive, hostile acts against their competitors. Such thought patterns do not seriously impair one's effectiveness as they do at lower levels; yet, they do require more vigilance and control than at the Responsible Level.

REACTIVE RATHER THAN PROACTIVE INTELLECTUAL FUNCTIONING

Because the Achievers' intellectual activity is primed to react to one crisis after another, little time is spent thinking proactively—to avoid problems in the future. This mode of intellectual functioning further complicates the process, while also confirming the syndrome itself.

The Achievement manager needs to heed the advice of David Grayson:

> Is it not the prime struggle of life to keep the mind plastic? To see and feel and hear things newly? To accept nothing as settled? To defend the eternal right of the questioner? To reflect every conclusion of yesterday before the surer observations of today? Is that not the best life we know?[12]

Activity Involvement

FRENZIED

Managers at the Achievement Level promote a sense of hurried, frenzied activity. Since the intent of such a pace is to increase the number of achievements, individuals at this level tend to subvert the quality of performance for quantity. Achievers compensate for the deficit by trying desperately to trade off the number of their achievements against their inherent value. Yet, even the frenzied pace itself can become boring. According to Dr. Ralph Greison in <u>The American Male</u>:

> It is characteristic of our big city organizational society that there's an agitated boredom that goes through everything. This looks like activity. Men are doing all kinds of things—except when you study what they're doing, they're performing avoidance of all kinds.[13]

Though the goal of such frenzied activity appears to be money and material objects, it is generally not money per se that fascinates the Achiever. Money is simply a symbol of success in the "numbers game" to which they have dedicated themselves. Seldom satisfied, Achievers seem to be in a never-ending struggle to acquire more and more wealth to fill a void that is consistently self-created.

POLYPHASIC ACTIVITIES

In their quest for accomplishment, managers at the Achievement Level often attempt two or three activities at once, and take great pride in so doing. Listening to motivational tapes in the car, studying while watching television, and taking reading material into the bathroom, are all examples of such polyphasic activities. Such multiple activity, though it may effectively utilize time, is nonetheless characteristic of functioning at the Achievement Level.

ROUTINE ACTIVITY

As with their thought patterns, Achievers often resort to ritualistic activities that have worked in the past. To insure success, they prefer to follow a set routine, only to become quite upset when unexpected interruptions disturb their preconceived agenda. Hence, they often find it difficult to switch from one activity to another.

IMPORTANCE OF GOALS, DEADLINES, PRIORITIES, AND RISKS

At this level, managers place high importance on setting goals, both short-term and long-term. However, because they are unrealistic in their estimate about the amount they can do and deadlines they can meet, they often feel frustrated in the process of achieving their goals. So even though they are willing to take risks, establish priorities, set goals, and meet deadlines—all positive activities—they do so for negative reasons. Managers at this level need to change their motivational patterns and perspective, not their activities.

Dimensions of the Achievement Level

Self-Discipline

MOTIVATED BY INTERNALIZED ANXIETY
Managers at this level are motivated to accomplish their goals by the fear of not achieving the results; in short, they fear failure. This is quite different from the desire for success that motivates people at the Responsible Level. Because Achievers depend upon anxiety to "inspire" or motivate them, they often feel more pressured than those at the Responsible Level.

INTOLERANCE OF AMBIGUITY AND UNCERTAINTY
Although less so than at other levels, Achievers also do not like ambiguity. Because their organizational skills are less developed than those at the Responsible Level, managers at the Achievement Level will, according to Gladstone, ". . .use any means possible to assure a positive outcome. They feel the need to 'play with a full deck' so nothing unexpected will occur."[14] Although aware of the benefits of long-range planning and the nature of complex problem-solving, these managers spend an inordinate amount of time hopelessly trying to eliminate ambiguity and uncertainty.

UNDERDEVELOPED PLANNING CAPABILITY
Even though Achievers may produce results comparable to the Responsible Level, the quality of their planning is not as effective. Managers at the Achievement Level are not as creative in their solutions and so have to rely on "hard work" and anxiety-driven drudgery to get the task completed. Though productive, they do not experience the sense of satisfaction they could if they planned more effectively. To quote a management cliché, if individuals at this level would "plan their work" and "work their plan," they could eliminate much of their experienced drudgery.

Relationships

OTHER-DIRECTED NEED FOR ESTEEM
Individuals at all levels want to have the respect of others. But at the Achievement Level, managers seem to be consumed by their frenzy to elicit such respect through their achievements. However, they have to feel that any form of recognition was warranted. This creates a never-ending struggle. Achievers feel they deserve praise only when they increase their achievements. Yet, receiving recognition becomes only a temporary source of satisfaction. Because of their insecurity about their own self-worth, they tend to exaggerate any negative feedback they receive. At the Responsible Level, people have a truer sense of their abilities and capabilities. Although responsible people are interested in the opinions of others, they are not destroyed by them or anxious about them. At the Achievement Level, managers often overact to even mild criticism. To retaliate, they sometimes create friction and distance with the source of criticism, even to the point of ending the relationship or quitting the job. Thus, because they lack a strong sense of self-worth, Achievement Level managers rely on others to provide a sense of esteem, and avoid those who offer negative feedback.

COMPETITION

The individuals at the Achievement Level automatically think that others want to compete with them—a socially reinforced view. According to George A. Morgan in <u>Prophetic Voices</u>:

> Our social fabric militates against relation. Competitiveness pervades everything we do and is taught from the time we are small children. Work and play are conceived of as a contest and race. . .we seize the one-half-truth that competition forces everyone to do his best (half-truth, because his best is by no means always the best in human terms), and completely ignore what this does to human meeting. Our fundamental stance is not to respond to others, but to outdo them, vie with them, beat them.[15]

Because of this pervasive need to compete with others, many Achievers feel the need to dominate most relationships, so that no one will be able to take advantage of them. The competition often becomes very apparent when managers at the Achievement Level encounter each other. Such an encounter may be a reflective experience of self, as the following description demonstrates:

> You feel hostile almost instanteously on meeting another hostile person. . .You are probably mirror images of each other. Each of you competes to be the talker, not the listener. Each of you competes not to learn from the other, but to teach and correct. Each of you strives so hard to receive the verbalized respect for each other. . .You unconsciously irritate each other by interrupting and hurrying the speech of the other. These conversations abound in such remarks as, "But you've already said that" or "If you would let me get a word in edgewise!" These are not conversations, they are battles, silly needless battles.[16]

This constant struggle against others produces the same physiological response as when one struggles against time or circumstances.[17]

Dimensions of the Achievement Level

WORK-RELATED EMPHASIS

For many managers at the Achievement Level, their primary human interactions and relationships are work-related. They seldom interact with individuals from whom they have little to gain. When Achievers are invited to purely social gatherings, they often feel that they are "wasting" their time because they are not "accomplishing" anything.

Managers at the Achievement Level often talk only to the "right" people, while low status people are ignored. This is not because of snobbery; it is simply that such individuals are not viewed as useful for the Achievement Level manager. In fact, the boredom and frustration felt in such "non-productive" associations is symptomatic of how de-humanized one's relationships have become.

Because Achievement relationships are goal directed, families and close personal friends are often ignored. As John Oliver Hobbes once remarked, "A man with a career can have no time to waste upon his wife and friends; he has to devote it wholly to his enemies."[18]

Like so many circumstances at the Achievement Level, this situation produces a paradox. One of the reasons for the free-floating hostility is a frustrated desire for love and affection, and yet, because of the Achiever's over-emphasis on acquisition, the circumstances for love-fulfillment are seldom available. As the Indian guru, Rajneesh once exclaimed, "It's difficult to love a running man!"[19]

Unfortunately, many managers at this level fail to realize that their professional and personal lives are reflections of one another. In Love or Perish, Dr. Smiley Blanton, noted:

> Life is all one piece. Men err when they think they can be inhuman exploiters in their business life, and loving husbands and fathers at home. For achievement without love is a cold and tight-lipped murderer of human happiness everywhere.[20]

When managers at the Achievement Level experience stress, their interpersonal behavior typically suffers the most. They may then use anger or depression to manipulate others to pay attention to them, or they may project their anger outward. Leo Tolstoy once observed:

> Who does not know men, inaccessible to truth or kindliness, who are always so busy that they never have a minute to ask themselves whether their work is not harmful. The most cruel men—your Neros and Peter the Greats—were constantly occupied.[21]

Thus, the over-emphasis on work and achievement-directed relationships can make life quite "serious" for the Achiever. For managers at this level the ability to have fun with others and to enjoy relationships for their own sake may be seriously hampered.

Physical State

PREDISPOSITION TO CORONARY DISEASE

As mentioned earlier, managers at the Achievement Level have a greater chance of an early death resulting from coronary disease. According to Friedman and Rosenman, the Achiever's "...ceaseless striving, his everlasting struggle with time...so frequently leads to his early demise from coronary heart disease."[22]

The increase in coronary problems for women in management positions may be directly attributed to the increase in stress resulting from the Achievement syndrome—a dramatic change from the not-so-distant past when heart disease was primarily a male disorder. The increase in female heart disease is the result of a change, not in terms of activities, but in the level of stress:

> ...most American women, at least in the immediate past, have remained in their homes and although have had many chores to do, relatively few were constrained to work under conditions whose essence consisted of deadlines and competition and hostility.[23]

For managers at the Achievement Level, changing their behavior patterns may be a matter of life and death. To do so, individuals need to alter their physical and mental habits. A New York physician, aged 49, five years after a severe heart attack, stated it this way:

> I began to appreciate how severe my sense of time urgency had been and how much of it was due to my aggressive overdrive to be too many things to too many people...I knew finally that my first aim had to be to survive and to survive in terms of beauty, life's beauty.

> I have learned to garden, to spend more time with my wife and children, and most important of all, to enjoy spending my time and in the fashion I did not do so before my attack.

> I know I haven't changed my basic personality just as a leopard doesn't really change his spots...But, I have learned to make various adjustments in my milieu so that my personality isn't challenged and aroused—it simply slumbers. After all, a sleeping tiger is as gentle as a sleeping rabbit, just don't challenge him by awakening him. And so I play a game with my basically hostile personality: I try to keep it 'asleep.' This isn't always easy...it amounts to a conscious and constant surveillance of everything I am doing and what I must stop doing. But what a small price to pay for the fun of living this new part of life...[24]

Dimensions of the Achievement Level

STRESS RELATED SYMPTOMS

At the Achievement Level, managers create a great deal of stress by adhering to the directive of "more and more accomplishment in less and less time." Consequently, they may suffer from such gastro-intestinal problems as indigestion and gas. In addition, Achievers sometimes have difficulty getting to sleep at night often worrying about the next day and fretting about what they should have done.

Skin disorders, such as acne in younger adults, as well as hives and skin rashes, may also be induced or complicated by the stress experienced at this level.

FATIGUE AND EXHAUSTION

Understandably, managers at the Achievement Level often feel "worn out" and exhausted from the day's activities. This is not so much a function of the results they produced, as much as it reflects the psychological energy and tension expended to get the job done. People at this level sometimes feel pushed to their limits and tire very easily, sometimes complaining of stiff muscles.

Yet, these recurring symptoms are regarded as "normal" with many managers at this level unaware of how their behavior patterns have induced their presence. Even so, these are early warning signals that action needs to be taken to eliminate some of the causes of reactive patterns to stress. One needs to become aware of the symptoms and results of stress.

Katherine Hathway suggests that people should listen more to their bodies:

> One reason, maybe, why Americans die so young in middle age—especially in cities—is because they do not know their own bodies. They force themselves to live and do things without any psychic acquaintance with their bodies. Their instinct is deaf to the language of the body, which would tell them how to live, if they would listen to it.[25]

DRUGS USED CONSCIOUSLY TO COPE WITH STRESS
To deal with symptoms of stress, individuals at the Achievement Level often, and very deliberately, use sleeping pills, tranquilizers, and stimulants and depressants. Such substances consist of both legal and illegal drugs in the form of coffee, aspirin, or alcohol, to marijuana or "speed." Alcohol has traditionally been the Achievers' primary coping substance—used to help them relax, to relate to others and to restore equilibrium. And yet, such use is not "abuse." At the Achievement Level, unlike previous levels, individuals

> . . .are conscious of what drugs or stimulants they take and are aware of their effects upon them and why they are taking them. They do serve to reduce tension and they are able to dispense with them when not under pressure. Above all, they are not dependent upon drugs to get them through a normal day and do not take drugs automatically when anything goes wrong.[26]

Spiritual Dimension

ETHICAL QUESTIONS
According to Loevinger and Wessler, individuals who have transcended the Conformist Level question why the rules exist, thus refusing to follow the rules simply because they are there.[27] At the Achievement Level, the motives and consequences of an act are much more important than they are at lower levels. In other words, Achievers feel worse if their unethical acts hurt others than they do if they had simply broken a rule. Thus, ethical concerns and the questioning of rules and values is high at the Achievement Level.

FEELING OF SPIRITUAL VOID
Reflecting a materialistic, bureaucratic culture, the Achiever tends to lack a sense of spiritual identification. Friedman and Rosenman warn of a world devoid of spiritual values:

> Perhaps our Western society will prove to have acted in a supremely wise fashion when it began to replace myths, rituals, and traditions with mechanizations, automation, and bureaucratic social security. Except for one thing: this is the first time in the experience of man on earth that a large group of individuals is attempting to live in so absolute a spiritual void. So far, our machines and computers click conscientiously away. Yet, how strangely sad we have become, as we search without hope for the color, the glory, and the grandeur that we think life should sometimes shed upon us.[28]

Our society does not revere or reward signs of spiritual growth, such as a dedication to serve others, or the development and maturation of self into a more realized whole. Thus, the Achievement Level is not typically attracted to such spiritual growth. Indeed, the act of "being" rather than "doing" may be perceived as threatening to the Achievement Level.

The Five Levels

	EMOTIONAL RESPONSE	INTELLECTUAL FUNCTIONING	ACTIVITY INVOLVEMENT
ACHIEVEMENT	Sense of futility. Harried. Insecurity. Hyperemotional.	Selectively unconscious. Rigid solutions utilized. Conceptual complexity. Polyphasic thought patterns. Reactive, not proactive. Cognitive preoccupation: acquisition.	Frenzied. Polyphasic activities. Routine activities. Importance on goals, deadlines, and priorities.
CONFORMIST	Stress and tension without cause. Fear, guilt, shame and inadequacy. Long recovery time. Intermittent hysterics.	Cognitive simplicity—"right/wrong". Intellectualizes rather than experiences. Circular worrying. Perfectionistic. Cognitive preoccupation: acceptance, appearance.	Pointless activities. Reduced risk taking. Need for praise.
SELF-PROTECTIVE	External causation. Emotional shifts. Hysterical behavior. Fear dominant emotion.	Blind to factual data. Difficulty with decision making. Chronic distortion of reality. Cognitive preoccupation: sex and aggression.	Avoidance of challenging activities. Little self-confidence. Work as anxiety-avoidance not a source of satisfaction.
UNCONSCIOUS	Unrelated to reality. Extreme shifts. Great stress and anxiety evident.	Difficulty in processing information. Obsessive thoughts. Gross perceptual distortion. Cognitive preoccupation: survival.	Ritualistic and compulsive behavior. Difficulty in changing. Extreme fear of attempting anything new.

SELF-DISCIPLINE	RELATIONSHIPS	PHYSICAL STATE	SPIRITUAL DIMENSION
High motivation—through internalized anxiety. Intolerance of ambiguity. Inadequate planning.	Other-directed need for esteem. Competitive. Work-related emphasis.	Predisposition to coronary disease. Stress-related symptoms. Fatigue and exhaustion. Drugs used to cope.	Concerned with ethical questions. Felt spiritual void.
Lack of flexibility. Need for clear definitions. Restricted internal motivation.	Drama roles. Retention of negative experiences. Psychological games.	Obese or thin. Sleep disturbances. Gastro-intestinal problems. Headaches. Skin problems. Physical tics/stuttering. Medical assistance necessary. Episodic drug abuse.	Ritualistic emphasis. Tyranny of "shoulds," "oughts," and "musts." Self-view as victim. Rules followed not questioned.
Obsessively ritualistic. Robot-like behavior. Opportunistic. Difficulty in learning.	Withdrawal, dependency, hostility. Unconcerned with agreements, commitments or rules.	Psychosomatic illness. No appetite/muscular soreness. Chronic drug abuse.	Non-ethical. Moral level: "Don't get caught".
Little self-control of motivation. Work contingent upon external conditions. Impulsive.	Unconsciousness in presence of others. Total communication breakdown. No concern for others. Little change from negative feedback.	Blank staring. Severe physical problems. Addictions.	Ethically or morally unconcerned. Fanatical behavior.

"I have grown to believe: that the one thing worth aiming at is simplicity of heart and life; that one's relations with others should be direct and not diplomatic; that power leaves a bitter taste in the mouth; that meaness and hardness and coldness are the unforgivable sins; that conventionality is the mother of dreariness; that pleasure exists not in virtue of material conditions, but in the joyful heart; that the world is a very interesting and beautiful place; that congenial labor is the secret of happiness; and many other things which seem, as I write them down to be dull and trite and commonplace, but are for me the bright jewels which I have found beside the way."[1]

—R.C. Benson

"The price of greatness is responsibility."[2]

—Winston Churchill

"Beauty, truth, power, God, all these come without searching, without effort. The struggle is to synchronize the potential being with the actual being, to make a fruitful liaison between the man of yesterday and man of tomorrow. It is the process of growth which is painful, but unavoidable. We either grow or we die, and to die while alive is a thousand times worse . . ."[3]

—Henry Miller

Chapter Six
THE RESPONSIBLE MANAGER

As we have learned in earlier chapters, responsibility is the key factor in psychological maturity. Capable of consciousness, man can make basic choices. Specifically, the choice whether to "be here" or not, represents a fundamental decision to accept responsibility for one's life. Yet, in the name of self-protection, we often choose to blame external factors even though it is self-defeating. To transcend this level, individuals need to acknowledge their fundamental choice and responsibility both for the quality and the reality of their experience.

As individuals mature, they begin to replace "prior programming" from childhood by confronting aspects of the Conformist Level. Not only are they now aware that they have a choice, they now come to the realization that as adults, the choices are indeed **their** choice. By taking responsibility for their actions, attitudes and emotions, such individuals transcend the Conformist Level. At the Achievement Level, people can be "successful" without being happy or having a sense of self-fulfillment. To mature, individuals need to realize that they create their own satisfaction, rather than relying on more tangible objects and achievements to produce that result.

Throughout all levels of growth, the key issue is responsibility. At the highest level of maturity, individuals manage every aspect of their lives with responsibility. Because of this central issue, the final level is called the Responsible Level. This is the same category described by Abraham Maslow as "Self-Actualized," by Carl Rogers as "Fully Functioning," by Harry Stack Sullivan as "Integrated," and by Eric Berne as "Winning," to mention a few.

The following is an attempt to isolate factors described by all the theorists and to provide a context for self-discovery. The implications related to these descriptions may also produce some radical consequences for business and organizations. According to Abraham Maslow:

> . . . these data are on the side of self-
> regulation, self-government, self choice
> of the organisms. . . This is in general

anti-authoritarian, anti-controlling. It means . . . not to intrude and to control . . . There is a greater stress on spontaneity and on autonomy rather than on prediction and external control.[4]

Thus, the challenge to organizations is not only to create an environment for individuals to grow into responsible individuals, but to allow these same people to function, and function well, without interference. With such a goal in mind,

> . . . people would be stronger, healthier, and would take their own lives into their hands to a greater extent. With increased personal responsibility for one's personal life, and with a rational set of values to guide one's choosing, people would begin to actively change the society in which they lived. The movement toward psychological health is also the movement toward spiritual peace and social harmony.[5]

Though attainable, such a goal is not without challenge, discomfort, and work. Yet, research indicates a universal, almost evolutionary desire, inherent in man, to grow, to actualize, and to improve. As Wasserman stated, "In every person, even in such as appear most reckless, there is an inherent desire to attain balance."[6]

Even so, because of ineffective parenting, schooling, and working conditions, modern society tends to stifle that growth. The Management by Responsibility philosophy aims to enhance growth and promote human development to create environments which nurture that potential implicit in ourselves.

American industry should not only assist workers and managers in self-understanding, but also provide a non-threatening environment in which individuals can confront themselves so change can take place. It will take the concerted effort of business and government to aid employers in promoting such a growth process. Yet, the choice is simple: grow and succeed, or stagnate

and fail, as other countries become more productive and more competitive. Meanwhile, American business flounders as anxiety produces work relationships that waste time, money, and human potential.

To assist in the growth process, the following dimensions of the Responsible Manager provide a "road-map" for those individuals who have been seeking direction for their lives. As Sir Richard Livingston so aptly put it:

> Knowledge of the first-rate gives direction, purpose, and drive; direction because it reveals an ideal to pursue; drive, because an ideal stirs to action.[7]

Dimensions of the Responsible Level

Emotional Response

Emotional Changes Have a "Cause"
Individuals at the highest level of development respond emotionally, sometimes intensely so. Yet, any change in their typically positive emotional state has a definite cause. Managers at this level do not experience tension or stress randomly. In other words, Responsible individuals experience emotions such as anger, tension, anxiety, fear, and disappointment, yet always for a reason. Responsible managers may become very angry when they find trust has been violated, or they may become tense when making an important presentation to company executives. They know why they feel as they do—as opposed to the free-floating anxiety or hostility that is prevalent at lower levels. They generally have a plan of action already formulated to do something about these uncomfortable emotions.

EMOTIONAL RESPONSES ARE OF SHORT DURATION
As discussed earlier, when individuals take responsibility for their reactions to events, their emotional responses pass quickly. At the lower levels of maturity, emotional responses can last for hours, and sometimes weeks. Managers at the Responsible Level often feel intense emotion; yet, the emotional reaction passes quickly.

NEGATIVE EMOTIONS TRIGGER ACTION
Although not experienced as much as in the lower levels, negative emotions motivate Responsible managers to change and to improve the situation in the future. Rather than being paralyzed by fear, worries, and conflict, managers at the Responsible Level, utilize these emotions to stimulate themselves to act. As Huxley states, the Responsible person struggles **for**, more than struggling **against**:

> Human life is a struggle—<u>against</u> frustration, ignorance, suffering, evil, the maddening inertia of things in general—but it is also a struggle <u>for</u> something . . . and fulfillment seems to describe better than any other single word the positive side of human development and human evolution—the realization of inherent capacities by the individuals and new possiblities . . . the satisfaction of needs, spiritual as well as material; the emergence of new qualities of experience to be enjoyed . . . [8]

EMOTIONAL STABILITY
Responsible managers display an emotional stability that is rare for many people. Because they are able to face negative situations confident of a positive outcome, they are able to remain conscious and, consequently, more effective. Even under tension and stress, individuals at this level are able to think clearly because they have their emotions under control.

Although Responsible individuals do not promote conflict situations, they are at a stage in their development where they realize that conflict is the determining factor for ongoing successful interaction. By so choosing, they are following the advice of an old Chinese Proverb: "If you are patient in one moment of anger, you will escape a hundred days of sorrow."[9]

Dimensions of the Responsible Level

POSITIVE EMOTIONAL STATES EXPERIENCED FREQUENTLY

At the Responsible Level, individuals experience more positive emotions than at any other level. They are able to accept themselves, other people, and situations as they are, and so are not constantly struggling to make reality fit their concept or image of how it **should** be. Rather, their choice of assuming responsibility enables them to experience the following range of positive emotions:

Enthusiasm/Optimism

According to Denis Waitley in his series, The Psychology of Winning, "The most readily identifiable quality of a total winner is an overall attitude of personal optimism and enthusiasm."[10] Responsible people maintain this sense of optimism because they react positively to any situation including failure, while concurrently rejecting a paranoid view of reality.

Thus, they view their world in an enthusiastic, positive and "inspired" manner. This is particularly noticeable in the work environment. Managers who are optimistic and enthusiastic tend to have staff members who reflect that image. Enthusiasm is contagious. Unfortunately, pessimism and the lack of enthusiasm are also contagious. Responsible people realize that they are role models and so reinforce positive behavior in others.

Satisfaction From Acceptance

One of the most important differences between people at the Responsible Level and those at the Achievement Level, is that Responsible people allow themselves to experience a great deal of satisfaction with themselves and with their life. This is not to say that they are complacent; they are not. It means that they allow themselves to feel satisfaction in the process of achieving their goals and objectives, not just at the completion.

Their satisfaction comes from giving up certain attitudes and behaviors that are quite common at lower levels. According to Maslow:

> In moments of here-now immersion and self-forgetfulness we are apt to become more "positive" and less negative in still another way, namely, in giving up criticism, (editing, picking and choosing, rejecting, judging, evaluating). This is like saying that we accept. We don't reject or disapprove or selectively pick and choose.[11]

So, for Responsible managers, satisfaction stems from an exchange. They choose happiness rather than an unrelenting struggle for achievement. They strive for a sense of self-fulfillment, instead of trying to always please others at all times. They want to live harmoniously with others instead of living life dramatically by repeating behaviors that were learned as children. They are conscious of the moment rather than being oblivious to much of what is happening around them.

There is always a trade-off, and some individuals learn these lessons the hard way. As Oscar Wilde remarked in De Profundis, "One of the many lessons that one learns in prison is, that things are what they are and will be what they will be."[12] For others, the exchange may come after reflecting upon one's life and the process of growth itself. The process of psychological maturation repeatedly involves giving up old behavioral patterns, relinquishing and rejecting some of the roles that one has learned. This sometimes can be painful and risky. Yet, each risk and new confrontation is more appropriate to the Responsible person's expanding world of increased capacity and opportunity. For the Responsible person, the greater the risk, the greater the satisfaction.

Sense of Humor
Since they have the ability to laugh at themselves and the situation, individuals at the Responsible Level generally have a very good sense of humor. Responsible managers can look at their failures without feeling defeated. They can retain a sense of humor even when confronting the unexpected or the disappointing. No longer attached to fear or to struggle, Responsible people have the advantage of being able to laugh at themselves and of learning from their past.

Feelings Of Self-Worth
Responsible managers do not depend on others for their feelings of worth. Proud of their uniqueness, they set their own standards for conduct and appreciation. As stated in the popular song title, "I Did It My Way," Responsible people believe strongly in themselves and feel an innate sense of worth.

According to Bonaro Overstreet, "Perhaps the most important thing we can undertake toward the reduction of fear is to make it easier for people to accept themselves."[13] Ironically, once we can accept ourselves we can give up the fear of being who we are and vice-versa. This sense of self-worth is based on self-awareness and self-acceptance. Only through such awareness and acceptance, can individuals rise to higher levels of maturity. In his excellent treatise of self-discovery, Man's Search For Himself, Rollo May states:

> The bewilderment—the confusion as to who we are and what we should do—is the most painful thing about anxiety. But the positive and hopeful side is that just as anxiety destroys our self-awareness, so awareness of ourselves even destroys anxiety. That is to say, the stronger our consciousness of ourselves, the more we can take a stand against and overcome anxiety.[14]

Thus, one of the first steps in the actualization process is to feel worthy as a human being. Accepting oneself allows the individual to be comfortable with his own potential and with the emergence of new possibilities from within.

Dimensions of the Responsible Level

Love

People at the highest level of growth are truly loving human beings. In fact, the ability to love is, itself, a measure of actualization. Through the process of accepting others, Responsible people help others to grow and change. According to Maslow,

> Love for a person permits him to unfold, to open up, to drop his defenses, to let himself be naked, not only physically but psychologically, and spiritually as well. In a word he lets himself be seen instead of hiding himself.[15]

This kind of love dispenses with wanting to change the other person. There are no "conditions" for love. Responsible individuals realize the perfection of others. Just as we love something intensely:

> . . . we are content to leave it alone. We make no demands on it. We do not wish it to be other than it is. We can be passive and receptive before it. Which is all to say that we can see it more truly as it is in its own nature, rather than as we would like it to be or fear it to be, or hope it will be. Approving of its existence, approving of the way it is, as it is, permits us to be non-obtrusive, non-manipulative, non-obstructing, non-interferring perceivers . . . Thus . . . the beloved person may be seen as already perfect, so that any kind of change, let alone improvements, is regarded as impossible or even impious.[16]

The Responsible Level is abundant with paradox. The less change and growth are demanded, the more likely they will occur. Love and total acceptance allows individuals the strength and courage to confront change and thus, to grow.

The sense of love is not just apparent in one's personal life. Responsible people seem to exude love and trust within all areas of their lives. Though obviously displayed differently at work, the sense of acceptance is nonetheless apparent to staff members. Not that Responsible managers are undemanding or unconcerned with productivity. They are—they accomplish their objectives in such a way that everyone's individual dignity is enhanced, thereby laying the groundwork for internalizing organizational goals. In this way, staff members **want** to do a good job.

Feeling Of Integration

A large part of self-acceptance for the Responsible person is the recognition and acceptance of one's dichotomies. According to Brouwer,

> Each human being is several selves . . . if there are conflicts among any of the roles, then discomfort arises. And such conflict brings with it such dynamics as tension, guilt feelings, and compensation.

> By definition, effective, consistent behavior is integrated behavior, while unintegrated behavior is the behavior of conflict.[17]

The acceptance of such dichotomies not only enhances a more positive view of oneself, it can also provide the impetus for actualizing one's potential. According to Carl Jung, "The greater the contrast, the greater is the potential. Great energy only comes from a correspondingly great tension between opposites."[18] A feeling of being an integrated whole provides people at the Responsible Level with a profound sense of self-worth, since each part of their nature contributes to that sense of oneness. As noted earlier, the Conformist experiences no such comparable sense of integration. He is victimized by his belief that definite behaviors and attitudes are appropriate for males, while a different set are appropriate for females. Unfortunately, for many males, " . . . 'feminine' means practically everything that's creative: imagination, fantasy, color, poetry, music, tenderness, languishing, being romantic, in general. All are walled off as dangerous to one's picture of one's masculinity."[19]

Whether we approve or understand it, the particular issue of sex-role dichotomies is becoming increasingly important as many men and women experience "culture shock" by living in a society where sex-role identities and behavioral models are changing rapidly. As women continue to advance into managerial and executive positions, it will become crucial for organizations to assist both men and women in understanding the roles they play. In this regard, Maslow was quite prophetic in his pronouncement:

> Only as men become strong enough, self-confident enough, and integrated enough can they tolerate and finally enjoy self-actualizing women-...women who are full human beings.[20]

Courage and the Sense of Confidence
At the Responsible Level, managers display confidence and courage, believing in themselves and what they are doing. Although fear can be used as a warning or as an impetus for action, it does not permeate the individual's emotional responses.

This sense of self-confidence enables the Responsible manager to feel independent and self-sufficient. Although such confidence may to others seem prideful or egotistical, this is not the case. At this level, managers display the courage to confidently face new events, and respond to success with a sense of humility. Responsible people are not "puffed up" in the Biblical sense, nor do they feel better than others as a result of success.

Such a sense of confidence enhances the Responsible person's positive motivation. At lower levels, individuals are motivated primarily by fear: the Unconscious fear reality; the Self-Protectives fear getting caught; the Conformists fear rejection; and Achievers fear the loss of esteem. At the Responsible Level, individuals are motivated primarily by desire. It is a positive rather than a negative emotional trigger. In his discussion of winners, Denis Waitley emphasizes the motivation of desire:

> ...fear and desire are among the greatest motivators...fear is destructive, while desire leads to achievement, success, and happiness. With this in mind, winners focus their thinking on the rewards of success and activity and tune-out fears of failures. We are all self-motivated, a little or a lot. Motivation is an inside job. Individuals are motivated by their fears, inhibitions, compulsions, and attractions...Winners focus on goals, desires, and solutions. We always move in the direction of our currently dominant thoughts. Since most of our fears are based on dark imaginings, it is vital for us to dwell on desired results...to look at where we want to go as opposed to that troubled place where we may have been or may still be hiding.[21]

Thus, Responsible people achieve their goals because they are motivated by desire. Because they focus on the positive results, they display a sense of courage and confidence rarely shown at lower levels.

Dimensions of the Responsible Level

Sense Of Tranquility And Peace

As opposed to the frenzied pace of the Achievement Level, Responsible managers have a sense of inner peace and tranquility. Living consonant with their internal laws and demands, their resulting fulfillment adds tranquility to their lives. Thoreau poetically describes this sense in his Journal:

> Sometimes we are clarified and calmed healthily, as we never were before in our lives, not by an opiate, but by some unconscious obedience to the all-just laws, so that we become like a still lake of purest crystal and without an effort our depths are revealed to ourselves. All the world goes by us and is reflected in our deeps.[22]

Such a calm reflective attitude affects one's relationships, and particularly, with the Responsible person, one's spiritual identification as well.

Appreciation Of Life, Art, And Nature

People at the Responsible Level have a deepened appreciation of music, art, the humanities, nature, and the subtleties of life in general. The old adage, "He never took time to smell the roses," is appropriate here. Responsible people are in tune with their senses and appreciate the world in which they live with a sense of awe.

In this way, Responsible people live life on a higher plane—a more aesthetic and spiritual existence than those realities that are created and experienced at the lower levels.

Intellectual Functioning

At the Responsible Level, intellectual functioning is at its peak. Not only is one able to process and input data effectively, but one is also able to take information and utilize it creatively, thereby maximizing current positive potential. Here, then, are aspects of intellectual functioning at the Responsible Level.

ABILITY TO INPUT AND PROCESS INFORMATION EFFICIENTLY AND EFFECTIVELY

At the Responsible Level, people are aware of their intellectual potential and consequent responsibility. As Nathaniel Branden points out, "A man who deals with the facts of reality on the conceptual level of consciousness has accepted the responsibility of a human manner of existence—which entails his acceptance of responsibility for his own life and actions.[23]

In this sense, Responsible managers are amenable to the input of new ideas, without prejudging or evaluating. Individuals at this level can truly listen and experience what another's words mean. Only then, when the data has registered, can it be processed, and finally utilized. Responsible people are very good at doing so:

> They let themselves be completely uncritical. They allow all sorts of wild ideas to come into their heads. And in great bursts of emotion and enthusiasm, they may scribble out the poem, or the formula, or the mathematical solution or work up a theory, and design the experiment.[24]

Thus, as well as inputting information from others and the environment, Responsible managers are able to let their own ideas flow. They are able to come up with ideas quickly and profusely while remaining open to all possible information. Then after processing the data, they are able to discard ideas that prove erroneous and to implement those that are effective.

Friedman and Rosenman insist that there are significant differences between their Type A (Achieving) and Type B (Responsible) patients, particularly in how such patients are able to think. The Type A person often thinks in rigid ways and is unable to "hear" certain information. Yet, the Type B (Responsible) person is

> . . . capable, at least at times, of freeing himself from the steel meshes of stereotypical thought and behavior. He does find the time to ponder leisurely, to weigh alternatives, to experiment, to indulge in the sort of dialectical reverie from which two or three or even four seemingly totally disparate events, facts, or processes can be joined to produce strikingly new and brilliant offshoots . . . [25]

Such thinking—so desperately needed in industry, commerce, and government—needs to be promoted. Responsible Level managers are open and flexible. Responsible managers are able to be objective, playing "fair witness" by perceiving the facts as they are. Judgment, evaluations, and consideration, all tend to blind a person and inhibit the thought process.

This is not to imply that Responsible managers are not able to make decisions effectively. They are able to "open" their minds to a tremendous amount of information by noting all possibilities, and yet can "close" their minds to make decisions. As George Bernard Shaw said:

> The open mind never acts. When we have done our utmost to arrive at a reasonable conclusion, we still, when we can reason and investigate no more, must close our minds for the moment with a snap, and act dogmatically on our conclusions.[26]

Once the decision is made, Responsible managers are able to act. If the situation proves to be detrimental or in error, they can simply pause, reflect upon alternative routes and solutions, and then act again. By so doing they effectively upgrade the quality of their thinking as its predictability rises.

Dimensions of the Responsible Level

EXPANDED CONSCIOUSNESS

Responsible managers not only have the ability to be conscious more often, they also seem to possess an expanded consciousness. This comes from choosing to be conscious, and then focusing one's consciousness. As W.H. Auden said, "Choice of attention to pay attention to this and ignore that, is to the inner life what choice of action is to the outer. In both cases, a man is responsible for his choice and must accept the consequences—whatever they may be."[27]

By focusing their awareness effectively, managers at the Responsible Level are able to think more clearly without distorting their ideas. Carl Rogers states in his book, On Becoming a Person, that to an individual who is open to experience, " . . . each stimulus is freely relayed through the nervous system without being distorted by any process of defensiveness."[28]

Because the Responsible manager can perceive without distortion, the ability to use both the right and the left hemispheres of the brain is enhanced. Thus, not only is factual data perceived more effectively, Responsible managers are also more intuitive. They have what Castaneda calls the ability to "see"things as they are:

> " . . . a special capacity that one could develop and which would allow one to comprehend the 'ultimate' nature of things . . . an intuitive grasp of things, or the capacity to understand something at once, or perhaps the ability to see through human interactions and discover covert meanings and motives."[29]

Those who are able to "see" at the Responsible Level, do so without being burdened by the past or distracted by future concerns. These are the people who truly have a sense of aliveness, who make the best of life. As John Jay Chapman writes:

> It is a rare matter when any of us at any time in life sees things as they are at the moment. This happens at times . . . that we become aware of what is going on about us, of feeling and of ideas in which we have always been living. These worlds are really in progress all the time, and the difference between one man and another, or the difference in the same man at different times, is the difference in his <u>awareness</u> of what is <u>happening</u>.[30]

At this level of maturity, people display the ability to transcend traditional world-views and to see beyond one's social milieu. This expanded view of reality requires discipline and openness, not to mention risk. Yet it is in these moments that realization of one's full potential occurs. According to Maslow, such a view means " . . . experiencing fully, vividly, selflessly, with full concentration and total absorption. . . . At this moment of experiencing, the person is wholly and fully human. This is the self, actualizing itself."[31]

As many of the mystics have reported, these are the moments of enlightenment. It was in such a rare, beautiful, exhilarating moment that Einstein's theory of relativity was created. And any moment can be such an experience. According to Thaddeus Golas, "Enlightenment is any experience of expanding our consciousness beyond its present limits . . . perfect enlightenment is realizing that we have no limits at all, and that the entire universe is alive."[32]

Such enlightenment does not simply "happen;" it appears to be a consequence of study, practice, and redefining one's self—sometimes for years. Responsible managers constantly increase their knowledge and wisdom through new experience, personal insight, feedback and decision-making. As a consequence, they are challenged by each new awareness and are able to correct errors and mistakes.

CREATIVITY

The Responsible person is intellectually highly creative. Such creativity allows people to see reality in new ways. D.H. Lawrence once described the creative process as a "spontaneous mutability, bringing forth unknown issues, impossible to preconceive."[33]

Unfortunately much of the American educational system has taught children not to think, not to be creative, not to question. Yet creative thought is essential for any organization and society. As Albert Einstein insisted in <u>Ideas and Opinions</u>, "Without creative personalities able to think and judge independently, the upward development of society is as unthinkable as the development of the individual personality without the nourishing soil of community."[34]

What fosters this creative approach is the ability to totally focus one's thoughts on the project at hand. When such a focused concentration occurs the experience seems timeless:

> . . . the creative person, in the inspirational phase of the creative furor, loses his past and his future and lives only in the moment. He is all there, totally immersed, fascinated and absorbed in the present, the current situation in the here-now, with the matter in hand. Certain prerequisites of creativeness—in whatever realm—has something to do with his ability to become timeless, selfless, outside of space, of society, of history . . . [35]

Thus, creativity is viewed as a function of consciousness. Yet, it is also a matter of choice. One has to choose to think creatively rather than to think in terms of the "easy" way, the most familiar, or in ritualistic ways common at lower levels. Katherine Butler Hathaway offers the following wise counsel:

> I invented this rule for myself to be applied to every decision I might have to make in the future. I would sort out all the arguments and see which belonged to fear and which to creativeness, and other things being equal, I would make the decision which had the larger number of creative reasons on its side . . . [36]

The poet and philosopher, Rainer Maria Rilke, repeatedly considered the mystery of the creative process. In his journal, he wrote: "I am learning to see. I do not know why it is, but everything penetrates more deeply within me, and no longer stops at the place, where until now, it always used to finish."[37] That inner knowledge, the intuitive sense, promotes the intellectually creative response.

Dimensions of the Responsible Level

POSITIVE THINKING AND PROJECTION

Responsible managers think, as well as feel, in positive ways. They take a point of view that things "will work out," viewing problems as opportunities that can challenge them to greater activity and growth.

Because they realize the effects of positive thought and action, they tend to project such views onto others and into life situations. By so doing, they assist others to mature. Typically, staff members respect managers at this level and aspire to be more like them. Because Responsible managers believe in the potential of others, staff members likewise strive to meet their expectations.

Yet, Responsible managers are not "Pollyanna" in their approach. They are realistic and able to adjust goals and thinking very readily. The positive nature of their thinking comes from recognizing who they are, deciding what roles they want to fill, and realizing that the future holds the key for unlocking their potential.

COGNITIVE PREOCCUPATION: SELF-FULFILLMENT

At the Responsible Level, all of life is seen as an experience to unfold potential. People at this level realize that what is viewed as "failure" are simply evaluations that the mind places on events. Taking on the role of a "learner," they view all of life as offering lessons for them. As Ralph Waldo Emerson admonished:

> Do not be too timid and squeamish about your reactions. All life is an experiment. The more experiments you make the better![38]

To view life experimentally helps eliminate the fear and hesitation prevalent at the lower levels. And yet, ironically, to do so takes the fear from the experience itself. Wanting to live completely, the Responsible person is mentally intent upon this process of fulfillment.

THOUGHTS STIMULATE ACTION

Rather than allowing fantasies and day-dreams to interfere with their thinking or action, Responsible managers control their thoughts and thus improve the action that is subsequently taken. In this regard, people at the Responsible Level listen to their own internal thoughts and use them to stimulate action. This is not the same blind obedience that the Conformists experience. Rather than responding to the "shoulds" or "oughts" of the past, the Responsible person listens from within to respond more authentically to the present situation.

WORLD-VIEW AS "PERFECT"

Because life is an experiment for Responsible individuals, they tend to view all events as "perfect," that is, as complete, unique, and necessary in their developmental process. Responsible people are not "perfectionists" nor are they complacent. They are simply able to accept reality for what it is—not what it should have been, or ought to be.

The idea that one's present experience is "perfect" allows people to grow. Paradoxically, the more one is able to accept life the way it is, the more positive one tends to become. In The Lazy Man's Guide to Enlightenment, Thaddeus Golas remarks:

> As you open your awareness, life will improve itself, you won't even have to try. It's a beautiful paradox; the more you open your consciousness, the fewer unpleasant events intrude themselves into your awareness.[39]

Activity Involvement

INTERESTED AND EXCITED ABOUT ACTIVITIES

Responsible managers are interested in what they are doing—whether it involves work or leisure activities. They do not do things just because they are "supposed" to: they are enthusiastic and their careers usually involve activities that they enjoy. In fact, for Responsible people, the distinction between what is defined as work and what is defined as play vanishes. As Mark Twain noted, "Work and play are words to describe the same thing under different conditions."[40]

This love of activity and the Achiever's excessive striving for recognition differ. Hugh Prather characterizes this distinction saying, "To live my life for results would be to sentence myself to continuous frustration. My only sure reward is **in** my actions and not **from** them.[41] For the Responsible person, the joy is in the doing, not just in the accomplishing. They like what they are doing and do what they like.

COMMITMENT TO EXCELLENCE

Responsible managers are committed to excellence. They enjoy their activities and feel challenged by their own standards. Committed to excellence, they will do a job completely—a pattern which at the Responsible Level becomes self-reinforcing. According to Erich Fromm,

> The more productively one lives, the stronger is one's conscience, and, in turn, the more it furthers one's productiveness. The less productively one lives, the weaker becomes one's conscience; the paradoxical—and tragic—situation of man is that his conscience is weakest when he needs it most.[42]

Responsible people seemed to have heeded Maslow's admonishment to his students: "If you deliberately plan to be less than you are capable of being, then I warn you that you will be unhappy for the rest of your lives. You'll be evading your own capacity; your own possibilities are true to their impulses that promote them further in their purpose of excellence."[43]

To the Responsible manager, work becomes more than a job: it becomes an exercise in attaining a sense of excellence and a feeling of competence. This commitment becomes a self-fulfilling prophecy. As Rainer Maria Rilke advised a friend,

> Do continue to believe that with your feeling and your work you are taking part in the greatest; the more strongly you cultivate in yourself this belief, the more will reality and the world go forth from it.[44]

Though committed to excellence, managers at this level do not use their accomplishments for self-aggrandizement. Typically, they do the opposite. As Mark Twain said, "Keep away from people who try to belittle your ambitions. Small people always do that, but the really great make you feel that you, too, can become great."[45] One can expect to feel more than simply good around a Responsible person; people at this level inspire others to realize their own potential.

Dimensions of the Responsible Level

COMPETENCE

Responsible managers are exceptionally competent and have strong feelings about their own adequacies. They take risks, yet do so in those areas in which they can learn. Responsible managers choose activities that typically bring a sense of competence, thereby reaffirming their feelings of success and well-being.

At this level, people take positive action to make things happen, rather than exhibiting a self-limiting mindset. They are not afraid of being successful—a fear which is often dramatically demonstrated at lower levels. In addition, Responsible managers are competent in many types of activities—those that require sudden bursts of energy as well as those that demand long-term perseverance.

FREEDOM FROM EXCESSIVE STRIVING

Unlike the Achievement Level, the Responsible Level is markedly free from excessive striving. At this level, people do not need to impress others with unwanted fame, or achievements, nor do they always have to be the "best" at everything they do. As William Gladstone stated, such a person:

> . . . does not need to limit himself to those activities and those relationships in which he knows in advance that he will succeed or be warmly accepted. He is also not afraid of being just average . . . He is not afraid of being less than the best at everything. He is not a perfectionist.[46]

RESILIENT IN FAILURE

At the Responsible Level, people are not ashamed of or discouraged by their failures. They are resilient and learn from their mistakes. At the lower levels, failure is often accompanied by a loss of esteem.

At the Responsible Level, managers do not take as long to recover from their setbacks and disappointments, often showing an inordinate ability to persevere. Successful people have always demonstrated this quality:

> One who fears limits his activities. Failure is only the opportunity to more intelligently begin again.[47]
>
> —Henry Ford

> A man should never be ashamed to say he has been wrong, which is but saying, in other words, that he is wiser today than he was yesterday.[48]
>
> —Alexander Pope

> The only people who don't have problems, are the people who don't do anything.[49]
>
> —Kemmons Wilson, Founder and Chairman of Holiday Inns, Inc.

> Disappointments should be cremated, not embalmed.[50]
>
> —Anonymous
> (Noted by Henry Haskins,)
> Meditations in Wall Street

Self-Discipline

At no other level are people able to discipline themselves as effectively and with as much satisfaction. At the Responsible Level, managers have a great capacity to project and accomplish what they want to do. The following are aspects of self-discipline.

INNER-MOTIVATION
At the Responsible Level, people do not require external rewards or fear of punishment to motivate them. Rather they are motivated by the desire to do a good job and to acquire a sense of accomplishment.

Managers at this level do not need to feel "inspired" to work on a project. In his study entitled, "The Common Denominator of Success," Albert E. Gray defines the key characteristics of successful people:

> Hard work is not the real secret of success, although in most cases it seems to be one of the requirements. The secret lies not only in what people did, but also in what made them do it. The common denominator of success of every person who has ever been successful is:

> The successful person has formed the habit of doing things that failures don't like to do.[51]

Responsible managers do not wait for others to tell them what needs to be done. They take initiative as a function of being responsible. As Kingman Brewster, Jr., former president of Yale University, said, "The higher the degree of responsibility, the greater the motivation"[52]

PATIENCE AND ENDURANCE FOR TEDIOUS TASKS
Responsible managers are able to do tedious tasks very effectively. Although they take breaks and need to feel refreshed at times, they nonetheless, can concentrate and perform well even under adverse conditions.

They can do so primarily because they are committed to the final result. As Earl Nightingale states, "Successful people have a strong purpose . . . strong enough to make them form the habit of doing things they don't like to do in order to accomplish the purpose that they want to accomplish."[53]

Dimensions of the Responsible Level

ABILITY TO EFFECTIVELY ORGANIZE AND PLAN

Responsible managers plan and organize their work and their lives more effectively than people at other levels. According to Nathaniel Branden, "The acceptance of responsibility for one's own life requires a policy of planning and acting long-range, so that one's actions are integrated to one another and to one's present and future."[54]

At this level, managers are able to reflect upon past performance, set future goals and objectives, and effectively plan to determine how they can accomplish the results. Denis Waitley, who concentrated much of his research in this area of Responsible behavior, found that

> winners in life have clearly defined, constantly-referred-to game plans and purposes. Their objectives range all the way from lifetime goals to daily priorities. And when they are not actively pursuing their goals, they're thinking about them—hard! They know the difference between goal achieving acts and those which are merely tension-relieving . . . and they concentrate on the former.
>
> The reason most people never reach their goals is that they don't define them, learn about them, or even seriously consider them as believable or achievable. In other words they never set them.[55]

A Responsible individual sets goals that are realistic, yet personally challenging. Indeed, as Branden notes, "The higher the goals one sets for himself . . . the more demanding the challenges he tends to seek . . ."[56] Because Responsible managers expect the most from themselves and from others, they usually do experience the best. They set goals and then carry out the action and procedures necessary to accomplish them. As simple as such a concept appears, it is unusual in many corporations.

FLEXIBILITY AND ADAPTABILITY IN BEHAVIOR

Responsible individuals are able to adapt to situations and behave in ways that the situation requires. They are not unpredictable; they are simply adaptable in their ability to deal with a great variety of individuals and situations.

Because they know they will be able to adapt to any changes necessary, they are able to face life more fearlessly. Thus, they welcome change. This attitude was expressed by Henry Ward Beecher in his book, Eyes and Ears:

> Our days are a kaleidoscope. Every instant a change takes place in the contents. New harmonies, new contrasts, new combinations of every sort. Nothing happens twice alike. The most familiar people stand each moment in some new relation to each other, to their work, to surrounding objects.[57]

A similar excitement occasioned by change is expressed by Kathleen Norris, in her book Hands Full of Living,

> None of us knows what the next change is going to be, what unexpected opportunity is just around the corner; waiting a few months or a few years can change all the tenor of our lives.[58]

By remaining flexible and adaptable, one lives more successfully in a world that constantly changes. Responsible people know this and act upon it.

ABILITY TO WORK HARD TO ACHIEVE RESULTS

Many writers, philosophers, and psychologists have noted the quality of Responsible people to work hard to make things happen. As George Bernard Shaw stated, "The people who get on in this world are the people who get up and look for the circumstances they want, and if they can't find them, make them."[59] Knowing that a great degree of satisfaction can come from producing results, people at this level enjoy working to their fullest capacity. Many writers have noted this characteristic of the Responsible Level:

The truth is that all of us attain the greatest success and happiness possible in this life whenever we use our native capacities to their fullest extent.[60]
—Dr. Smiley Blanton

The happiness that is genuinely satisfying is accompanied by the fullest exercise of our faculties and the fullest realization of the world in which we live.[61]
—Bertrand Russell

On any level of intelligence or ability, one of the characteristics of self-esteem is a man's eagerness for the reward, for the challenging, for that which will allow him to use his capacities to the fullest extent—just as the fondness for the familiar, the routines, the unexacting, and the fear of the new and the difficult, is virtually unmistakable indication of a self-esteem deficiency. In the realm of his work, the primary desire of a man of self-confidence is to face challenges, to achieve and to grow; the primary desire of a man lacking in self-confidence is to be "safe."[62]
—Nathaniel Branden

He who likes cherries soon learns to climb.[63]
—German Proverb

The mode in which the inevitable comes to pass is through effort. Consciously or unconsciously we all strive to make the kind of a world we like.[64]
—Oliver Wendall Holmes, Jr.

Enthusiasm finds the opportunities and energy makes the most of them.[65]
—Anonymous

Anyone who proposes to do good must not expect people to roll stones out of his way, but must accept his lot calmly if they even roll a few more upon it.[66]
—Albert Schweitzer

Dimensions of the Responsible Level

Relationships

People at the Responsible Level have productive and intimate relationships with others. Their interpersonal skills, combined with their willingness to be open with others and the freedom to be themselves, allow them to establish closeness with others that is not seen at other levels. Rather than living out a "drama" with others, Responsible people are authentic and allow others to be as they actually are, without projecting their own fears and desires. The following are aspects of Responsible relationships.

CAPACITY FOR INTIMACY

Responsible individuals achieve a sense of balance in all areas of life: in work, love and play. Attempts to satisfy all needs and aspirations in only one area at the exclusion or diminution of the other two, can produce negative results. As Sigmund Freud noted, "Just as a cautious businessman avoids investing all his capital in one concern, so wisdom would probably admonish us also not to anticipate all our happiness from one area alone."[67] Unlike people at the Achievement Level who tend to "over-invest" in work, the Responsible Level person places great importance on love and closeness.

At this level, people are very concerned about others. They have the capacity for intimacy that can only be present when people allow themselves to be vulnerable and are willing to share themselves with others. Moreover, Responsible people can also be trusted with the vulnerability of other people, thereby imbuing trust as the basic modality of their relationships.

Such trust implies that individuals are not involved with "power games." As Carl Jung notes:

> Where love rules, there is no will to power, and where power predominates there love is lacking. The one is the shadow of the other.[68]

The very nature of a power struggle, which defines so many relationships, is contrary to the give and take required of the intimate relationship. Giving to another person from a position of choice and desire is very different from demanding as a test of control. According to Rollo May in <u>Man's Search for Himself</u>:

> To be capable of giving and receiving mature love is as sound a criticism as we have for the fulfilled personality. But by that very token it is a goal gained only in proportion to how much one has fulfilled the prior condition of becoming a person in one's own right.[69]

To receive love and to graciously accept from others is a rare ability. Often one feels obliged or embarrassed when others offer love. Yet, the people who have the most to give others are those who are best able to receive love. By establishing intimacy with others, Responsible people afford themselves a tremendous opportunity for further growth. It is only through others, that one can become truly himself.

114

Dimensions of the Responsible Level

UNCONDITIONAL POSITIVE REGARD FOR SELF AND OTHERS

"You can't love anyone until you love yourself," is a familiar refrain that could not be a more accurate statement of the Responsible Level. According to Harry Stack Sullivan:

> When the satisfaction and the security of another person becomes as significant to one as is one's own satisfaction and security, then the state of love exists . . . Under no other circumstances is a state of love present.[70]

At this level, people have a full sense of identity that includes a recognition of both positive and negative factors. Nonetheless, they can accept those factors they do not like, without diminishing their sense of positive regard. R.D. Laing feels we must stop our self-destruction and self-hate, before we will be able to love and accept others:

> Perhaps men and women were born to love one another, simply and genuinely, rather than to this travesty that we call love. If we can stop destroying ourselves we may stop destroying others. We have to begin by admitting and even accepting our violence, rather than blindly destroying ourselves with it, and therewith we have to realize that we are as deeply afraid to live and to love as we are to die.[71]

By accepting their natures, Responsible people cherish their sense of individuality. Because they are humble, they are able to admit their mistakes. They realize they do not know everything and thus are capable of learning from others.

Managers at this level become more authentically real: they are who they are—not who they pretend to be. In that regard their relationships become more authentic as well. A full sense of identity allows one to identify with others. According to Maslow, the discovery of one's identity means:

finding out what your real desires and characteristics are, and being able to live in a way that expresses them. You learn to be authentic, to be honest in the sense of allowing your behavior and your speech to be the true and spontaneous expression of your inner feelings. Authenticity is the reduction of phoniness toward the zero point.[72]

Because they are authentic, Responsible people truly enjoy being with others. Detached from the "drama" that marks relationships at the lower levels, they are able to assist others in their growth. Buddha's description of a "master" seems to reflect such a state:

> The master endures
> insults and ill treatment
> without reacting,
> for his spirit is an army.
>
> He is never angry
> He keeps his promises.
> He never strays. He is determined.[73]

Since people at this level view others as a reflection of self, they do not become as upset with others. They literally live by the "Golden Rule." All of the world's major religions teach such a behavioral model because their founders were able to see others clearly, realizing that their experience of others was a manifestation of self.

Dimensions of the Responsible Level

THE ABILITY TO COMMUNICATE SUCCESSFULLY
People at the Responsible Level are able to communicate successfully with others—by listening effectively and conveying their ideas to others. This capacity stems from taking total responsibility for the communication process. According to Denis Waitley, they

> . . . specialize in truly effective communication, taking one hundred percent of the responsibility not only for sending information but for listening for the real meaning from every person they contact. They know that paying value to others is the greatest communication skill of all.[74]

Responsible people are skillful communicators. They have learned to perception-check, and to "be heard." Most importantly they are genuine. They are interested in what the other person has to say and as a consequence encourage others to speak. As Oscar Wilde profoundly expressed:

> Christ, like all fascinating personalities, had the power of not merely saying beautiful things himself, but of making other people say beautiful things to him.[75]

Though they communicate successfully, this skill does not necessarily mean the Responsible person agrees with everything that is being expressed. Yet, at this level managers are not afraid of conflict. They realize that as part of every human relationship conflict can be a productive, as well as a destructive aspect of the relationship. As Kahlil Gibran advised, "A disagreement may be the shortest cut between two minds."[76]

Although not promoted by Responsible people, such disagreements enable them to see other viewpoints, and to more objectively evaluate their own.

THE ABILITY TO BE AN EFFECTIVE LEADER AND AN EFFECTIVE FOLLOWER
Because others respect them, Responsible people are often leaders. They realize that the true purpose of life is to serve others. At this level of maturity, one realizes that serving others can be accomplished both by being a leader and a follower.

True leaders practice their art by relating productively to their group and by acting upon the realization that their true purpose is to promote the common welfare. Responsible managers are empathetically involved with staff problems and yet are firm in having them take responsibility for their solutions.

As followers, Responsible people have the ability to compromise and cooperate. They are uncritical, and simply suggest various approaches without arguing or demanding. They do not wait for others to solve their problems. Rather, they suggest solutions, or simply take the initiative themselves.

SPECIAL RELATIONSHIP PROBLEMS

There is a mistaken notion that people at the Responsible Level do not have personal conflicts. This is not the case. Although their relating skills are excellent, others sometimes feel quite threatened by people at the Responsible Level and thus create particular relationship problems.

People at this level realize the futility of the Conformist Level dictum, "You should like everyone, and everyone should like you." Even the most loving, caring, successful person in the world will not be liked by all people. Abraham Maslow's studies of self-actualized people underscore the paradox confronting the Responsible person:

> We surely love and admire all those persons who have incarnated the true, the good, the beautiful, the just, the perfect, the ultimately successful. And yet they also make us uneasy, anxious, confused, perhaps a little jealous, or even envious, or a little inferior, clumsy . . .

> By being who they are, they make us feel aware of our lesser worth, whether or not they intend to. If this is an unconscious effect, and we are not aware of why we feel stupid or ugly, or inferior whenever such a person turns up, we are apt to respond with projection, as if we were the target. Hostility is then an understandable consequence.[77]

Thus, at the Responsible Level, people need to be aware that others, because of their own insecurities, may need to project negative images.

Physical State

A FEELING OF WELL-BEING

People at the Responsible Level have a general feeling of well-being. Though they may become ill, they seldom have chronic illness or patterns of disease. Because they take responsibility for the other dimensions of their lives, they tend to be physically healthy.

Many psychologists, human development specialists, and medical researchers, are becoming increasingly aware of the impact of psychological and emotional factors on one's physical health. Freud saw this connection and related illness to an absence of love:

> A strong egotism is a protection against disease, but in the last resort we must begin to love in order that we may not fall ill, and must fall ill, if in consequence of frustration, we cannot love.[78]

Later psychologists studying human actualization have noted the same connections. Here are some of their observations:

> Most psychiatrists and many psychologists and biologists now have come simply to assume that practically all disease without exception, can be called psychosomatic or organismic. That is, if one pursues any "physical" illness far enough and deep enough one will find inevitable intrapsychic, interpersonal and social variables that are also involved as determinants.

> Increasing psychological health . . . can probably also increase longevity and reduce susceptibility to disease.[79]
> —Abraham Maslow

Dimensions of the Responsible Level

Winners understand the psychosomatic relationship—psychic and soma; mind and body—that the body expresses what the mind is concerned with. They know that life is a self-fulfilling prophecy; that a person usually gets what he or she actively expects. Your fears and worries turn into anxiety which is distressful . . . the production of hormones and antibodies change; resistance levels are lowered and you become more vulnerable to disease and accident. Conversely, since your mind and body are trying to comply with your instructions and achieve a condition of "homostasis" or balance, if your mental expectancy is healthy and creative, your body will seek to display the general feeling with better health, energy, and a condition of well-being![80]
                                —Denis Waitley

There is a burgeoning amount of evidence to support the notion that people even choose things like tumors, influenza, arthritis, heart disease, "accidents" and many other infirmities, including cancer, which have always been considered something that just happens to people.[81]
                                —Wayne Dyer

Your physical health and your mental health are closely associated. Recent research is finding that many mental illnesses have physical correlations and that there is a close relationship between chemical and biological processes and mental behavior. Actually your physical condition is both a cause and mirror of your mental condition.[82]
                                —William Gladstone

Though more research is necessary to isolate causal factors, there is enough evidence to suggest a high correlation between stress and illness. The implication for business is very clear: increasing emotional and psychological maturity could assist in reducing absenteeism, industrial accidents, and even death.

HIGH ENERGY LEVEL
People at the Responsible Level have a low degree of internal conflict: that is, they are not "at war" with themselves. Thus they have more energy than the average person. As Sarah Bernhardt said, "Life begets life. Energy creates energy. It is by spending oneself that one becomes rich."[83]

The high energy level may be related to several factors. Exercise and eating high energy foods may be a major factor. Happiness itself may be energy producing. Who has not experienced a sense of exhilaration from being happy? E.F. Benson noted, "When one is happy, there is not time to be fatigued; being happy engrosses the whole attention."[84]

Since Responsible people are constantly growing, the growth process of confronting barriers is also energy-producing. According to William James,

> . . . a single successful effort of moral volition, such as saying 'no' to some habitual temptation, or performing some courageous act will launch a man on a higher level of energy for days and weeks, will give him a new range of power.[85]

The energy produced when confronting one's fears successfully, as well as conquering a detrimental habit can be tremendous. Often, individuals feel both relieved and a sense of release when they acknowledge a lie or a withold from those close to them. Typically, they feel "like a thousand pounds has been lifted." Since Responsible individuals are honest in their relationships, they are able to utilize their energy in more productive ways.

REGULAR SLEEPING, EATING, AND BREATHING CONDITIONS

At the Responsible Level, people experience the absence of any problems associated with irregular habits related to sleeping, eating, and breathing. Although problems in such areas may or may not be related to mental stress, usually at this level people do not suffer from the following symptoms:

- —insomnia
- —drowsiness
- —heartburn
- —indigestion
- —excessive gas
- —nausea
- —constipation
- —diarrhea
- —severe acne
- —weight instability
- —rapid breathing
- —asthma

To re-emphasize, being ill or lacking energy does not mean that an individual is acting irresponsibly. Responsible individuals simply do not typically experience such symptoms. These symptoms may be indicative of lower functioning in one or several dimensions of one's life.

RAPID RATE OF RECOVERY FROM ILLNESS OR ACCIDENT

Though individuals at the Responsible Level usually are not as ill or accident-prone as others at lower levels, when they do experience some physical setbacks, their rate of recovery is much faster. Because of their generally good health and because of their positive mental attitude, the body responds quickly and recuperates. Again, it should be explained that this is **generally** the case. In some diseases the detrimental effects are long-term. Therefore, slow recoveries may be indicative of other physical causes.

TAKE RESPONSIBILITY FOR HEALTH

People at this level take responsibility for maintaining and keeping their health. Specifically, their sleeping and eating habits are regular. Their foods are high in protein. They do not use legal or illegal drugs to excess, or to cope.

They also exercise. As the old proverb states, "Those who do not find time for exercise will have to find time for illness." Whether they jog, swim, walk, or play racquetball, Responsible people are involved in a regular exercise program to keep fit. By so doing, they typically ease some of the pressure in other areas of their life. Regular exercise can and does relieve some of the tension and anxiety inherent in our complex society.

Dimensions of the Responsible Level

Spiritual Dimension

RECOGNITION OF THE IMPORTANCE OF SPIRITUAL VALUES AND ACTION

Individuals at the Responsible Level incorporate spiritual aspects into all areas of their lives. They may or may not be involved in organized religions. They realize that a spiritual experience can be found everywhere. To people at the Responsible Level:

> . . . the sacred is in the ordinary . . . It is to be found in one's daily life, in one's backyard, in one's neighbors, and friends, and families . . . To be looking elsewhere for miracles is . . . a sure sign of ignorance that everything is miraculous.[86]

Responsible people are able to transform their experiences into a cohesive whole and are able to incorporate the lesson to be learned from each experience.

HIGH ETHICAL STANDARDS AND PRINCIPLES

At the Responsible Level, individuals adhere to ethical standards. They appear to know what is inherently right and inherently wrong. Unblinded by cultural bias, individuals at this level place a great deal of importance on values. Because they are so keenly aware of what is important to them, they are able to make ethical decisions more quickly and with more certainty.

Responsible people are aware that their actions do, in fact, have real consequences. At lower levels of maturity, people act as though they can get away with their negative behavior. Responsible people know that in some way, they will pay themselves back for acting unethically. According to Nathaniel Branden,

> . . . a man who acts against his own moral convictions will suffer a sense of impending disaster. Whether the moral values a man accepts are rational or irrational, man cannot escape the knowledge that, in order to deal with reality successfully, in order to live, he needs some sort of moral principles to guide him; he cannot escape his nature as a conceptual being. And implicit in this knowledge, is the awareness, (however dim, however confused) . . . that ethical principles are a practical necessity of his life on earth. A corollary of this awareness is his expectation that moral and immoral actions have consequences, even if he cannot always predict them. If he takes actions which he regards as good, he expects to benefit existentially or psychologically; if he takes actions which he regards as bad, he expects to suffer . . . although this expectation is often evaded and repressed. Thus, what he is left with, if and when he betrays his own standards, is the sense of some unknown danger, some unknown retribution, waiting for him ahead.[87]

This sense of impending doom is largely responsible for the anxiety and guilt-ridden behavior typical at the lower levels of maturity. Since Responsible individuals act in accord with their ethical standards, they are able to experience more positive emotions and a more positive mental outlook.

SPIRITUAL ACTS MOTIVATED BY LOVE, NOT FEAR

Just as Responsible people are motivated in a work environment by the desire to do a good job, rather than a fear of being fired or ostracized, so, too, are they motivated spiritually. Rather than performing good deeds because they fear the consequences of hell, or eternal damnation, they act positively because of a love of God and their fellow man. They realize fear is a negative motivation.

Bonaro Overstreet, in his excellent dissertation, Understanding Fear in Ourselves and Others, shed some light on the consequence of acting ethically out of fear:

> One give away symptom by which fear is disguised as goodness is it's tendency to define virtue in negative rather than positive terms: in terms of refraining from rather than in terms of productive outreach; of resisting temptation rather than affirming life.[88]

As Nicholaus Birdyar wrote in Towards a New Epoch, "Fear is never a good counselor and victory over fear is the first spiritual duty of man."[89]

Since they have overcome their fear, Responsible people take affirmative action to express their love of God. They act, rather than restrict the actions of themselves and others. They realize that life is a series of choices—either affirmative or negative choices. According to Maslow:

> At each point there is a progressive choice and a regression choice . . . To make the growth choice instead of the fear choice a dozen times a day is to move a dozen times a day toward self-actualization. Self-actualization is an on-going process; it means making each of the many single choices about whether to lie or be honest, whether to steal or not to steal at a particular point, and it means to make each of these choices a growth choice. This is a movement toward self-actualization.[90]

At the Responsible Level, one makes ethical choices because that is what brings satisfaction for self and others. Ultimately, at this level of maturity, love of self and of others becomes one.

121

Dimensions of the Responsible Level

LIVE BY THE "GOLDEN RULE"

All of the world's great religions incorporate some form of the "Golden Rule." The Responsible person lives by the Golden Rule, realizing that individual growth stems from serving others. As managers they serve their organizations, their boss, their peers, and their staff members. As family members, they serve their loved ones and friends. As citizens, they go "outside themselves" to serve their country, their society, and their world.

Maslow noted that self-actualized people integrate serving self with service to others:

> The empirical fact is that self-actualizing people, our best experiencers, are also our most compassionate, our great improvers, and reformers of society, our most effective fighters against injustice, inequality, slavery, cruelty, exploitation (and our best fighters for excellence, effectiveness, competence). And it also becomes clearer and clearer that the best helpers are the most fully human persons. What I may call the bodhaisattic path is an integration of self-improvement and social zeal, i.e., the best way to become a better "helper" is to become a better person. But one necessary aspect of becoming a better person is via helping other people. So one must and can do both simultaneously.[91]

This aspect of growing through others is no more apparent than in true friendship. According to Don Marquis:

> There is nothing we like to see so much as the gleam of pleasure in a person's eye when he feels that we have sympathized with him, understood him, interested ourself in his welfare. At these moments something fine and spiritual passes between two friends. These moments are moments worth living.[92]

DEDICATED TO A MISSION

Individuals at the Responsible Level are dedicated to something outside of themselves. Indeed, they often dedicate their lives and work for something that for them has become a "cause." At this stage, work becomes more than "just a job"—it is a labor of love. Seldom is there a work/play dichotomy for the Responsible human being.

Transcendence of the commonplace into a mission typically involves a dedication to a particular purpose of serving fellow man. To serve others becomes the spiritual directive. Albert Camus said, "The aim of life can only be to increase the sum of freedom and responsibility to be found in every man and in the world."[93]

In this vein, the primary mission of the Responsible person is to teach others this sense of responsibility. This is the spiritual goal of the parent, the teacher and the manager. Each role provides the opportunity to guide others to grow independently for their own good. This is also the greatest act of leadership: According to The Art of Leadership, by Ordway Tead:

> Respect for the personality of others, a strong sense of dignity and intrinsic worth of each person, a realization that all men are similar and on an equal footing in more ways than they are different; all this is essentially a religious and democratic outlook in the best and deepest sense.[94]

The Responsible person enacts this deeper, more profound spiritual mission of serving others.

LITTLE FEAR OF DEATH

Unlike most people, individuals at the Responsible Level do not fear their own deaths. Perhaps because they have lived life so fully, or because they have learned not to fear the unknown, they live more spiritually enriched lives that are not overshadowed by fear of their own impending deaths. Perhaps the underlying reason is paradoxical: those who fear death the most are those who are most afraid of life. As Anais Nin wrote:

> When I was analyzing I observed clearly that the fear of death was in proportion to not living. The less a person was in life, the greater the fear. By being alive I mean living out of all the cells, all the parts of one's self. The cells which are denied become atrophied, like a dead arm, and infect the rest of the body. People living deeply have no fear of death.[95]

Because they live life fully, Responsible people tend to view death as a transition, not an end point. As Bob Toben states in Space, Time, and Beyond, death can be viewed as a simple "change of cosmic address."[96] Though many will state that they believe their souls are immortal, at the lower levels of maturity, the response to death appears to be based on a stronger sense of finality. At the Responsible Level, death is the transition. As Waitley describes, winners have a

> . . . spiritual power woven intricately into every fiber of their being. Winners understand the mortality of their bodies, and as a result are able to age gracefully. They do not necessarily accept death as the final gun in the game of life. They see it as a transition which although they may never come to fully comprehend its meaning, they do not fear, they anticipate its eventual arrival. Winners plant shade trees under which they know they'll never sit.[97]

Since Responsible people do not fear punishment or seek reward at their deaths, they live life ethically and spiritually now. Paradoxically, the "future" reward will be a consequence of their life's actions, not a result of negative denial.

The Five Levels

	EMOTIONAL RESPONSE	INTELLECTUAL FUNCTIONING	ACTIVITY INVOLVEMENT
RESPONSIBLE	Short duration. Negatives trigger action. Stability. Positive emotions experienced often.	Ability to input and process data. Expanded consciousness. Creative. Positive projection. Thoughts stimulate action. World viewed as perfect. Cognitive preoccupation: self-fulfillment.	Interested and enthusiastic. Commitment to excellence. Competence. Freedom from excess striving. Resilient in failure.
ACHIEVEMENT	Sense of futility. Harried. Insecurity. Hyperemotional.	Selectively unconscious. Rigid solutions utilized. Conceptual complexity. Polyphasic thought patterns. Reactive, not proactive. Cognitive preoccupation: acquisition.	Frenzied. Polyphasic activities. Routine activities. Importance on goals, deadlines, and priorities.
CONFORMIST	Stress and tension without cause. Fear, guilt, shame and inadequacy. Long recovery time. Intermittent hysterics.	Cognitive simplicity—"right/wrong". Intellectualizes rather than experiences. Circular worrying. Perfectionistic. Cognitive preoccupation: acceptance, appearance.	Pointless activities. Reduced risk taking. Need for praise.
SELF-PROTECTIVE	External causation. Emotional shifts. Hysterical behavior. Fear dominant emotion.	Blind to factual data. Difficulty with decision making. Chronic distortion of reality. Cognitive preoccupation: sex and aggression.	Avoidance of challenging activities. Little self-confidence. Work as anxiety-avoidance not a source of satisfaction.
UNCONSCIOUS	Unrelated to reality. Extreme shifts. Great stress and anxiety evident.	Difficulty in processing information. Obsessive thoughts. Gross perceptual distortion. Cognitive preoccupation: survival.	Ritualistic and compulsive behavior. Difficulty in changing. Extreme fear of attempting anything new.

SELF-DISCIPLINE	RELATIONSHIPS	PHYSICAL STATE	SPIRITUAL DIMENSION
Inner-motivation. Ability to organize and plan. Flexible and adaptable. Works to capacity.	Capacity for intimacy. Unconditional positive regard. Ability to communicate. Ability to lead and to follow. Special relationship problems.	Well-being. High energy. Regular sleeping, eating, and breathing. Rapid recovery. Takes responsibility for health.	Actions congruent with values. High ethical standards. Motivated by love, not fear. Live by the golden rule. Little fear of death.
High motivation—through internalized anxiety. Intolerance of ambiguity. Inadequate planning.	Other-directed need for esteem. Competitive. Work-related emphasis.	Predisposition to coronary disease. Stress-related symptoms. Fatigue and exhaustion. Drugs used to cope.	Concerned with ethical questions. Felt spiritual void.
Lack of flexibility. Need for clear definitions. Restricted internal motivation.	Drama roles. Retention of negative experiences. Psychological games.	Obese or thin. Sleep disturbances. Gastro-intestinal problems. Headaches. Skin problems. Physical tics/stuttering. Medical assistance necessary. Episodic drug abuse.	Ritualistic emphasis. Tyranny of "shoulds," "oughts," and "musts." Self-view as victim. Rules followed not questioned.
Obsessively ritualistic. Robot-like behavior. Opportunistic. Difficulty in learning.	Withdrawal, dependency, hostility. Unconcerned with agreements, commitments or rules.	Psychosomatic illness. No appetite/muscular soreness. Chronic drug abuse.	Non-ethical. Moral level: "Don't get caught".
Little self-control of motivation. Work contingent upon external conditions. Impulsive.	Unconsciousness in presence of others. Total communication breakdown. No concern for others. Little change from negative feedback.	Blank staring. Severe physical problems. Addictions.	Ethically or morally unconcerned. Fanatical behavior.

"Actually, management authority has been eroding in recent years. There is an authority vacuum whose symptom is cynicism, and the one way to counteract this cynicism and restore proper authority is to demand responsibility from each member of the work force.

Responsibility is a hard task master, however. The worker who is asked to be responsible for what he does is going to expect that the manager will think through what he is doing and be able to explain his actions and behavior. The boss does not have to be perfect; he definitely does not have to be likeable; but he must appear to be doing what he is paid for: planning, outlining objectives, deciding priorities, setting assignments and standards—in short, assuming full responsibility for his own performance.

In the last analysis, the key factor in making people fully utilized, instead of just a potential resource, is to build into the work force—including management—the demand for responsibility, the discipline and the incentive of responsibility."[1]

—Peter F. Drucker
People Are Our Greatest Asset

"Few things help an individual more than to place responsibility upon him, and to let him know that you trust him."[2]

—Booker T. Washington
Up From Slavery

Chapter Seven

THE MBR SYSTEM: PART ONE—DELEGATION

At the Responsible Level, managers realize the way to foster productivity and to maintain a high level of satisfaction is to assist others in their growth. As staff members continue to grow, they challenge their manager to grow as well. Thus, by assisting others, managers are automatically providing increased opportunities for their own growth.

The Management By Responsibility process is based on one law of human dynamics:

> "The purpose of a manager is to serve others."

Of course, "serving others" does not mean "helping" or "rescuing." To serve others is to assist them in realizing their 100 % responsibility for their own success and satisfaction. To do so, the manager needs to create an environment which supports success rather than creating failure. Furthermore, "serving others" is not restricted to staff members; it also includes co-workers, one's supervisor, and the organization as a whole.

By constantly asking, "Am I serving myself and everyone involved?" or "Are my actions going to create more harmony or dissonance?", the Responsible manager can begin to eliminate "stamp collecting" and common business games. Such behavior is counter-productive to organizational goals because it creates dissonance between staff members and impedes individual growth. To be effective as a staff, individual members need to work harmoniously. This requires cooperation and a concerted, unified effort to achieve staff goals.

In staff situations, competition among individual members can be positive or negative. Competition between individuals or departments at the expense of the overall purpose of the organization can be destructive to the department and to the organization as a whole.

For example, the purpose of a football team is to win the game. If, rather than cooperate, individual players compete with one another for stardom, the team often ends up losing. Team members can become self-righteous by silently disagreeing with the play that was called by the quarterback and undermining its success by only putting forth partial effort. They will be "right" and yet the team will fail to make the first down. While competition during practice sessions can assist each player to actualize more of his potential, competition during the game can be a destructive force.

Similarly, in the work environment, when staff members not only set individual goals but share the methods they have found to be more effective in accomplishing their goals, they will be more individually and collectively productive. Unfortunately, many departments foster the "zero-sum" game: "What you win - I lose." This is particularly noticeable when the manager, like the quarterback, proposes an approach to a problem and staff members disagree. Unlike football players in a huddle, it is the responsibility of staff members to state, as objectively as possible, why they do not agree. Yet, if the final decision is made contrary to staff opinion, it remains the responsibility of staff members to carry out management decisions as completely as possible so as not to undermine the organization's efforts.

So unlike football, where decisions are made quickly and unilaterally, staff members must voice differing opinions and discuss alternative options. Like football, however, when those decisions are made, it is the responsibility of the staff member, to carry out the functions related to the decisions, without complaining or setting up the situation to be "right" about failure. Of course, this position assumes that the directives and policies are ethical. If one is continually compromising his ethical standards, the situation will need to be confronted directly and if nothing changes, different employment may be necessary.

So to encourage a feeling of teamwork and a spirit of cooperation, the manager must create an environment that is based on clear perceptions. Staff members need to know what their specific duties are, what their authority level is, and how their efforts contribute to the attainment of organizational goals.

Office friction can be eliminated or substantially reduced when the manager clarifies the functions to be performed and the results to be produced. Defining the job and clarifying the goals become the two major functions of management, whose overriding purpose is to serve others through the accomplishment of these functions and goals. To complement the Management By Responsiblitity system, one starts by defining the job to be done.

Defining the Job

During the last decade, job performance appraisals and various types of periodic evaluations have become popular. Yet, the popularity has generally been confined to personnel departments and upper management. Worker resentment over such procedures does not seem to actually be directed toward the process itself. Rather, the resentment stems from being evaluated on precise performance criteria, while the job itself remains ambiguously defined.

To avoid such resentment, the following steps are suggested.

Step One: Clarifying the Job Functions

The Management By Responsibility system begins by clearly defining the job to be done. This includes the functions to be performed, the authority one has to carry out those functions, and the priorities of the functions themselves. The following diagram illustrates the initial step:

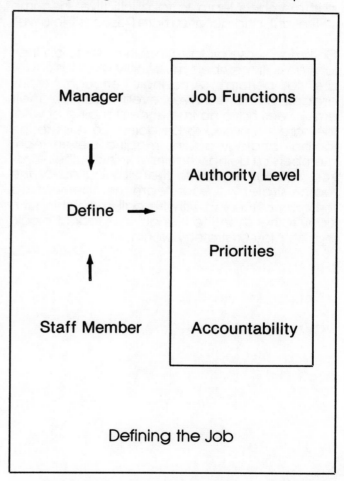

As a matter of mutual concern, the manager and staff member, **separately and in writing**, specify the functions that the staff member should perform as part of the job. The definition should be as detailed as possible. Vague job descriptions stated in a paragraph that concludes with " . . . and other duties as assigned," are not specific or explicit enough.

When the functions are not clearly defined, resentments build both for the staff member and for the manager. Often they take the form of such familiar and destructive psychological games that begin with "That's not my job!" and "Who told you to do that?" Even when there is no overt resentment, the reluctance to perform job functions, coupled with very little recognition, can be debilitating for staff members. Only when job functions are specifically established can staff members learn to take initiative, become self-reliant, and act at a more Responsible Level.

Common sense dictates that in order to do their jobs all staff members must know what tasks they are to perform. Amazingly enough, many organizations survive even though their employees have no true understanding of what they are supposed to be doing. To refer to the football analogy again, imagine eleven team members all doing what they "think" is their function, without regard to the play called or the team's strategy. If each team member wanted the glory of running with the ball or catching the pass, rather than the less glorious task of blocking, no play or strategy would work.

Task confusion can similarly affect department functions. In one retail store, the sales personnel did not feel it was "their job" to clean the glass counters or to return merchandise to the racks after customers had tried on clothes. They kept waiting for the janitorial staff to provide these functions. The janitorial staff felt that their function included only such duties as general cleaning, primarily when the store was closed. The purpose of serving customers was forgotten as each group accused the other of not "doing their job." Predictably, the net result cost the store a great deal of business to everyone's disadvantage.

To avoid this exercise in futility, the first part of the MBR system involves the manager and the staff member **writing** their individual perceptions of the functions that are part of the staff member's job. They do this separately to distinguish those functions that are commonly recognized from those that are discrepant. When such discrepancies appear, the process of negotiation must take place to formulate a commitment. The manager and staff member must mutually agree on those functions that are part of the staff member's job.

The list resulting from such negotiations is not permanent or immutable. This process does not exclude the fact that situations change, requiring staff members to perform certain functions not included on the original list. It is a desirable trait for a staff member to willingly cooperate when new functions arise. In a similar fashion Responsible managers do not assume that their position authorizes them to "order" staff members to perform such functions. Requests are far more effective.

A manager and staff member need to negotiate in good faith in order to formulate functions that are realistic. The manager needs to avoid "dumping" the workload, and the staff member needs to assume initiative for performing necessary functions of the job.

The number of job functions listed will vary depending on the type of job and the diversity of functions performed. A general office manager, who does everything from answering sales calls, to bookkeeping, to directing work flow, may have several pages of distinctly different functions. A bookkeeper assigned to one division may have only one page.

Though this process may take some time, it only needs to be updated periodically once it is completed. When job functions are clarified, hiring new personnel will be much easier, as will be assisting the newly hired staff member in knowing what is to be done as part of the job.

Step Two: Defining the Authority

After achieving precise definition and agreement on job functions, the next step is to determine the authority with which the staff member can carry out those functions.

Vaguely defined authority is the cause for some of the most serious psychological games played on the job. Frequently, staff members say, "My boss gives me as much authority as I'm willing to take." This approach seemingly works—that is, until there are problems. When something goes wrong, the same boss who previously had a laissez-faire attitude shouts, "Who told you that you could make that decision? Why didn't you come to me first?"

This problem underlies the familiar story of the manager who introduces his staff member to friends at a cocktail party: "Group, I'd like you to meet Greg Johnson. Greg is the most responsible person on my staff . . . whenever anything goes wrong, he's responsible!" The failure to clearly define authority, **in writing**, inhibits staff members from operating at higher levels of maturity.

Rarely do staff members know precisely the authority they have to make decisions or to carry out their functions. So staff members continue to go to their managers to make decisions that they are capable of making themselves, or, conversely, they make decisions for which they should have had prior approval.

AUTHORITY LEVELS

Authority typically exists on four levels:

1. Complete Autonomy: The staff member makes the decision or carries out the function, without checking with anyone or reporting the action taken.

2. Act and Report: The staff member makes the decisions or carries out the function, and then submits a report to the manager or peers. The report may be verbal or written, simple or complicated. The reporting procedure should be discussed and agreed upon in advance. The report may also be issued to individuals outside the department, and may even involve a formal presentation.

3. Act Only After Consultation: The staff member makes the decisions or carries out the function, but only after consulting with management or other staff members. At this level, it is generally acknowledged that the staff member can make the decision without the overt consent and agreement of management. And yet, because of the nature of final accountability, management always reserves the right to reverse the decision, although such action would be rare.

For example, vice-presidents can propose new methods and operational procedures, yet the president must always be consulted. Not to allow vice-presidents that freedom would stifle their creativity. The president may or may not agree with the proposed change, and has an obligation to say so. Before such changes can become a permanent part of the ongoing company policy, however, the president may have to approve the change.

Another example concerns hiring and firing. The manager may want to be consulted before department heads hire new personnel or dismiss members of their staff. And yet, the basic decision will rest with the department head.

4. Act Only After Approval: The staff member makes a decision or carries out the function only after receiving management approval. This approval may be oral or written and may involve more than one person or department. Some functions and decisions will always remain at this level. Major decisions such as those involving large expenditures and policy changes may remain at this level so that the manager always remains in control.

Although some decisions and functions must necessarily remain with management, many decisions and functions can be delegated to staff members by increasing their level of authority. Increasing the level of authority is a function of the staff member's experience, motivation, level of responsibility, and past success.

Each time staff members are given more authority to make decisions and to independently carry out their functions, it involves both trust and a certain amount of risk on the part of management. To inappropriately trust a staff member who does not have the ability or who is not positively motivated may be akin to organizational suicide!

To adequately delegate authority, managers must be keenly aware of their staff members' abilities, past experience, and motivational level. Thus, the importance of implementing and maintaining a working system to establish authority levels should not be underestimated.

The process of defining levels of authority is the same as defining job functions. Both the manager and the staff member separately list the perceived authority level and then meet to negotiate any discrepancies. The following form may be used in this process:

Responsibility Definition Worksheet

Functions Performed As Part Of Job *	Authority Level**			
	1	2	3	4
1. _____				
2. _____				
3. _____				
4. _____				
5. _____				
6. _____				
7. _____				

*Functions should be clustered and ranked so that the top 20% are noted. These are the most crucial functions for success on the job. Evaluate the key factors that are expected to make the greatest contribution to earnings and for which goals and performance standards are set.

**Authority Levels: 1 - Complete Autonomy   2 - Act and Report   3 - Act Only After Consultation
4 - Act Only After Approval.

The maxim, "The best decisions are made at the lowest possible level," is a necessary condition of effective, responsible management. Most staff members want to make decisions that affect their jobs. The wise manager allows them to do so, knowing that they usually have better information with which to make valid decisions. Given the increased authority they have merited, staff members tend to "own" their decisions. Thus, positive results are much more likely to occur. The further benefit of increased job commitment can only enhance organizational well-being.

Staff members generally would like to participate in decisions that affect their jobs. At least, they should be consulted and their suggestions given a great deal of consideration. After all, they are much closer to the situation than their managers.

This is not to say that managers should "abdicate" the ultimate authority for decision-making. Responsible managers simply allow staff members more authority to make decisions and to carry out their functions. This is directly proportional to the ability, experience and willingness of the staff members to do so.

At first, some staff members may balk at being asked to assume more responsibility. They may quibble, "But I'm not the boss. Why should I make those decisions or do that job?" Staff members, particularly those operating at the Conformist Level, are fearful that any mistakes will be held against them when raises or promotions are given. In these instances, trust may take some time to establish. Staff members may even test their managers to determine sincerity. Only by allowing the staff members to correct their own mistakes and by actively soliciting their suggestions, can managers instill a high level of trust.

Agreement through mutual negotiations is the key to defining and establishing authority. Forcing staff members to take on more authority, whether it is done overtly or covertly, often builds resentment and could even lead to psychological games of "Stupid," "Kick Me", "Harried", or "Let's Make the Boss Sorry" to prove to management that additional functions or increased authority is not desired.

When both parties perceive that they have a choice, the desired result is more likely to occur. That is why managers and staff members check the perceived level and then negotiate. In that way, all concerned parties are committed to agreed upon authority levels.

Even though misunderstandings regarding authority levels are the primary source of negative feelings and psychological game playing, very few organizations provide a system for clearly establishing the level of authority. The cost for not doing so is staggering. The ambiguity of authority levels leads to ineffective and inefficient operating procedures. Organizations will run much more smoothly when authority levels are established, defined, and agreed upon in advance.

The third requisite of job definition is to establish the priority level assigned to a particular function and assignment. On some jobs where the priorities are constantly shifting, new agreements to determine what are **now** the top priorities, need to be formulated.

Even in jobs where priorities remain fairly constant, managers may view some functions as top priorities, while the staff members may regard these same functions as less crucial. For example, in many sales offices, managers place a much higher priority on the neatness of the office than do the sales personnel. Unless all parties can negotiate on the importance of neatness, the manager can play "Martyr": "Why doesn't anyone else clean up around here?" In contrast, the sales personnel can feel justified in their position of "I'm only being paid to sell." The net result is a disorganized office, frustrated managers and sales personnel, as well as disgruntled customers. Everyone loses.

It is crucial that management discuss **what** they feel are top priorities and **why** they feel they are so important. It is also essential that management listen openly to staff members. Not only may differences be uncovered, but management may also find that staff member's perspectives are more accurate.

As with establishing functions and authority levels, managers need to attend to areas of priority discrepancies. Once divergent perspectives are discovered, each participant should openly and objectively verbalize their positions, while keeping an open mind about the validity of the contrary view. Perceptions may be easily checked by such questions as, "Then you feel that 'X' is a top priority for the following reasons . . . Is that right?" Or, "Let me see if I understand your point of view. Because of these factors . . . you feel that this is top priority. Is that correct?"

In sum, the objective throughout the whole process of job definition is to arrive at clearly defined agreements about functions, authority, and priorities. In the initial stages, this process may be time-consuming. However, once the job is clearly defined, it will only need to be updated periodically. This is usually accomplished during regular quarterly reviews.

Creating effective job descriptions requires successful delegation on the part of the manager. The following section is provided to assist in effective delegation. Once managers have defined the job, a determination can be made as to **who** can best perform the job functions.

The Delegation Process

Managers at the Responsible Level realize the importance of delegating job functions and the authority to carry out those functions. Managers at lower levels tend to avoid delegation for a number of reasons. The following are typical excuses these managers use to justify not delegating effectively:

1. **"If you want something done right, you have to do it yourself."** This position allows one to be "right" about being busy. Responsible managers work "smarter not harder."

2. **"My staff members are already too busy."** They may be, because they have to get decisions from management that they are in a better position to make themselves. Typically, the best decisions are made at the lowest possible level.

3. **"My staff members lack the experience."** The only way staff members become experienced is to be given responsibility and the opportunity to perform new functions.

4. **"Mistakes are too costly."** Managers need to be certain that they have adequate controls to prevent costly errors. If staff members learn from their mistakes, they will grow. Managers need to realize that staff members may make the same mistakes they did before they became managers.

5. **"It takes less time to do it myself."** This may be true in the short run, but not on a long-term basis.

6. **"My staff members are unwilling to take responsibility."** Managers encourage this attitude by constantly rescuing their staff members, i.e., solving their problems for them. Responsible managers allow staff members to take the responsibility by allowing them to suggest solutions.

7. **"I enjoy making my own decisions and keeping busy."** Responsible managers do not make the mistake of being just busy, rather than being productive. Results do not lie. Being frenzied is not indicative of Responsible management.

Two recurring situations are symptomatic of poor delegation: (1) a manager's functions and the hours necessary to perform them far outnumber those of staff members, and (2) the insistence on the part of staff members to have management make decisions that they could better make themselves.

Effective delegation involves more than assigning tasks and giving orders. It is based upon **mutual commitment**, rather than a "You will do this and you will like it," managerial approach. Where delegation is successful, psychological games are avoided. Responsible managers concentrate on producing results and satisfaction, not drama.

In his book, <u>No-Nonsense Delegation</u>, Dale McConkey details specific roles for both the manager and the staff member in the process of delegation:[3]

Role of the Manager in the Delegation Process

1. To communicate clearly the functions being delegated.

2. To specify the level of authority.

3. To encourage staff participation in the process.

4. To review results, not methods.

5. To show trust and positive expectations.

6. To give credit, not blame.

7. To solicit recommendations.

8. To give support to staff members.

9. To be consistent.

10. To develop staff members.

Role of the Staff in the Delegation Process

1. To take initiative.

2. To relate positively to the manager.

3. To ask for realism in delegation.

4. To establish personal and professional goals.

5. To determine objectives to accomplish goals.

6. To assist in determining means for feedback.

7. To report to the manager.

8. To carry out the delegation.

9. To continue in self-development.

10. To provide Responsible Staff Action.

"Responsible Staff Action" is the key if each staff member is to take total responsibility. It eliminates the drama of the staff member playing "Victim" and waiting to be "Rescued" or "Persecuted." Developed by the Air Force over a quarter of a century ago,[4] it is as applicable today in any organization as it was then.

The following adaptation should assist in clarifying this key concept:

Responsible Staff Action

Responsible Staff Action is the study of a problem—and the presentation of a solution—in such a form that the manager may simply indicate approval of the completed recommendation for action.

1. Get Approval
Staff members need to be certain that formulating a solution for this particular problem is a high priority item.

2. Work Out The Details
Staff members should present a solution in a form that is complete, with all the details worked out in advance. Actually, the more difficult the problem is, the more tendency there is to present the problem to managers in piecemeal fashion. It is the responsibility of staff members to work out the details.

3. Consult With Others
Staff members should not consult with their managers in determining the details of their action plan unless necessary. Instead, if they cannot determine these details by themselves, they should consult with other staff members, departments, or orgaizations. In far too many problem situations, the typical impulse of inexperienced staff members is to be "rescued" by asking their managers what to do. This occurs more often when a difficult problem produces frustration. It seems so much easier to ask managers what to do and wait for the answer. Staff members must resist the impulse to be "rescued."

4. Advise The Manager Of A Specific Plan Of Action
It is the function of staff members to advise their managers what ought to be done, not to ask what **they** ought to do. Managers need answers, not questions.

It is the job of staff members to study, analyze, check, restudy, and recheck until they have come up with a single proposed action—the best one of all that they have considered. Their manager may then approve or disapprove the recommended action. In most instances, this will require a single document prepared for the signature of the manager, without accompanying comment. As one manager put it, "Don't give me the labor pains, just deliver the baby."

5. Present A Single, Coordinated Proposed Action
In presenting a solution, staff members should not make long explanations or write detailed memoranda. Viable solutions are self-evident. Except for record purposes, writing a memo **to** one's manager does not constitute Responsible Staff Action. Writing a memo **for** one's manager to be sent to someone else does.

Staff members should place their views before their managers in **finished** form so that they can make the recommendations their own views by simply signing their names. If the proper result emerges from the "finished" solution to a problem, managers will usually recognize it at once. If managers need comment or explanation, they will ask for it.

The requirements for "Responsible Staff Action" do not negate the possibilities of a "rough draft" or an oral presentation. However, such preliminary forms must not be presented as "half-baked" ideas or used as a means of shifting to the manager the burden of formulating the action. The action plan must be **complete** in every respect, with all the previous steps followed.

6. Test For Responsibility
Staff members should test whether they are willing to assume total responsibility for their proposal by asking, "If I were the manager, would I be willing to put my name on this action plan, and, thus, take total responsibility on its being correct?" If the answer is "no" or "perhaps," they should take it back and re-work it until they are willing to assume total responsibility.

Responsible Staff Action may result in more work for staff members, yet provide more freedom for managers. This is as it should be, since it accomplished three important things:

1. Managers are protected from incomplete ideas, long memos, and premature oral presentations.

2. Staff members are in a better position to implement the ideas they have formulated.

3. Staff members grow individually by taking responsibility.

When staff members formulate proposals using Responsible Staff Action, they begin to operate at the Responsible Level. In addition, the action plan is typically far more effective since staff members are much more familiar with the problems and the means to solve them.

Constant staff requests to be "rescued," are examples of "delegation up." In most organizations, staff members delegate their problems to their managers, who, in turn, delegate their problems to their managers, and so forth. At each level, managers need to ask, "Whose problem is this anyway?" A manager should either solve the problem immediately with the staff member or let the staff member suggest an approach through Responsible Staff Action.

Effective delegation, like effective goal setting, involves the recognition of mutual benefits. If the manager does not outline the benefits of staff members assuming responsibility in solving their problems, then the staff will continue to try to be rescued or they will persecute their managers because their problems have not been solved **for** them.

Once the job has been defined by delegating functions, authority and priorities, then goals and objectives need to be established. This is the second part of the MBR process. The next chapter on goals, objectives, and performance standards focuses on the techniques involved.

"If you don't know where you're going, you can't get there. And you can't get anywhere until you know who you are."[1]

—Seneca

"What is my goal in life? What am I striving for? What is my purpose?" These are questions which every individual asks himself at one point or another, sometimes calmly and meditatively, sometimes in agonizing uncertainty or despair. They're all old, old questions which are asked and answered in every century of history, yet they are also questions which every individual must ask and answer for himself his own way."[2]

—Carl Rogers
On Becoming A Person

"Goal: Something desirable; something to be achieved; an expectation; an end to be reached; a target to strive for or to aim at."[3]

Webster's New World Dictionary
Of The American Language

Chapter Eight

THE MBR SYSTEM: PART TWO—GOAL SETTING

The first phase of the MBR system clarifies the job to be done. The second phase establishes goals and objectives. Quite simply, a goal is defined as a result to be produced. Organizational, departmental, and individual goals need to be clearly established—both those that are long-term as well as short-term.

Unfortunately, many corporate managers act like the pilot on the intercom who says, "I have some good news and some bad news: The bad news first—we're lost over Texas. The good news is that we're going five hundred miles per hour."

In a similar fashion, many departments are speeding along at 500 m.p.h. without a clear direction. Staff members work furiously, yet no one seems to know what short or long term purpose is served by such a furious pace. Once the direction is known, it is much easier to get there. As the title of David Campbell's book suggests: <u>If You Don't Know Where You're Going, You'll Probably End Up Somewhere Else!</u>[4]

Management must clearly establish the direction. After the direction is clarified, managers, together with their staff members, need to establish specific goals to be accomplished. These goals and objectives, as well as performance expectations, need to be clearly communicated to all concerned.

To accomplish goals, individuals need to make commitments. Commitments are based on taking total responsibility, rather than on "wishing" and "hoping" that everything will work out as planned.

Many firms think they have an MBO (Management By Objectives) program. Actually they have an MBW program. At the end of the year, the manager plays a persecutor by saying, "But you stated that you were going to produce 1000 widgets and you only produced 800!" The staff member retorts, "Well, I wish I could have, but . . ." The manager, too, wishes that 1000 widgets would have been produced. That's MBW: Management by Wishes!

The only real question when asking for a commitment is: "Are you willing to do what is necessary to produce the result?" In other words, is the person truly committed to taking total responsibility? If there is not a definite, affirmative response, then the intention is a wish, not a goal.

The entire MBR system is based on making and keeping commitments. Commitments are made to produce results. These results may be tangible or intangible; easy or difficult. They are, nonetheless, results.

To formulate goals, commitments must be made. To be accomplished, goals must be perceived as mutually beneficial for all parties involved. If an individual fails to see a benefit for accomplishing the goals, the likelihood of producing results is slim. In this context, a commitment may look like this:

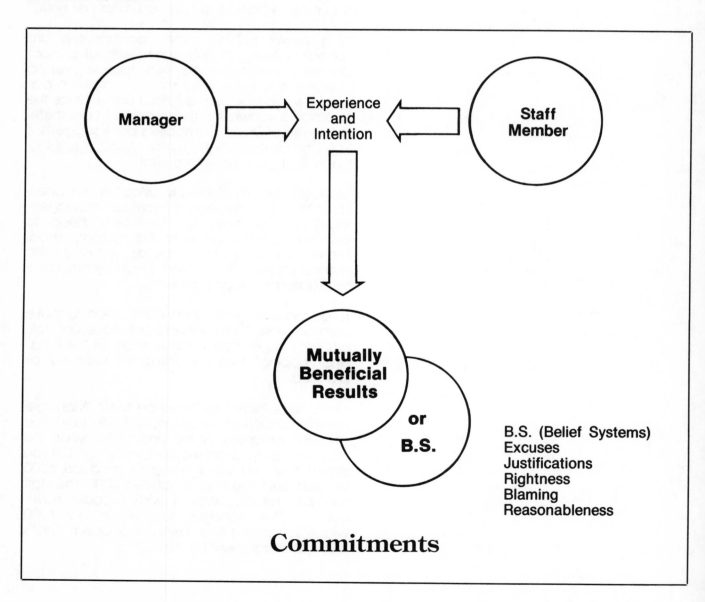

B.S. (Belief Systems)
Excuses
Justifications
Rightness
Blaming
Reasonableness

Commitments

Life is RESULTS or B.S. You've either produced the result on time, as agreed, or you produce the B.S. as to why you haven't
RESULTS DON'T LIE.

The best agreements are Win-Win . . . I win **and** you win. If it's Win-Lose, or Lose-Win, the agreement will **not** work.

If results are not produced, either the individuals involved did not take total responsibility, (and perhaps never intended to), or they did not perceive a benefit for them in the accomplishment of the goal.

Interestingly enough, corporations, like individuals, are either producing results or are producing excuses as to why they did not produce the results. When results are not produced, the mind automatically produces the "reasons" why. The mind focuses on the "B.S."—the "excuses" and "justifications"; it pleas for "reasonableness," stands on "rightness," and ends up "blaming" other people, circumstances, and events.

All of these responses to not producing results bring people down to lower levels or maturity. The internal dialogue—the mind chatter—attempts to make non-productivity reasonable. And yet, the level of satisfaction one experiences is directly proportional to the extent that commitments are kept to one's self and to others. Thus, job satisfaction depends upon one's willingness to make commitments and then to produce the results.

The basic commitment to the organization and to one's immediate supervisor is to be productive. One is paid to produce results. Strangely enough, that comes as a shock to some staff members. Somehow, they have the mistaken notion that they should be paid simply for coming to work everyday. Others believe that doing as little as possible will bring them the greatest satisfaction. Both approaches indicate lower levels of functioning. Unfortunately, these people did not realize that they, themselves, are the only ones who ultimately lose, because they are the ones with very little satisfaction and even less self-pride and dignity. Staff members who attempt to do less than others end up with less satisfaction than everyone else. Each individual is ultimately the only source for their individual job satisfaction.

For many, it is difficult to accept that they are totally responsible for the results they produce individually. It is harder still to acknowledge that one is also totally responsible for the results produced by the staff. Thus, managers are 100% responsible for commitments they make based on the performance of their staff.

For example, a manager of a life insurance office stated that he felt no responsibility if his agents failed to meet their goals. He said, "If they don't produce what they said they were going to, how am I to be held accountable? It's not my responsibility that they didn't produce their volume. I base my projections on what they say they will produce. When my boss calls me and the final results are due, I'm not responsible if they didn't do what they were supposed to do! It's not my fault!"

Though common, the life insurance manager's rationalization misses the point. When staff members do not produce the results to which they committed themselves, it may not be the manager's **fault** and yet that does not negate responsibility. Total responsibility asssumes that one is the cause of one's experience.

In other words, did the manager do everything necessary to produce the result? In the example cited, the manager failed to keep his commitment with his boss, because his agents failed to keep their commitment with him. Yet, each of us has only one perspective from which reality is experienced.

When asked what he would have done to insure their success, the manager responded, "I would have held special meetings if I noticed that they were falling behind their projections. I would have worked with them privately. I would have made certain their leads were good. I would have provided excellent training programs to assist in problem areas." He realized that if they failed to produce the results, it may have been because he did not take any of the aforementioned actions.

Slowly, the manager began to realize that when the agents did not keep their commitments, it was **his** responsibility. Conversely, he recognized that if they had kept their commitments, he would have assumed total responsibility when his boss congratulated him on outstanding performance that year.

If individuals fail to produce the result to which they have committed themselves, it is because they did not do everything necessary to do so. Yet, instead of acknowledging their choice for not doing so, they feel the need to justify their actions, make the result reasonable, defend themselves, and come up with excuses. Unfortunately, most corporations and managers encourage excuses. Of course, if staff members cannot come up with enough excuses and justifications themselves, management often creates committees to help them!

Such excuses are very time-consuming. If a staff is producing the results and meeting their goals, there is not much to communicate, other than to congratulate each other. If the staff is not producing results, special meetings proliferate. Long memos are written to justify not reaching goals. Committees and task forces are formulated to investigate the situation. Such meetings and long memos simply assist those involved in failing to produce results to feel justified and self-righteous. Yet, there is very little personal or professional satisfaction.

To experience satisfaction, each staff member and the manager need to take total responsibility for making commitments that will work.

Commitments are contracts. The goal, of course, has to be perceived as being mutually beneficial. A benefit may be for a desired reward, rather than performing out of fear of particular consequences. Either can be motivating; yet the desire, rather than fear, is usually more effective because it is a positive internal motivation. As such, it does not require the manager to be constantly "supervising" to get the job done.

For example, a famous producer of Broadway shows met with the actors and stated that his goal was to produce the finest musical the world had ever known. He stressed the mutual benefit for all involved and what it could mean to their careers if they were involved with such a successful company.

He then stated that to reach the goal would require several commitments, most important of which was to have rehearsals that started on time and for which each person came prepared. To the surprise of the cast, he went on to state the consequences of not being committed. If the leads showed up late or were unprepared, they would see their understudy in the rehearsal. If it occurred a second time, they would view the performance from the wings that evening. If they chose to be late or unprepared a third time, they would no longer be part of that production.

Some of the "stars" felt the producer was simply stressing a point and later found themselves out of work. Their understudies went on to become some of the biggest box office successes Broadway has ever seen. The producer manifested his goal, and in fact realized his results by producing one of the world's finest musicals.

Too often managers respond to the fear of the consequences, rather than to the reward of success. Fear is typically related to those who seek immediate gratification at lower levels of maturity. As the Indian guru Rajneesh states, "Success is a consequence, not a result."[5] Success is a consequence of living successfully. It is a manifestation of wanting to do the best job possible for one's self, for the staff, and for the organization. At higher levels, the motivation to do a job well is not based on the fear of being fired or of not being accepted; rather it is the motivation to be a successful, happy, actualized human being.

The primary goal of management is to discover, hire, and maintain staff members who are willing to make commitments to accomplish their goals because they are motivated by a sincere desire to do what is best for themselves and others in any given situation.

When commitments are made to accomplish a particular goal, each individual involved needs to assume a position of 100% responsibility. It is **not** a "50-50" proposition!

Whenever a goal is accomplished all parties involved assumed 100% responsibility, even if some of the parties involved did most of the actual work. Part of assuming 100% responsibility is hiring successful, responsible staff members and then proceeding to create an environment conducive to growth. Everyone involved must take total 100% responsibility or the result will not be produced.

If the manager and the staff are not reaching their goals, it is because each, individually, is not taking total responsibility.

If a manager keeps making commitments with staff members who consistently fail to keep them, there are several possibilities:

1. The manager may be manifesting his or her own negative beliefs about others, i.e., "If you want something done right, you have to do it yourself."
2. The manager may be using certain staff members as scapegoats—people who are blamed or held responsible when things are not going well.
3. The staff members may not **really** want to be on the staff. They may have psychologically "quit" a long time ago.
4. The manager may have psychologically "fired" certain staff members and yet allowed them to continue to work for the organization out of a desire to avoid confronting the situation.

Remarkably, in most cases, one usually knows upon making a commitment whether he or she will do what is necessary to keep the commitment. Making commitments with no intention of completion makes total nonsense out of even the most well-intentioned Management By Objectives programs! In a typical scenario the manager calls the staff member into the office and says, "Can you produce 1000 widgets by this time next year?" The staff member responds, "Yes, that seems reasonable," all the while saying to himself or herself, "1000 widgets? Is the boss kidding? I'll be lucky to produce 850!"

The moment the commitment is made to produce the results, the staff member begins to create excuses as to why it will not be completed. It may take a year to come up with enough reasonable justifications and excuses, and yet the process started at the time when commitment was made.

Chances are very likely that the manager also knew that producing 1000 was not likely. The staff member was asked to commit to a 1000 figure in the hope that perhaps 850 might be produced. The problem with formulating goals based on lies is that the result is not produced. In-

stead, the predictable result is frustration, feelings of dissatisfaction, resentment or discouragement. So, one emphatic way to lower staff morale is to compel staff members to commit themselves to unrealistic goals.

In contrast, however, in setting goals with employees at the Achievement Level, it is the role of management to ask staff members to lower their goals so that they are more realistic and attainable. In working with Conformist employees, managers may determine that the goal is too conservative. Goals that do not provide a challenge are not desirable. Typically, the greater the risk, the greated the satisfaction.

There is a very fine line between what is challenging and what is realistic. The goal must be enough of a challenge to provide satisfaction upon its successful completion, and yet, it must not be so high as to be perceived as impossible. It is also crucial that the goal be negotiated, rather than pre-determined by a management committee. Most staff members want to be asked about what they can produce. People become committed to those results where they have perceived a choice. Feeling forced into making a commitment often leads to non-productive or even counter-productive behavior.

Because of the importance of goals in a work environment, it is important to turn our attention to the process of establishing realistic or challenging goals.

The Successful Goal-Setting Process

Step One: Getting S.M.A.R.T. About Goals

To accomplish them, one needs to become SMART about goals. SMART stands for: Specific, Measurable, Acceptable, Realistic, and Truthful.

Specific: One needs to be very specific about goals and the objectives necessary to accomplish them. The more specific the goals and objectives, the more likely that results will be produced. Consider the significant difference between, "We want to have the best sales volume in the history of this company," and "Our goal for this year is 80,000 units to be sold by July 1."

To enhance job productivity, specific goals should be negotiated with each staff member individually and as a group. What are the specific results that need to be produced in the next year, month or week? Time spent in developing goals is time well-invested. Furthermore, goals should be stated in positive terms, rather than negative ones. For example, a positive goal, such as "I will budget departmental funds effectively so that we can purchase . . . " is much better than a negative one, such as "I'm going to stop unnecessary expenditures and waste in the office." Goals should also begin with a strong statement of intention, such as, "I will . . . " This usually assists in establishing a definite commitment.

Measurable: The results should be stated in measurable terms. If goals are not measurable, they are probably an ongoing purpose, a wish or a dream. Typically, organizational "goals" are actually mission statements.

"To increase customer satisfaction" is an overall organization mission. A mission or purpose is ongoing—more can always be done. Conversely, a goal is a measured result which enacts the purpose. For example, "To increase the orders by 15%," may reflect an increase in customer satisfaction.

"To increase staff morale next year," again is too vague and unmeasurable. How could an increase in staff morale be measured? To do so, there may be specific, measurable goals about decreasing turnover and absenteeism or goals related to positive responses on employee job satisfaction questionnaires.

Acceptable: Are the goals and the objectives to be accomplished acceptable in light of ethical considerations? One may have a goal to double one's income in two years. That is specific and measurable, yet one needs to determine whether the means to accomplish this goal are ethically acceptable.

Frequently in the corporate arena questions of ethics are not raised. All too often, an individual has a goal to become promoted, and then sets about to have the person in that position fired. At lower levels of maturity, people fail to realize that they pay themselves back when they act unethically.

Realistic: Is the goal realistic? Responsible mature individuals consistently set realistic goals for themselves. If goals are not realistic, the consequence is personal dissatisfaction. Each individual is the only one who can determine whether or not goals are realistic. What is realistic for one person may be totally unrealistic for others.

In formulating goals, it is always important for the manager to ask staff members if they feel their goals are truly realistic. Most managers have the mistaken notion that motivation produces success.

They feel if they could "just motivate" their staff, they would become far more successful. The reverse is often the case: success produces motivation. The more successful the individual is, the more motivated the individual is to become successful. To create a staff of successful people, their goals must be realistic. If they fall short, both the manager and the staff member must determine whether their goals were realistic in the first place.

Truthful: Is the goal the truth? Remember, results don't lie. If the goal is not the truth, a great deal of time and energy will be wasted. To determine the truth one needs to ask two questions: "Do I have the ability?" and "Am I willing to take total responsibility to accomplish this goal?"

Step Two: Determining Ability

One either does or does not have the ability to produce the result. Only the individual knows whether he or she has the ability.

If people set goals for which they do not have the ability, the goal is immediately transformed into a "wish" or a "hope." For example, a woman stated that her goal was to become a grandmother within the next five years. She somehow failed to recognize that she did not have the ability to produce that result! What she had was a "hope" not a goal.

Most people, however, do not have to worry too much about ability. They have incredible ability to produce results. Yet, most fail to realize that it is not the lack of ability that impedes progress; it is an unwillingness to take the responsibility to make it happen.

Step Three: Assuming Responsibility

The crucial factor in accomplishing goals is responsibility. Like ability, one is or is not willing to take total responsibility. A partial willingness by definition, is unacceptable.

The crucial question to ask oneself is: "Am I willing to do what is necessary to produce the result?" The truth is inherent in the result. If one is willing to do what is necessary, the result will be produced. The question of responsibility is also very important for managers to ask themselves when setting goals with staff members. Is the manager willing to do what is necessary to insure that the staff member accomplishes his or her goals? That question virtually assures a realistic goal!

Step Four: Determining The Objectives and Action Plan

What are the steps necessary to produce the result?

If one has the ability and is willing to take total responsibility, then the overall goal needs to be broken into meaningful objectives accompanying an action plan complete with due dates. Inherent within any goal is both the desire and the willingness to act. In other words, a goal is something one wants to obtain or maintain. It is also something sufficiently compelling to prompt the action necessary to achieve it.

Too often, staff members fail to recognize the specific action that is necessary.

Implementing the MBR System

Once the goals are formulated and commitments are made, the most essential phase toward accomplishing the result has been initiated. Periodic reviews of the goals, broken down into easily attainable short-term objectives, will be necessary. Typically, monthly or quarterly reviews to determine whether the staff is on-plan or not, will be essential to the continued success of the MBR system.

If a staff member's results are not according to plan, the goal or objectives may have to be revised or commitments may have to be reaffirmed. The staff member and/or the manager may have to take some particular action to get back on course. The Responsible manager realizes that **now** is the time to take action, not four months from now. If one waits, it may be too late. That is why periodic reviews are crucial to individuals, as well as departmental and corporate, success.

An overview of the MBR system follows:

PHASE ONE: Defining The Job

A. INITIAL STAFF MEETING
1. Explain the MBR process; its purpose and benefits.
2. Distribute and explain "Responsibility Definition Worksheet."

B. RESPONSIBILITY DEFINITION MEETINGS
1. Manager and staff member compare "Responsibility Definition Worksheets."
2. Negotiation of functions, authority levels, and priorities.

PHASE TWO: Establishing Goals

A. GOAL-SETTING STAFF MEETING
1. Establish purpose and yearly staff goals.
2. Explain how to write goals, objectives and performance standards.
3. Distribute the Goal Setting Worksheets.
4. Explain the nature of taking 100% responsibility and formulating commitments.
5. Make certain goals are both realistic and challenging.

B. INDIVIDUAL GOAL-SETTING
1. Manager and staff member negotiate goals, objectives and performance standards.
2. Goals are broken into quarterly and monthly objectives.
3. Feedback mechanisms are established.

PHASE THREE: Providing Feedback

A. QUARTERLY REPORTS, INDIVIDUAL OBJEC-
TIVES
1. Prepared by staff member.
2. Review of goal progress.
3. Review of responsibility definitions.
4. Note problems and obstacles; create action plans and renegotiate goals if
necessary.
5. Acknowledge positive performance.

B. RESULTS REVIEW—SIX MONTH STAFF
MEETING
1. Review of staff goals by manager.
2. Create staff action plan, renegotiate
goals if necessary.
3. Acknowledge positive performance.

C. ACTION PLANNING INTERVIEWS
1. Staff member submits "Responsible Staff
Action" of problem areas.
2. Negotiation of agreements with
managers.
3. Specific action plans formulated and
committed to by staff member and
manager.

D. FINAL RESULTS REVIEW
1. Preparation of final "Results Statements"
to be used in Results Review by staff
member.
2. Manager and staff member meet and
discuss yearly review of progress.
3. Development plan formulated.
4. Manager writes yearly appraisal.

E. RESULTS REVIEW STAFF MEETING
1. Results noted, problems and obstacles
discussed.
2. Acknowledgements given, rewards
where possible.
3. Schedule individual meetings to update
responsibility definitions and new goals
for upcoming year.
4. Begin MBR system for the new evaluation
period.

One technique to assist staff members to create a specific action plan is to use a goal pyramid. A major goal is written on a 3" x 5" card. Staff members are then asked "What are we going to have to do to accomplish this result?" That question will probably create three or four more cards. The same question is asked again and again, until an entire pyramid of cards is created with each card more specific and detailed than the previous level. Each card is then assigned a due date and a staff member who will make a commitment to produce the result. Other staff members may be utilized as resource people, but only one name appears on each card. Spending just a few moments to create the pyramid can save hours in the long run.

This technique is also valuable to determine staff goals and action plans. Follow this by breaking goals down into specific objectives and plans of action that need to be taken. Finally, place names and dates on the cards, so that progress can be determined and assigned. In this way, the staff can spend time reporting on what has been accomplished rather than justifying what has not!

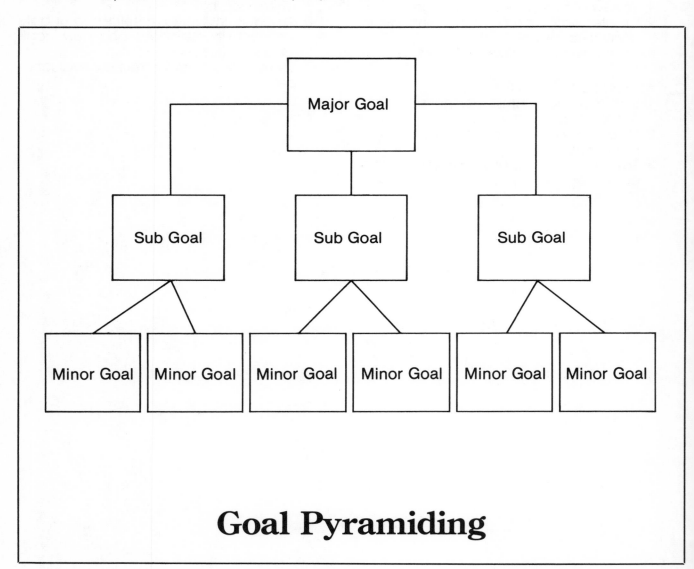

Goal Pyramiding

A Results Review concludes the MBR system. Typically, this total review takes place a year from the original formulation of the goals. The major question to be asked during the Results Review is, "What are the results **actually** produced?"

If possible, management should link the production of results and performance with a reward system. Management needs to reward results rather than rewarding "efforting" at producing results. There are no prizes for "doing your best." What speaks clearly and loudly is results, not wishes, dreams, or efforts.

In sum, to produce results and to accomplish goals, the manager needs to be SMART about the goals themselves. Then a commitment has to be formulated based on the ability and willingness to take total responsibility. Finally, an action plan must be created to follow through on the commitments.

Management must establish a firm, positive stance on goal-setting by involving staff members as well. In addition, feedback should be provided to increase the probablility of success and to assist everyone in acting at a more Responsible Level.

"A man's true greatness lies in the consciousness of an honest purpose in life, founded on a just estimate of himself and everything else, on frequent self-examinations, and a steady obedience to the rule which he knows to be right."[1]

—Marcus Aurelius

"Once we become more positive about ourselves, we will be much more successful than we ever dreamed of being. Your identity and your success go hand-in-hand. Many people sacrifice their identities by not doing what they really want to. And that's why they are not successful. Being successful is accepting yourself, expressing yourself, and setting goals that are right for you."[2]

—Lila Sewell

"Self-examination, if it is thorough enough, is nearly always the first step toward change. I was to discover that no one who learns to know himself remains just what he was before."[3]

—Thomas Mann

Chapter Nine

MANAGEMENT EFFECTIVENESS: AWARENESS, CHOICE, AND CHANGE

Now that we have diagnosed all the levels of growth from sickness to health, from rigidity to adaptability, from immaturity to maturity, we should have a good understanding of how to assess our own behavior in relation to the various levels.

But "understanding" human growth and development does not mean that one will change. Awareness does not bring about change; it can only provide choice, as the following diagram shows:

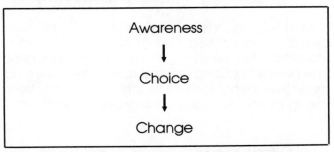

Awareness of the various levels creates a choice. You may continue to operate at lower levels, or you may choose to act more responsibly as a person and as a manager. To do so, one needs to examine present behavior—both the positive and negative aspects—and then take responsibility to create the changes necessary. As Erich Fromm stated in <u>Man for Himself</u>,

> As long as anyone believes that his ideal and purpose is outside him, that it is above the clouds, in the past or in the future, he will go outside himself and seek fulfillment where it cannot be found. He will look for solutions and answers at every point except the one where they can be found—in himself.[4]

To more adequately assess our "ideal and purpose," we need to examine our attitudes and behavior and then accept ourselves in light of our new awareness.

Assessing Strengths and Weaknesses

Responsible behavior requires that we become aware of our individual strengths and weaknesses and then accept both. This awareness is essential for growth. As Carl Rogers noted:

> . . .as the individual becomes more open to, more aware of all aspects of his experience, he is increasingly likely to act in a manner we would term socialized. If he can be aware of his hostile impulses, but also of his desire for friendship and acceptance, aware of his own purpose, aware of his selfish desires, but also aware of tender and sensitive concern for another, then he behaves in a fashion which is harmonious, integrated, constructive.[5]

But accepting one's weaknesses and deficiencies is not easy. Because of a sensitivity and a tendency to overreact to negative feedback, one needs to guard against rationalizations and defensive behavior which inhibit change from taking place. As Cardinal Mercier so eloquently put it:

> So few men have the courage to question themselves in order to ascertain what they are really capable of becoming, and so few have the will to become it.[6]

Ultimately, such self-evaluation and consequential feedback will provide a more realistic self-concept and operational mode. Though it may not be apparent at first, awareness of both positive and negative aspects of self should increase self-confidence. An adequate self-evaluation should address all of life's dimensions:

Emotional Reaction:
- How long does it take me to get over negative reactions?

- How often am I feeling negative?

- How much courage do I have to create meaningful change in my life?

- How much hostility and anger is apparent?

- Do I maintain a sense of humor, especially where self is concerned?

Intellectual:
- How creative am I in my problem-solving ability?

- How often do random thoughts or daydreams get in the way of my being effective?

- Do my ideas seem rigid to others?

- How involved am I in intellectual pursuits, i.e., reading, lectures, and learning?

Activity Involvement:
- Do I prioritize my activities to create a sense of balance?

- Can I stay on a project that is long and tedious?

- Do interruptions or delays cause problems?

Self-Discipline:
- How disciplined am I? Do I exercise regularly? Do I say "no" to unhealthy foods and cigarettes? Am I moderate in my use of alcohol and drugs?

- Am I resilient in failure?

- Am I internally motivated by desire or do I wait for others and circumstances to motivate me?

Relationships:
- How substantial is my ability to give and receive affection and loyalty?

- How strong are my relationships with my family? Do I spend enough time with them? Am I loving enough?

- How are my leadership qualities?

Physical State:
- How long since I've had a good physical examination?

- How healthy am I?

- How much stress do I endure? Do I exhibit any stress-related symptoms?

- What am I doing to make myself healthy?

- How much time do I spend each day devoted to physical health?

Spiritual Dimension:
- How much am I concerned with ethics and issues of morality?

- How would I rate my spiritual life?

- Do I live by the Golden Rule?

- Am I aware of my mission in life?

We need to do everything we can to increase our level of self-awareness—careful to face the negatives without going through denial or rationalization. Growth takes place through such awareness. As Virginia Wolfe noted in <u>The Common Reader</u>,

> The man who is aware of himself is henceforward independent; and he is never bored, and life is only too short, and he is steeped through and through with a profound yet temperate happiness. He alone lives, while other people, slaves of ceremony, let life slip past them in a kind of dream. Once conform, once do what other people do because they do it, and a lethargy steals over the finer nerves and faculties of the soul. He becomes all outer show and inward emptiness; dull, callous, and indifferent.[7]

In addition to such self-reflection, you should avail yourself of as much testing and direct feedback as possible. Many organizations provide assessment centers, as do outside consultants. Typically, these involve paper and pencil tests ranging from personality tests, motivational inventories, strength assessments, and ability tests. These should be utilized to provide additional sources of information.

Moreover, you should ask directly for feedback from your staff, spouse, children, and friends, all of whom can be a tremendous source for your growth. Listen as they provide you some insight, not all of which you will find pleasant—nor should you. However, be careful not to become defensive or to rationalize your behavior. In other cases, you may have to ask "leading" questions to elicit feedback, since some people may be reluctant to say anything because of your authority position. Appropriate questions would include, "Am I doing anything that may be related to this problem?", or, "Would you be willing to share how you could see me improve?" Such questions should make the other person feel more at ease in providing effective feedback.

The O–M–R Formula

Once you have received feedback from several sources, you need to create specific action plans for self-improvement. To do so, you should follow the O-M-R method. "O" stands for the **Outcome**: What are your goals? What kind of person do you want to be? What type of manager do you want to become? Focus on the outcome and avoid any limitation imposed by the **Methods** involved, (the "M"), or the **Resources** (the "R") currently available to you.

For example, avoid saying "I'd like to...but I can't afford it." Focus on "Outcome" first. In addition, keep asking, "Is this an Outcome or is it a Method or a Resource?" For example, to say you want to be a millionaire may not be an Outcome—it may be the method or resource that allows you to live a particular lifestyle. But, what is that lifestyle?

Confusion and imposed limitations will restrict the choices available to us. As Pearl Buck wrote in her book, To My Daughter, With Love, "Once the **what** is decided, the **how** always follows. We must not make the **how** an excuse for not facing and accepting the **what**.[8]

Having decided what kind of person you want to be, the kind of lifestyle you want to live, and the kind of manager you want to be, focus on the methods you could use to create the changes you want. Be creative, but then become very specific. As John Dewey once warned, "We cannot seek or attain health, wealth, learning, justice, or kindness in general. Action is always specific, concrete, individualized, unique." Thus, the action plan which spells out the methods, must be very detailed and realistic.

Having determined some of the methods, turn your attention to the resources available. How much time will it take? How much money? Do others need to be involved? Be realistic and honest about your resources. Is it the lack of resources or your use of the resources available to you that creates the restriction?

To more adequately determine the Outcome and Method for managerial skills, note the following description of how managers utilize their skills at each level of functioning. As you read this section, approximate your behavior in each management dimension and then follow the same O-M-R format to create an action plan.

Assessing Your Management Style

To review your management style, you need to determine the behavior and approach you use along the following dimensions of management:

1. Your Basic Management Philosophy

2. Your Use of Power

3. How Goal-Setting is Accomplished

4. How You Delegate

5. How You Resolve Conflict

6. Your Performance Evaluation Methods

7. Your Leadership Style

Managers at the five levels of maturity operate very differently along these management dimensions. Just as with life dimensions, one may operate at the Conformist Level when goal-setting and yet be at the Responsible Level in the use of power. These variables, however, are interdependent, and an awareness of them, coupled with an honest self-appraisal can be an important step in producing the necessary changes.

Such changes are important in many ways. To become effective as managers, individuals must change who they are, not just what they do. As Brouwer states:

> . . .it is manifestly clear that change in self-concept as a function of executive growth has a payoff. . .To twist an old adage, it isn't what you know that finally counts; it's who you are.[10]

Thus, changes within self can and do affect the entire environment. Managers who operate at a particular level tend to have members of their staff who reflect their image. After reviewing research on leadership impact, Christopher Argyris concluded that ". . .subordinates tend to use the same leadership style that their boss tends to use regardless of the training they receive."[11]

Changes in the manager will, then, have a profound impact upon the work group. Stated inversely, if managers do not like what they see in their staff members, they should look very closely at their own behavior. To assist in that process, descriptions of managerial dimensions at each level follow.

Basic Management Philosophy

The manager's basic philosophy encompasses (1) the view of the staff, (which, of course, is typically self-projection); (2) the emphasis the manager places on concerns for productivity and the corresponding concerns for people, and, (3) the manager's basic operational approach at each level. Each level of development has a particular impact on basic management philosophy.

THE UNCONSCIOUS LEVEL:
Managers at the Unconscious Level view their staff as trapped and without the power to change their position. As a reflection of their own feelings, they see the situation as fundamentally hopeless. Unconscious managers are neither concerned with productivity nor with the people they supervise. They tend, rather, to withdraw from their staff and avoid becoming involved with issues or policy decisions.

THE SELF-PROTECTIVE LEVEL:
True to McGregor's "Theory X" manager, the Self-Protective manager views staff members as lazy and incompetent. Because they view productivity and people concerns as mutually exclusive, they think that people do not want to be productive, and so, feel compelled to use force and coercion to get the job done.

Because managers at this level are so intellectually blinded by their own beliefs, they see no exceptions to their pessimistic view of staff members. If they do see an exception, they use the exception to prove, rather than disprove the rule. Thus, they feel justified in taking such an authoritarian stance.

THE CONFORMIST LEVEL:
Conformist managers feel that their staff members are weak, and, therefore, have to be protected from those in authority. Although such a manager would probably deny it, the Conformist believes the staff to be incompetent. Because they want to be accepted by others, these managers rate people concerns as more important than concerns of productivity. They tend to enjoy "rescuing" staff members from unrealistic demands and thus become involved in morale issues. Since it is less risky than change, these managers maintain the status quo, following the "we've always done it that way" dictum.

THE ACHIEVEMENT LEVEL
Achievement Level managers view their staff as moderately and occasionally productive, and yet feel they need to be manipulated to increase their productivity. As at the Conformist Level, these managers see a conflict between productivity and people concerns. Yet, the Achievement Level manager reacts just the opposite by emphasizing results, sometimes at the expense of personal concerns. Due to a lack of planning and effective delegation, they tend to "manage by crisis", a syndrome that reinforces their reactive approach and their constant impatience.

THE RESPONSIBLE LEVEL:
Unlike the lower levels, Responsible managers view their staff as productive and creative. This positive self-projection is constantly reinforced by staff members who want to meet their manager's high expectations. These managers see no conflict between concerns with productivity and people concerns. For them, the two concepts become integrated. They realize that for staff members to feel a sense of self-worth and to have high self-esteem, they need to be productive. Likewise, the best way to manage an effective and productive office is to foster growth within the staff.

Their positive view of staff members, and their integration of productivity with human concerns leads to a management style based upon involvement. Feeling that "people support what they helped to create," they look for ways to maximize staff involvement and participation by delegating decision-making, authority, and accountability.

Use of Power

The use of power denotes how managers use and misuse power and influence within the organizational setting—a factor closely associated with the manager's basic philosophy and leadership style.

THE UNCONSCIOUS LEVEL

Reflecting their own feelings of impotence, managers at the Unconscious Level avoid the use of power. Their low level of power orientation becomes apparent when staff members ask them to make decisions or request interpretations of corporate strategy, and they retort, "I'll see what I can do." Because they usually do nothing, they are viewed as incompetent and weak by most people within the organization.

THE SELF-PROTECTIVE LEVEL

Unlike their Unconscious peers, Self-Protective managers use power to dominate and control others. They have a high need for power, sometimes bemoaning the fact that the organization fails to give them enough latitude to get the job "done right." Since they use their authority to demand obedience from others, they use fear to motivate others. As would be expected, they are often viewed as dictatorial and ruthless by their staff.

THE CONFORMIST LEVEL

As a result of childhood experiences, Conformist managers have an aversion to power, seeing it as a form of manipulation. Because they are unwilling to use the power inherent to their position, they often fail to receive the respect from their staff they so desperately seek. Their need to be liked presents still another problem. Staff members will complain bitterly about unpopular decisions which the Conformist manager makes. In an attempt to maintain harmony, the manager then makes an exception thereby creating the impression that he or she is indecisive, inconsistent, and shows favoritism.

THE ACHIEVEMENT LEVEL

Managers at the Achievement Level have a high need for power. They use power as a method of personal aggrandizement and for personal gain. Achievement managers are known throughout the organization as "empire builders." Power, itself, becomes a symbol of success.

Unlike Responsible managers, Achievement Level managers are not as skilled in their use of power. Because they tend to be more impulsive and erratic, others often see them as exploitive and aggressive.

THE RESPONSIBLE LEVEL

Responsible managers also have a high need for power, but they use it to influence and have impact on the organization for the benefit of all concerned. Thus, their motive is altruistic, rather than self-serving.

Managers at this level are controlled in their use of power and so are viewed as fair, consistent, and just. Because their power is not personalized they are seen as a source of strength to others.

Goal-Setting

Goal-setting refers to the manager's basic approach to setting goals and formulating objectives with staff members. It also encompasses the process of negotiating staff commitment to take responsibility to reach their goals.

THE UNCONSCIOUS LEVEL

Managers operating at the Unconscious Level seldom set goals for themselves, much less with their staff members. To avoid any risk, they often rely on precedent or policy to determine results. Staff members who want to get something accomplished often feel frustrated and "give up." Thus, there is very little commitment to goals on the part of the staff.

THE SELF-PROTECTIVE LEVEL

As an extension of their view of authority, Self-Protective managers feel that staff involvement would be a sign of weakness and inadequacy. They, therefore, set goals **for** their staff, not **with** their staff. Because staff members are not consulted or "sold" on the goals, they feel little commitment to follow through and, in some cases, may even sabotage the attainment of the goals.

THE CONFORMIST LEVEL

Managers at the Conformist Level often abdicate their goal-setting responsibility to their staff. Such permissiveness is based on the assumption that their staff may not like them if they make too many demands upon them. Since the staff is in control, there is low to moderate commitment to the goals.

THE ACHIEVEMENT LEVEL

Though Achievement Level managers still determine goals for their staff, they utilize a "sales-consultative" approach. They feel that if they can "sell" their goals and get their staff to recognize the logic of their approach, the staff will become committed. Because managers at this level are often persuasive and respected as successful, they receive a moderate to high commitment to their goals and objectives.

THE RESPONSIBLE LEVEL

True to their emphasis on staff involvement, Reponsible managers work with staff members in the goal-setting process. The synergy which results from involving the people affected by the goals enhances the creativity and hence the value of the objective-setting process. Such involvement produces the highest levels of commitment.

Delegation

Delegation refers to what is delegated, how it is delegated at each level, and the consequences of the delegation process.

THE UNCONSCIOUS LEVEL

Managers at this level fail to delegate successfully because they do not want to become involved with staff members. Thus, they fail to discuss functions, priorities, and levels of authority. They assume that staff members were told everything they needed to know when they were hired. Because of their non-participative approach, the net result is non-productivity.

THE SELF-PROTECTIVE LEVEL

Self-Protective managers often only delegate those functions that they themselves dislike, or those which offer no opportunity for self-promotion. When they do delegate, it is often with the implied threat that, "you will do this or else."

As a means of control, managers at the Self-Protective Level discourage staff members from being creative or from taking any authority for decision-making. Using harsh, punitive measures for stepping outside of the narrow limits of acceptability, they create a fear of making mistakes.

THE CONFORMIST LEVEL

Since Conformist managers do not want to impose or make demands on others, they are seldom effective in the delegation process. They rarely delegate authority to make decisions, so staff members often come to them to make decisions. Such rescuing causes the manager to become more overworked, prompting feelings of persecution. Because managers at this level have trouble prioritizing their own work, they are unsuccessful in assigning priorities and meaningful tasks to others.

THE ACHIEVEMENT LEVEL

Managers at the Achievement Level often fail to delegate specifics, assuming that staff members should know what to do and how to do it. Because they are often impatient and crisis-oriented, they often wait to the last minute to delegate, sometimes causing the staff to work overtime. Moreover, they often change priorities mid-stream, creating even more confusion. Their erratic approach creates a sense of urgency and frustration for their staff.

THE RESPONSIBLE LEVEL

Responsible managers know the capabilities of their staff members and what motivates each member. Through negotiation, they delegate the functions to be performed as well as the priority of each. After assessing staff capability and experience, they give staff members the maximum authority possible to make decisions and carry out their functions. Because of this approach, Responsible managers promote teamwork, a sense of harmony, as well as an internalized recognition of the accountability of each staff member.

Conflict Resolution

Conflict Resolution depicts how managers typically approach conflict situations, how they attempt to resolve or avoid conflict, the value they give to personal goals and relationships, and finally, how their approach typically would be viewed by others.

Applying Kenneth Thomas' approach, conflict can be understood on a grid system with the concern for relationship along one axis and the concern for personal goals along the other.[12] Similar to Blake-Mouton's Managerial Grid, the conflict resolution grid utilizing the five levels of development would look like this:

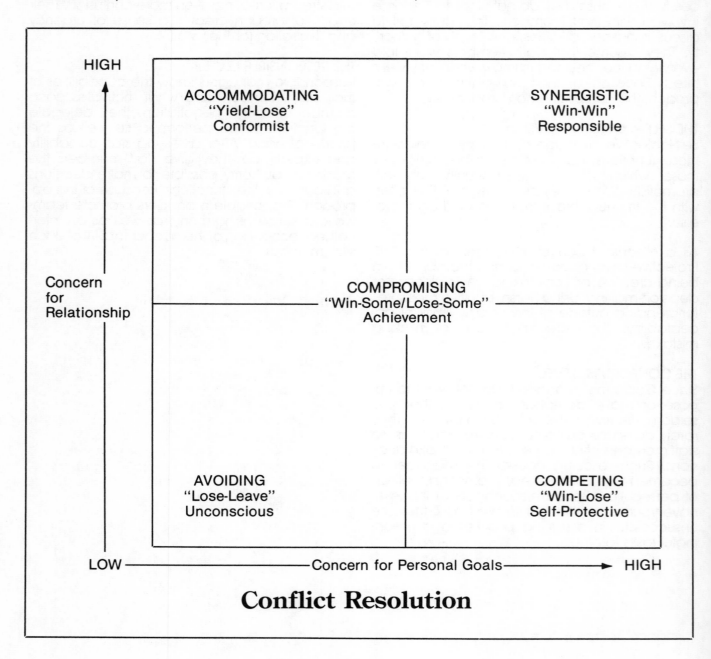

Conflict Resolution

THE UNCONSCIOUS LEVEL

Managers at the Unconscious Level avoid conflicts, either by remaining passive, or by detaching themselves physically or psychologically when conflicts threaten to arise. Since they do not care a great deal about their relationship with another person or whether their personal goals are being met, (since they seldom know what their goals are), they operate from a "lose-leave" position. Because they see the conflict as hopeless, they avoid direct confrontations or personal involvement by preferring to lose or by leaving the situation. Characteristically, they remain withdrawn and detached.

THE SELF-PROTECTIVE LEVEL

Unlike their Unconscious peers, managers at this level strive to win at all costs. Since managers at the Self-Protective Level are primarily concerned with "getting their own way," they strive to reach personal goals and are willing to sacrifice their relationships as a necessary cost of the conflict which ensues. Conflict is viewed as a means to demonstrate their power and strength. To lose would be an outward indication of weakness. So managers at the Self-Protective Level protect their social status either by not tolerating differences of opinion or by being devious in reaching their personal goals. Thus, their approach to conflict is often seen as aggressive and dogmatic.

THE CONFORMIST LEVEL

Whereas Self-Protective managers strive to reach personal goals at all costs, Conformist managers strive to protect their relationships. Because Conformists view conflict as a risk to the stability and durability of any relationship, and because they strive to maintain harmony at all costs, they approach conflict by being accommodating. They will yield their personal position or lose rather than risk any harm to their relationship. Since conflict is seens as detrimental to the staff, managers at the Conformist Level use any number of techniques to avoid open confrontation including tabling important issues, denying that conflict exists, procrastinating, or simply "giving in" to the demands of others. Because of their approach, they are often viewed as timid and hesitant in conflict situations.

THE ACHIEVEMENT LEVEL

Managers at the Achievement Level approach conflict as a combination of the two previous levels. They use a compromising, "you-win-some and you-lose-some" approach to conflict situations. Although appropriate in many situations, such a tact is still a variant of "win-lose." Inherent within the approach is the automatic assumption that one party has to lose. Thus, Achievement Level managers attempt to lessen the effect of losing by limiting the gains available to the other party. In using this approach, these managers maximize their gains through persuasion and manipulation. As such, they often are accused of spending a great deal of time formulating "power plays" and determining strategy to put themselves in better positions.

THE RESPONSIBLE LEVEL

Managers at the Responsible Level use a synergistic approach to conflict, an approach which recognizes that "the whole is greater than the sum of the parts." They know that individuals working together in unison, can accomplish more than individuals working separately. Managers at the Responsible Level view conflict as natural and ultimately as promoting the group process of teamwork. Striving to create a "win-win" situation, Responsible managers want to hear all views and spend their time reflecting upon the means by which all goals can be met. They realize that if a relationship is to remain truly productive and satisfying, then each party's goals must be met. To do so, they listen well, and are candid and creative in their problem-solving approach. By utilizing such a synergistic approach they are able to increase the level of commitment and the quality of decision-making that takes place. Thus, Responsible managers use conflict to enhance the relationship by determining how all members can ultimately reach their goals.

Performance Evaluation Methods

Performance evaluation methods encompass managerial attitudes toward formalized performance evaluations as indicated by the frequency with which managers provide such evaluation and the effectiveness of both positive and negative feedback.

THE UNCONSCIOUS LEVEL

Managers operating at the Unconscious Level avoid performance reviews. The very act of reviewing performance requires an involvement with staff members and a concern about productivity—both of which are shunned at this level. If these managers are required by their organizations to provide reviews, they usually wait until the last minute, or until asked for the third time to present the data. Furthermore, they look for ways to avoid significant contact, often by having staff members fill out their own forms, using adjective checklists or by rating every item at a moderate level to avoid explanation.

THE SELF-PROTECTIVE LEVEL

Managers at the Self-Protective Level use formal performance appraisals very infrequently. When they do, their appraisals are used to display their authority. Seldom giving positive recognition, managers at this level focus their attention on past mistakes and failures—a negative approach which is punitive in nature. Self-Protective managers look for staff members to blame and for ways to decide penalties so the same situation does not recur. In this regard, it is not uncommon for Self-Protective managers to "sacrifice" a staff member as an "example" to bring others into "line." Thus, their staff members often hate performance appraisals and become very defensive.

THE CONFORMIST LEVEL

As opposed to the Self-Protective Level, managers at the Conformist Level follow the dictum, "If you don't have anything nice to say, don't say it at all." As a projection of their own fears of receiving negative feedback, they often feel that members of their staff are too fragile to be confronted by their weaknesses and so performance evaluations are often avoided. When providing positive feedback, they tend to use vague, cliche-ridden, terms, (i.e., "You're doing a great job"), yet they are perceived as being "phony" or a "push-over" by the staff which in many cases takes advantage of their good nature.

THE ACHIEVEMENT LEVEL

Unlike the lower levels, managers at the Achievement Level typically provide frequent performance reviews. True to their reactive method of thinking, however, they wait for positive or negative performance to determine when and how appraisals are given. Positive feedback is usually provided in a group setting, and yet tends to be more of a "pep-talk" than a direct means for personal acknowledgement. Negative feedback tends to be related more to achievement factors, such as missing due-dates and failure to reach objectives than to any other factors. In many cases, staff members resent the "love 'em and leave 'em" syndrome prevalent at this level. When the objectives are being met or are in process, Achievement Level managers display a great deal of involvement and provide feedback frequently. However, once the goals have been reached, Achievement managers tend to ignore their staff members by going on to yet a new crisis or problem area.

THE RESPONSIBLE LEVEL

Responsible managers provide feedback on a frequent, regular basis. They view performance appraisals as an integral part of their managerial functions, and as a learning experience for their staff. Moreover, they encourage two-way evaluation techniques. They are evaluated by their staff members as well as giving reviews to their staff members.

As a reflection of their own positive feelings about themselves, managers at the Responsible Level are readily able to acknowledge positive performance by providing realistic, genuine feedback. Negative performance evaluation sessions are candid, yet constructive in tone and feedback. Rather than spending time blaming or labeling, managers at this level emphasize developmental action-plans to correct the situation.

Leadership Style

Leadership style refers to how managers view themselves in relation to the group, how decisions are made, and how managers view the leadership role. The following areas show differences in the leadership approach displayed at each level.

THE UNCONSCIOUS LEVEL

Because managers at the Unconscious Level avoid contact and involvement, others do not see them as leaders. As a result, "informal" leaders necessarily emerge from the staff to become the true decision-makers. When Unconscious managers are asked to make decisions or to act in a leadership role, they often point to policy or refer decisions to their superiors. Repeated declarations that their "hands are tied" soon convince staff to look elsewhere for leadership.

THE SELF-PROTECTIVE LEVEL

Intent upon justifying their roles, Self-Protective managers demand strict and rapid compliance with their orders. Having made their decisions, usually without consulting anyone, these managers demand obedience to their wishes. Thus, they insist on closely supervising their staff members. Self-Protective managers view themselves as strong and dominant in their roles as leaders. Anything or anyone who threatens this self-view is dealt with swiftly and directly.

THE CONFORMIST LEVEL

Because of their basic, non-assertive nature, managers at the Conformist Level provide very little direction for others. They view their role as leader to provide for the social needs of the group, making certain that "everyone is getting along." In addition, they concern themselves with providing basic maintenance needs such as assuring that everyone has sufficient supplies. They equate leadership with boosting morale and protecting their staff from minor annoyances.

THE ACHIEVEMENT LEVEL

Viewed as a strong, powerful, and sometimes inspirational leader by others, the Achievement Level manager strives to maintain such an image. Yet, because of their essential disregard for maximum involvement and commitment, Achiever managers are not as effective as they could be. They lead by "exception," maintaining an "open-door" policy, so that they can "fight fires" when necessary. Since staff members realize they do not need to make decisions, they often wait for the leader to do so. Managers at the Achievement Level tend to view themselves positively as leaders, as flexible and adaptable, even though such a perception is not shared by many others on their staff.

THE RESPONSIBLE LEVEL

Managers at the Responsible Level make the best leaders. Ironically, they often do not see themselves as such, tending rather to view themselves as a team-member whose position enables them to contribute special resources, thereby promoting task attainment. Their leadership behavior accounts for studies that show that morale increases within a group as the degree of direct leadership decreases.[13] In such a setting, employees feel more "self-responsible," and so are more committed to results. Through involvement and participation, Responsible Managers stimulate their staff toward the synergistic achievement of common goals.

External Factors Affecting Management Style

After reviewing the dimensions of management, one must acknowledge that factors outside of the individual must also be taken into account. The organizational climate itself may determine at what level the manager can appropriately operate. Factors within the situation, such as time constraints and emergency issues, may override other considerations. The staff members' level of maturity will also have a great impact upon the manager's style.

Not to recognize all the factors inherent within any given situation is to not see all the facts. At the Responsible Level, however, managers can "choose" to adopt a particular approach, aware that the approach is appropriate with a person at that level of maturity, and yet are adaptive to the situation when conditions change or the staff member matures. Such flexibility is similar to that advocated by Paul Hersey and Kenneth Blanchard in their "Situational Leadership" approach. Responsible managers take into account the maturity level of their followers and adjust their leadership style to follow suit. According to Hersey and Blanchard,

> ". . . as the level of maturity of the follower continues to increase in terms of accomplishing a specific task, the leader should begin to reduce task behavior and increase relationship behavior. This should be the case until the individual or group reaches a moderate level of maturity. As the follower begins to move into an above average level of maturity, it becomes appropriate for the leader to decrease not only task behavior, but relationship behavior as well. Now the follower is not only mature in terms of the performance of the task, but also is psychologically mature."[14]

So, to be ultimately effective in management, one needs to consider the organization's style, the particular situation, the maturity level of the staff, and factors within the individual manager.

After reviewing these management dimensions, and factors within your environment, note at which level you perceive yourself operating most of the time. Now write your "Outcome" in a positive fashion. Rather than stating, "I want to stop avoiding conflict situations because I'm afraid of the result," say, "I will confront unpleasant situations or conflict because I know that it will enhance my relationship if done with a positive attitude to serve all involved." Assign yourself seven goals to work on in one month. Read them often—at least several times a day—and then act. As Goethe wrote:

> How can you come to know yourself?
> Never by thinking—always by doing. Try
> to do your duty and you'll know right
> away what you amount to. And what is
> your duty? Whatever the day calls for.[15]

But, of course, in order to act, you must risk a change in behavior. This is perhaps the greatest single factor that impedes progress. The next section can help maximize the potential that has always been yours.

	BASIC MANAGEMENT PHILOSOPHY	USE OF POWER	GOAL-SETTING
RESPONSIBLE	View of staff: Productive and creative. Productivity and people concerns integrated. Method of operation: Involvement with staff through delegation and participation.	**Altruistic** - used for common good. High need to have impact and to be influential. Viewed as fair, just, and strong.	Inclusion of staff in goal-setting process. Promotes creativity in objective setting. High level of commitment.
ACHIEVEMENT	View of staff: Moderately productive, yet need for manipulation. Productivity concerns emphasized. Method of operation - Management by crisis - inadequate planning and delegation.	**Personal Aggrandizement** - used for personal gain. High need - to build "empires". Viewed as exploitive and aggressive.	Sales consultative approach - "Sells" staff on goals. Moderate to high level of commitment.
CONFORMIST	View of staff: Weak, need to be protected. People concerns emphasized. Method of operation: Maintenance of status quo.	**Aversion** - power seen as domination. Low need - unwilling to exercise power. Viewed as indecisive and inconsistent.	Abdication of goal-setting to staff. Permissive - feels staff won't like them if they push. Low to moderate commitment.
SELF-PROTECTIVE	View of staff: Incompetent, lazy. Productivity and people concerns are mutually exclusive. Method of operation: Coercion and force.	**Domination** - power used to control. High need - used for authority to demand obedience. Viewed as dictator, ruthless.	Sets goals **for** staff not with staff. Feels to let staff be involved is sign of weakness. Low commitment - sabotage.
UNCONSCIOUS	View of staff: Powerless and trapped. Productivity and people concerns are unimportant. Method of operation: withdrawal and non-involvement.	**Powerlessness** - power is avoided. Low need - perceives self as weak and ineffective. Viewed as incompetent.	Avoids goal-setting. Will rely on precedent and policy. No commitment.

DELEGATION	CONFLICT RESOLUTION	PERFORMANCE EVALUATION METHODS	LEADERSHIP STYLE
Delegates maximum authority, functions, priorities **with** staff. Aware of staff capabilities and motivations. Creates team-work, harmony and accountability.	**Synergistic, (win/win).** If relationship is to last, all goals must be met. Candid, creative, problem-solving approach.	Frequent, regular basis. Used as learning experiences. Positive-realistic, genuine feedback. Negative-constructive and candid.	Leader views self as team member. Encourages others to contribute. Self-view: a contributor of special resources.
Does not delegate specifics. Last minute delegation, changing priorities, improper planning. Creates urgency, confusion, frustration.	**Compromising (win some/lose some).** Attempts to soften effects of losing by limiting the gains. Persuasive, manipulative approach.	Frequent, though based on positive or negative performance. Used to increase performance. Negative - based on productivity failures, due-dates etc.	Maintains "open door" policy. "Management By Exception", fire-fighting when necessary. Self-view: Flexible and adaptable.
Seldom delegates effectively. Unable to assign realistic priorities and meaningful tasks. Creates staff wanting to be "rescued".	**Accommodating (yield/lose).** Relationship - primary importance. Conflict viewed as destructive of relationships. Hesitant, timid approach.	Infrequent. Used to build morale. Positive - cliché -ridden. Negative - avoided - staff viewed as fragile.	Provides little direction for others. Acts as support person to provide social and technical needs. Self-viewed: Morale booster and provider.
Delegates only functions they dislike. Creativity and decision-making discouraged. Creates fear of making mistakes.	**Competing (win/lose).** Personal goals - prime importance. Social survival at stake - to lose means weakness. Aggressive, dogmatic approach.	Infrequent. Used to display authority. Positive - seldom given. Negative is punitive and to determine fault and blame.	Expects strict and rapid compliance with orders. Insists on close, constant supervision. Self view: Strong and dominant.
Does not delegate - staff should know what to do. Non-participative. Creates non-productivity.	**Avoiding (lose/leave).** Hopelessness - no win, total avoidance. Withdrawn and detached approach.	Non-existent. Avoidance of all feedback. If forced by organization will have staff make out their own or prefer adjective checklists.	Avoidance of any contact. If necessary, resorts to policy or to refers to superiors. Self-view: weak, "my hands are tied".

Risking Change

Having reviewed your strengths and weaknesses, both personally and professionally, the most difficult part remains. Are you willing to risk change? Are you willing to become that person who is your ideal self? Many of us are as fearful of success as we are of failure.

As John Newman states in his PACE seminars, the self-concept acts as a set dial on a thermostat.[16] Just as a thermostat has a "comfort zone" to act as a signal to either turn the furnace on or to shut it off, our self-concepts also have a comfort zone. The diagram below illustrates this concept.

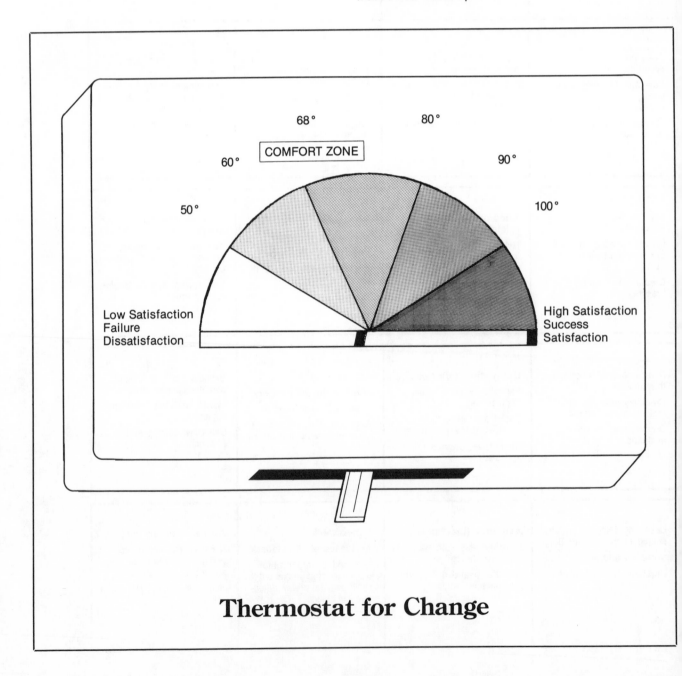

Thermostat for Change

If our experiences fall far below our self-concept, we strive to change the situation to restore the balance. For example, if our self-view is positive, loving and successful, and then we undergo a divorce, lose our job, or experience a similar setback, we will strive very hard to restore equilibrium. If unable to do so, our self-concept may be lowered and a new comfort zone established.

Unfortunately, the same mechanism works in reverse. When people become more successful or happy than they have been, they may become very uncomfortable. As Henry S. Haskins reported in <u>Meditations on Wall Street</u>:

"When our affairs are succeeding beyond expectation, when we are being benefited by our foresight and contrivance and apparently are becoming a considerable person, a mean little thought bares its teeth and says: "Watch yourself: This is not going to last."[17]

Because our minds are so addicted to manifesting our strongest beliefs, we may unconsciously sabotage our success and happiness by saying, "Everything is going too well. . .Something is bound to go wrong." As a self-fulfilling prophecy, we then unconsciously create situations that justify our fears.

Such fear of success is often a manifestation of being comfortable with our lives the way they are. Though we experience negative aspects, at least they are knowable and offer a form of security. As Lillian Smith wrote in <u>The Journey</u>,

"We build up our defenses slowly, brick by brick, cementing them with our fear and anguish; and then, when they are no longer needed, we cannot bear to tear them down. We have leaned on them too long. Our lives have been shaped to fit them, psychic muscles have stiffened against them, emotions have learned to flow under them, our vocabulary has entwined itself around them until they are almost hidden from us."[18]

To become aware of our own potential is often awesome, yet simultaneously replete with wonder, doubt, and fear. Very often people operating consistently at the Responsible Level are no different from others, apart from displaying an uncommon courage to release their inherent potential. Maslow concluded that:

". . .we fear our highest possibilities, (as well as our lowest ones). We are generally afraid to become that which we can glimpse in our most perfect moments, under condition of great courage. We enjoy and even thrill to the godlike possibilities we see in ourselves in such peak moments. And, yet we simultaneously shiver with weakness, awe, and fear before these same possibilities."[19]

The first question we must ask ourselves is "Are we willing to become our ideal self?" This may mean overcoming our doubts and rising above our reluctance to experience discomfort. As Shakespeare wrote in <u>Measure for Measure</u>, "Our doubts are traitors,/And make us lose the good we oft might win,/By fearing to attempt."[20]

Indeed, becoming more congruent with our ideal self is often uncomfortable. Yet as John Kennedy stated during his presidency,

"There are risks and costs to a program of action. But they are far less than the long-range risks and costs of comfortable inaction."[21]

Part of realizing the nature of change is to stop waiting for the right circumstances and to stop expecting that self-development will be easy. In The Business of Life, William Feather wrote, "Conditions are never just right. People who delay action until all factors are favorable are the kind who do nothing."[22]

We need to weigh the cost of changing or not changing. Essentially, such change requires a commitment to better one's life and career. To be true to such a worthy cause is the very nature of self-fulfillment. Many authors, philosophers, and psychologists have explained the process of facing discomfort to risk change and can offer some inspiration:

"Willing endurance of suffering and grief is the price that you have to pay for conscious fidelity to any cause that is vast enough to be worthy of the loyalty of a lifetime."[23]

—Josiah Royce
William James and Other Essays
on the Philosophy of Life

"It would be unfair of us to suggest that this re-engineering will be an easy process or a painless one. It must go on for a period of years . . . You will find that it requires great persistence rather than a dramatic sort of courage; the measures to be adapted frequently run directly counter to impulses that have become natural to you. Tyrannizing habits that have been in command of you for decades will not yield to mere armchair resolutions or a few days of desultory attention. In our experience, the battle of new habits against old may have to continue indefinitely."[24]

Friedman and Rosenman
Type A Behavior and Your Heart

". . . You must push yourself beyond your limits all the time . . . what was impossible before is perfectly possible now and perhaps your total success is only a matter of time. In this affair the only possible course that a warrior has is to act consistently and without reservations. You know enough of the warriors' way to act accordingly, but your old habits and routines stand in your way."[25]

Carlos Castenada
A Separate Reality

"Any change, even a change for the better, is always accompanied by drawbacks and discomforts. Having decided to achieve a certain task, achieve it at all costs of tedium and distaste. The gain in self-confidence, in having accomplished a tiresome labour, is immense."[26]

Arnold Bennett
The Arnold Bennett Calendar

"Ways of belief, of expectation, of judgement and attendant emotional dispositions of like and dislike, are not easily modified after they have once taken place."[27]

John Dewey
Human Nature and Conduct

Having resolved to risk change, to face the discomfort, and to willingly persevere, it would be well to keep in mind the old Irish proverb: "Nodding the head does not row the boat." At this point in your life and in your career—

The time is **now**. The choice is yours.

Action Plan for Change

List below ways in which you want to change and a detailed Action-Plan to produce the result.

AREAS OF CHANGE   ACTION-PLAN

1. _____   _____

                                   _____

                                   _____

                                   _____

2. _____   _____

                                   _____

                                   _____

                                   _____

                                   _____

3. _____   _____

                                   _____

                                   _____

                                   _____

4. _____   _____

                                   _____

                                   _____

                                   _____

                                   _____

5. _____   _____

                                   _____

                                   _____

                                   _____

6. _____   _____

                                   _____

                                   _____

                                   _____

"It is, I believe, the destiny of America to produce the first of a new species of man."[1]

—Wyndham Lewis
America and Cosmic Man

"Our success (in America) is not inevitable. Our ability to compete rests on our ability to organize human beings in such a way as to generate opportunity and results, rather than impasses, stagnation, bureaucracy, and wasteful friction."[2]

—Richard Tanner Pascale and Anthony G. Athos
The Art of Japanese Management

"Deep in his gut the American manager thinks people aren't important to productivity, that it's just a question of more capital or new technology. He's got to learn that people are the key and that we've got to unleash the untapped talent of workers."[3]

—Jerome Rosow
President, Work in America Institute

Chapter Ten

WHERE DO WE GO FROM HERE? THE AMERICAN DILEMMA

Examination and self-assessment—of past and present levels of behavior, and of the relationships among maturity, responsibility, and effective management—are only useful to the extent that they allow us to focus on the future and provide an impetus for change. Changes are taking place so fast that it is difficult to comprehend them, much less direct them.

And yet, change is constant, virtually mandating that we react to such changes positively. John Dewey, in his treatise <u>Reconstruction in Philosophy</u>, provides excellent advice:

> "Since changes are going on anyway, the great thing is to learn enough about them so that we will be able to lay hold of them and turn them in the direction of our desires. Conditions and events are neither to be fled from nor passively acquiesced in; they are to be utilized and directed."[4]

This chapter will explore the challenges that change presents for the future manager and will examine some of the possible solutions to create a better system. Our very survival—not just our way of life—may depend upon how we are able to meet those challenges.

The Challenges of the Future

Changes Within American Society

As is true for all industrial countries, the very fabric of American society is being questioned and challenged. Certain trends can be seen throughout the decades of the fifties, sixties, and seventies. The future will foster a continued concern for issues of human rights, for an increase in the quality of life, and for employees at all levels of the organization being involved in the decision-making process.

Although other societies will experience pressure on these same issues, the U.S. will be confronted time and time again, since many of the initial struggles took place within the American system. The future promises to be an era of extreme cultural unrest. Since resources will be limited, various groups will vie for power to determine who will gain the most. As human rights issues face decreasing resources and increasing numbers of people in the work force, American managers will feel the powerful impact and the resulting stress. Pressures from external sources, special interest groups, and governmental regulations will profoundly impact the role of managers.

In addition, the trend to demand more quality of life from the job will continue, even though the traditional trappings of what that means will change. In the not-so-distant past, work was valued for its own sake. As part of our heritage from our Pilgrim forefathers, work and activity was thought to be intrinsically worthwhile, and as a measure of spiritual well-being. During the last two decades work values have changed drastically. Now there is a greater emphasis on what work should provide. More and more employees want an opportunity for fulfillment, interesting work, challenge and growth. And yet, they feel that work should not interfere with their leisure time or strain family relationships. In view of the restricted resources to provide such a quality of life experience on the job, managers will feel an incredible challenge.

In response for increased quality of life, more workers are demanding a greater role in the decision-making process. Because employees are both better educated and older, their increased level of experience makes it appropriate to ask for a greater role in self-determination. According the The Managerial Challenge

> "Greater competence will permit increased decision-making at lower levels. The capability to make these decisions will, in turn, increase pressure for the right to make decisions. One of the major tasks for both the present and the future will be to push decision-making responsibility down to the lowest practical level without abdicating accountability or control."[5]

Since there will be fewer managerial positions available, such decision-making at the employee level will necessitate increased training and the acceptance of responsibility.

Changes Within the Nature of Work Itself

Continued technical advances will revolutionize the nature of the job itself for millions of workers. Since such advances require new training and re-education, organizations will need to provide new opportunities for workers to learn new skills.

Additionally, workers and managers alike will need to become extremely flexible in their approach to the job. More and more career changes may become necessary during one's life as technology and information changes so rapidly.

Changes Within the Organizational Structure

Since the individuals who compose organizations change, the nature of the organization itself will change. The future will see the organization remaining more static than it has been in the past. More and more managers will refuse to move to new locations, fewer new positions will be available, and the internalized motivation for upper mobility itself will be under severe scrutiny.

In addition, because resources will be more scarce and world competition more acute, managers will be held more accountable for the results they produce. Both their efficiency and effectiveness will be determining factors for their continuation and for their compensation. Thus, the structure of organizations will become as lean as possible to produce maximum results. No longer will supervisory and management positions be held as rewards for faithful employees. Decisions as to who will become managers and who will stay in those positions will be much more stringently defined and regulated by organizations.

Alternative Solutions

Look Within, Not From Without

In order to provide a new motivational strategy, American managers need to re-think basic constructs. To do so, we can utilize other approaches as examples, yet the new strategy must be decidedly "American" in nature. Thus, it needs to be based on fundamental concepts inherent to our way of life: opportunity for upward mobility, a Judeo-Christian ethic, individualism, equality, and free enterprise.

Increased levels of productivity in other nations have provided the impetus to examine our own system of management and to change in response to the challenge. The American managerial system—a streamlined adaptation to the post-Industrial Revolution—tends to divorce the "person" from the "job." This depersonalization is what employees at the Responsible Level object to most vehemently and is the one issue that must be dealt with most dramatically. Richard Pascale and Anthony Athos in their book, The Art of Japanese Management, state that in the traditional American structure,

> ". . . the person, as laborer, became an objectified and standardized component of the production process. Not surprisingly, this view of 'labor' tended to divorce man as a social and spiritual being from his 'productive' role at work. . . This concept has persisted in Western thinking to this day and it is one of the sources of our present problem.[6]

Many books and hundreds of articles have been written explaining how the Japanese and other industrial nations have included the social and spiritual need fulfillment as part of the job and as a function of working for a particular organization. Increased levels of productivity and positive identification with the organization have spurred many American executives to speculate on the inherent deficiencies of this nation's corporate entities.

Unfortunately, many firms have "borrowed" the techniques used in foreign countries, hoping that such techniques will "fix" their people and their problems. Such approaches seem doomed to fail for many reasons. Yet, one factor predominates—external systems will not change internal beliefs that are the crux of the problem. According to Pascale and Athos,

> ". . . technology, techniques, and innovative ways of thinking move across national boundaries more readily than ways of perceiving, believing, and behaving. We face a tough task in changing how we manage because we are a large part of the problem. We must change who we are, as well as what we do."[7]

Thus, organizations have implemented Quality Control Circles and techniques borrowed from other countries, as panaceas and as a desperate struggle to "do something." Yet, they have failed to recognize that the fundamental change must come from within the organization and, most importantly, within the managers themselves.

Ironically, the cultures we taught to move ahead technologically into the 20th century, are the very cultures that are showing us that we need to take one step back and learn to be more contemplative and holistic in our view of work. Such a new view needs to be more spiritual in nature.

This is exactly what Maslow predicted:

> "If we learn to give greater trust as autonomous, self-governing, and self-choosing individuals, then we...must shift our image over to a more Taoistic one...Taoistic means asking rather than telling. It means non-intruding, non-controlling. It stresses non-interferring observation rather than a controlling manipulation. It is receptive and passive rather than active and forceful...In prescribing 'what is best for them,' it looks as if the best technique for finding out what is best for them is to develop techniques for getting them to tell us what is best for them."[8]

Paradoxically, it appears that Maslow may have been the father of Japanese Quality Control Circles! As managers we need to recognize the value and worth of listening to Responsible employees. Involvement from within the organization to improve conditions and profits is often far more effective than instituting techniques and methodology from the outside. The resulting self-direction does not mean that we have relinquished our power as managers. Rather, by so doing, we have enhanced our power for the good of all within the organizational structure. Such involvement of the employees in the structure of the organization itself will re-shape the organization into a more efficient and effective unit. The Eastern mind needed to learn about techniques to increase efficiency and now it is up to the Western mind to learn about human beings, their development, and the respect they deserve as **total** beings, not just work units.

Maximize Employee Potential

Increasingly in the years ahead management will have to become more concerned with developing employees within the organization. Since job mobility will be restricted and fewer supervisory positions will be available, more employees will remain in their present positions. Rather than viewing such conditions as problems, Responsible managers realize the opportunity and potential of assisting employees in maximizing their potential.

In order to be effective in this process, managers will be required to realize the level of maturation of employees and respond accordingly. As employees continue to mature, more difficult assignments and greater responsibility can be given, thus instilling a sense of pride and independence.

The following are guidelines to assist in such a process.

DO NOT EXPECT TOO MUCH FROM EMPLOYEES AT LOWER LEVELS

One of the greatest mistakes executives, personnel directors, and trainers make is designing systems and procedures based on assumptions that are correct for individuals at the Achievement and Responsbile Levels, but are incongruous with the needs and aspirations of employees at the lower levels. Many employees at the Self-Protective and Conformist Levels do not want to be involved in decision-making, preferring to be told what to do, how to do it, and when it has to be done.

Because of their fear of making mistakes or their negative view of work in general, such employees need close, supportive and yet, firm supervision. They need to be informed as to the consequences of negative behavior and rewarded for positive activities. To place too much responsibility and independence upon them is to unwittingly promote failure.

As the individuals begin to feel more comfortable and trusting of the organization, more authority, accountability, and responsibility should be provided. Flexible job descriptions and new assignments can then foster positive changes. In addition, a simple delegation notation when formulating assignments can be a graphic illustration of what is expected. The following form can assist in clarifying one's expectations when assigning projects:

DELEGATION LEVEL
Check Appropriate Box

☐ 1. **Explore:** Go on a fact-finding mission. Present the facts objectively. I will determine what is to be done.

☐ 2. **Present Alternatives:** Present the alternatives available and objectively list the positive and negative factors of each. I will decide which alternative we will take.

☐ 3. **Make a Recommendation:** Formulate a specific action plan for my approval.

☐ 4. **Implement Action Plan—After Approval:** Inform me of your intended action plan, but delay any action until you receive my approval.

☐ 5. **Implement Action After Consultation:** Get my feedback on your intended action before you implement your plan. Be open for suggested changes.

☐ 6. **Act and Report:** Implement your action plan. Keep me informed as to how it turns out.

☐ 7. **Act With Authority:** Implement your action plan. Communicate with me only if you experience severe problems. Otherwise, no further communication with me is necessary.

PRIORITY LEVEL
☐ (A) Urgent and important.
☐ (B) Important, but not urgent.
☐ (C) Moderate importance.
☐ (D) Low priority.
☐ (E) Pending—(When you get to it).

Using such forms and techniques can help employees to respond accordingly. By assigning tasks and authority relative to the individual's level of maturation, employees will feel more harmonious with themselves and their environment. As Carl Jung stated:

> "Man is not a machine in the sense that he can consistently maintain the same output of work. He can only meet the demands of outer necessity in an ideal way if he is also adapted to his own inner world, that is to say, if he is in harmony with himself. . .Conversely, he can only adapt to his inner world and achieve unity with himself when he is adapted to the environmental conditions."[9]

The harmony created by having the functions, authority, and accountability of one's job congruent with one's ability, level of maturity, and motivation creates an environment in which growth can take place. Not to do so manifests resultant frustration and resentment.

DO NOT EXPECT TOO LITTLE FROM EMPLOYEES AT HIGHER LEVELS.

Becoming increasingly more common is the American business community's failure to adjust to individuals operating at a mature level. Different approaches need to be based upon what psychologically mature individuals deem important in their career roles. A sense of autonomy, the freedom to make decisions, accountability for their actions, a sense of satisfaction with a job well done, and a feeling of dignity that comes from correcting errors—these are all key motivators. Unfortunately, such opportunities are sadly lacking in many organizations. Chris Argyris researched the factors found in typical organizations, and compared them with what fully mature individuals want on their jobs. The findings show basic incongruities between the impact of formal organizational principles and growth factors in a healthy personality:

"If the principles of formal organizations are used as ideally defined, employees will tend to work in an environment where
(1) they are provided minimal control over their workaday world,
(2) they are expected to be passive, dependent, and subordinate,
(3) they are expected to have a short time perspective,
(4) they are induced to perfect and value the frequent use of a few skin-surface shallow abilities, and
(5) they are expected to produce under conditions leading to psychological failure.

All these characteristics are incongruent to the ones healthy human-beings are postulated to desire. . . .They are much more congruent with the needs of infants in our culture. In effect organizations are willing to pay high wages and provide adequate seniority if mature adults will for eight hours a day behave in a less than mature manner!"[10]

Since many jobs are designed for less mature individuals, controls are often established that would be appropriate for the Self-Protective or Conformist manager, and yet the same controls are viewed as demeaning and de-motivating for Achievement and Responsible Level individuals. Mature individuals often react by reverting to lower levels of functioning while on the job by doing as little as possible, and demanding maximum return. They then "save" their energies and creativity for their personal endeavors. According to Harry Browne,

". . .most employees have no real incentive to use their intelligence in their jobs. So they reserve their mental energy for their hobbies, personal relationships, and other things outside the office. In fact, with normal compensation systems, an employee often uses most of his initiative figuring out how to work less without losing his job."[11]

What has worked in the past does not work as well in today's world. Motivation based upon the promise of tangible rewards or upon the fear of losing one's job or status within the group, simply does not provide the motivation at higher levels of maturity. If managers desire employees to work at a more Responsible Level, the motivation context must change to provide increased identification with the job. The motivational approach must help, not hinder, individual growth. As Douglas McGregor stated,

"Unless there are opportunities at work to satisfy these higher level needs, (self-fulfillment), people will be deprived, and their behavior will reflect this deprivation."[12]

The question becomes one of how to motivate people to act at a more Responsible Level, where the promise of tangible reward and increased esteem fail to motivate as it does at the Achievement Level and where fear is not the motivator it is at the lower levels. Daniel Yankelovich feels that Responsible

> "...employees want recognition of their worth as individuals as well as for what they do on the job. Ideally, people would prefer to work in small groups in which they can form close human ties. Many want more responsibility and authority early in their career...Most people want a chance to learn new things, to find interest in their work, to be with pleasant and agreeable people, and to find new ways to express themselves on the job."[13]

In short, Responsible employees want a sense of psychological well-being. By studying the necessary components of this sense of well-being, researchers have clearly established several factors:

1. A sense of positive self-esteem.
2. A clear sense of identity.
3. A confirmation that one's actions make sense to others.
4. A set of concrete goals and values.
5. A feeling of personal power and self-worth.
6. A sense of stimulation to avoid boredom.
7. A feeling that one's world is reasonably stable.
8. A pervading sense of meaning and coherence in one's life.[14]

Yet, the individual cannot by himself create such a world. Such feelings can only take place in relation to others. The entire work environment needs to change to foster this sense of growth.

Abraham Maslow, in his studies of self-actualized individuals, noted that change within the organization itself must take place:

> "...I have no doubt that the standards of practice which has worked well in large organizations needs modification and revision of some sort. We'll have to find some way of permitting people to be individualistic in organizations."[15]

For years, the American free enterprise system with its corollary values have urged people to grow to the Achievement Level. It must now make an equally "giant step for mankind" by supporting an environment that urges people beyond achievement—to the Responsible Level.

Emphasize the Three "R's" of Motivation: Responsibility, Recognition, and Reward

By having individuals assume more responsibility there needs to be pay-offs in terms of recognition and rewards. Work relationships need to be formulated so all individuals know the area of responsibility over which they have complete control and then receive maximum reward for doing so.

Because of the restriction of tangible rewards and symbols of success, greater emphasis will have to be placed upon reward mechanisms that are intangible. And yet, this is consistent with the shift in values that has taken place in recent decades. Because of a shift in basic values, many workers now respond differently to the realities of the work place. Daniel Yankelovich has studied this change in values and has found a striking shift for the "New Breed." In the period from 1945 to 1970, Americans, in general, valued a strong work ethic. According to Yankelovich, during that era,

> ". . . individual aspirations for success and the socio-economic trajectory of the society toward even greater growth fitted together harmoniously. The individual wanted what the society was prepared to reward. When people worked hard, earned money, and spent it unstintingly on consumer goods, it brought them self-esteem and the approval of others as well as material comfort. Crucially important, people were able to feel that they were advancing the goals of the larger society as well as fulfilling themselves . . . 'Success' meant . . . a ten dollar-a-week raise in pay, buying a new Oldsmobile, having a son or daughter accepted at Michigan State, moving to Scarsdale, or throwing a successful Tupperware party."[16]

Understood within the context of Management By Responsibility, the "New Breed" has begun to transcend the Achievement and Conformist Levels. Materialistic success is no longer synonomous with self-fulfillment. However, the goal of self-fulfillment remains problematic. There are few cultural norms, and even less support within the work environment. Thus, the reality of self-fulfillment still eludes many Americans.

In an attempt to actualize their potential, the "New Breed" has experimented with a gambit of new structures and behaviors:

> "In the pursuit of the elusive goal of self-fulfillment, Americans today restlessly uproot themselves. They shuttle from one end of the continent to the other. They break up perfectly good marriages and form new ones. They leave one job for another. They change careers. They redecorate. They diet. They jog. They read Gail Sheehy's book Passages to find out how they are doing in comparison with others in their age group. Self-assertively they wonder out loud whether they are being assertive enough. Complaining of other people's narcissism, they elbow other egos out of the way to make room for their own. Obsessed with self-fulfillment they pull the plant from its soil over and over again to make sure its roots are healthy."[17]

Because there are no outward symbols that say "I have arrived"—"I am now fulfilled," the New Breed relentlessly and unsuccessfully searches for that which is not possible. New values operating in an old paradigm only create struggle. Perhaps those now waging such a struggle will come to realize that fulfillment is always a process, not a goal.

To realize that reward is more than money, we need to transcend achievement as the only measure of worth, and give up the inherent "hurry sickness," impatience, and striving so prevalent to the Achievement Level. Americans, so proud of their fast-paced, "throw-away" life-style will need to learn to take pride in themselves as a nation, to assist individuals in their process of growth, to conserve their natural resources, and to appreciate the human dignity that is inherent in their national system. We will have to learn to reduce our pace and to take more time in learning about our employees.

This will take time. For, as Barett Wendell pondered many years ago,

> "I wonder whether the feverish ebb and flow of energy that makes up our lives here is human or only Trans-Atlantic. Calm, steady, regular, healthy, normal progress from day to day seems almost out of the question. Temperance in life is a virtue almost unknown. Over-reaction and crushing reaction seem the rule."[18]

Albert Einstein noted the same difference in European and American life-styles. In his Ideas and Opinions, he speculated:

> "The American lives even more for his goals for the future, than the European. Life for him is always becoming, never being."[19]

To counteract such an emphasis on achievement as the primary form of self-worth, Pascale and Athos recommend in The Art of Japanese Management,

> "American managers, as a group, need to reduce their pulse rate . . . They need to drink in their organizational experience and discern more deeply what makes things work. From that, wisdom can come."[20]

Implement the Management By Responsibility System

One of the most direct solutions is to implement an MBR system throughout the organization. This involves three stages: (1) the adoption of the MBR philosophy as the operational strategy of the organization, (2) providing the MBR training for all employees so that they realize why they are being asked to assume responsibility, and how they can do so, and (3) consistent follow-up and reinforcement of the MBR philosophy through continued courses as well as organizational policy and procedures. Though the actual implementation will vary from organization to organization because of size and purpose, the following are some useful guidelines and suggestions.

STAGE ONE: MBR AS THE OPERATIONAL STRATEGY

Although the MBR philosophy can be successfully implemented within a department or a staff, in order to be maximally effective, it should be operational throughout the entire organization. Since the MBR system will affect everyone in the organization, all levels should be involved in the implementation process, not just upper or middle management. Workers, as well as their supervisors, need to be aware of and support the benefits of being involved, of being committed to excellence, of being more responsible, and of being willing to communicate problems and then working on them cooperatively to arrive at viable solutions. In this way, employees at all levels of the organization can work together productively for common goals, rather that playing psychological games and blaming externals when mistakes are made.

Implementing the MBR system requires full support and an on-going commitment to MBR principles. Without such support the system could falter or die. Such a commitment entails a belief that employees acting at more mature levels are more productive and have more job satisfaction, not to mention higher quality personal lives. This requires investment in the organization's most valuable resource: the people who work there. When employees become aware of the options that are available to them and realize the responsibility they have to themselves and to their co-workers, they will work cooperatively for common goals to fulfill the organizational purpose.

Furthermore, the existing organizational structure and personnel should be utilized to implement the MBR system. Such a process will entail planning, organization, and involvement at many levels to determine what and who is available to make the system work. The first step may be a needs assessment and the identification of organizational problems. The MBR system can be identified as a partial solution to those problems or needs, after listening to recommendations and determining a willingness to act upon them.

STAGE TWO: MBR TRAINING FOR ALL EMPLOYEES.

Now that the entire MBR seminar has been video-taped to provide a cohesive and extensive training of the MBR principles and philosophy, it is possible for facilitators from within the organization to provide training for all employees in this philosophy.

Involving top management and staff is crucial to the success of the entire system. They need to be aware of the benefits of the MBR system and their role in the implementation process. Emphasis must be placed upon defining organizational purpose, strategic planning, involvement of staff throughout the organization, and communication of organizational direction.

There is also a crucial need to involve employees in the MBR training. They need to be aware that "management" means managing their own lives so that they can be happier and more successful. Otherwise, employees operating at lower levels of maturity may view the MBR system as another management "trick" to get more work out of them. Initially supervisors may be confronted with negative attitudes of cynicism, mistrust, and skepticism from these employees. As the MBR training is provided and employees become involved, these suspicions should be alleviated and replaced by trust and identification both with the organization and the MBR system itself.

STAGE THREE: CONSISTENT FOLLOW-UP AND REINFORCEMENT OF THE MBR SYSTEM

After management and staff members complete the MBR training, systems need to be designed to provide constant reinforcement. This involves periodic reviews of job descriptions, goals and objectives, as well as performance appraisals that follow MBR principles of effective feedback. Certain organizational policies and procedures may need to be altered to be consistent with MBR philosophy. In addition, employee and management task force groups could be formulated to review all aspects of the organization to promote maximizing human potential at all levels. Such groups could be maintained on a permanent basis to act as review guides for problems, as well as productivity committees to increase the success of the organization.

Such follow-up is based on the concept that implementing MBR training is not a goal or an end in itself. Such training is part of an on-going purpose of assisting all employees in achieving their goals more effectively and in actualizing their human potential. Reinforcement of the MBR system shows an organizational commitment to create new opportunities for human development at work.

Through follow-up the MBR system can be the means to integrate individual and organizational goals. When the goals and aspirations of employees are perceived as divergent and at odds with those of the organization, a dysfunctional disparity occurs that is detrimental both for the employees and the organization. The MBR philosophy can provide the environment for the integration of individual and organizational goals to take place.

In additon to organizational reinforcement through internal systems, on-going training can be provided, using the MBR philosophy as basis for increasing skills. Training Systems, Incorporated, has developed additional follow-up courses to reinforce the MBR system. They are as follows:

- Effective Goal-Setting
- Effective Delegation
- Action-Planning Interviewing. (Problem-Solving Skills)
- Team-Building
- Conflict-Resolution Skills
- Leadership Strategies
- Client-Centered Selling
- Effective Time Utilization

Many organizations have their own "in-house" training programs that only need to be modified slightly to emphasize the philosophy of responsibility. In addition, an orientation program for new employees and a course for newly-hired or potential managers could use segments from the MBR Video Program to stress a commitment by the organization to assist employees in their development.

In short, providing follow-up and reinforcement of the MBR principles will take a great deal of hard work, by a number of truly dedicated people. It will take support, perseverance, and a realization that any kind of significant change may be accompanied by stress and some fear of the consequence.

PROBLEMS IN THE IMPLEMENTATION PROCESS

As with any new system or organization approach, there will often be problems in changing from one organizational mode of operation to another. The following are some of the problems that may be experienced.

MBR May Not Receive Universal Support

Managers at the lower levels of functioning, who live in the past and rely on force and threats to get the job done may not be, nor should they be expected to be, supportive of the MBR system and philosophy. For them the process of involving staff members in defining job functions, authority levels, performance standards, and goals, is seen as a loss of power and control.

The MBR system will be given wide support, however, by those managers who realize that old ways of controlling employees are ineffective with the new work force. Such managers realize that a constantly changing environment and a restricted economic system with limited availability of resources, demands truly committed, responsible employees.

Implementing MBR Can Be A Long And Challenging Process

As with any new approach, complete implementation of the MBR process can be a time-consuming process. Managers at all levels of the organization need to realize that it will not happen instantly. And yet, this is how it should be. Implementation will take time if MBR is to meet the specific needs of the specific organization.

The impact that MBR has within the organization on the effectiveness and productivity is an ongoing process that grows from within and cannot be imposed from the outside. What makes the MBR system work is people. It is what happens **inside** the individual and between people. Yet, the process of creating a positive environment that produces more job satisfaction and success is not something you **see**; it's something you **feel**. It is the intuitive awareness you feel when you walk into a well-run, organized office as compared with a poorly-managed office.

MBR May Be Seen As A Threat By Some And A "Cure-All" By Others

Initially some managers and employees may be threatened by the MBR philosophy because they may feel that it puts too much control and authority into the hands of those being managed. Conversely staff members may fear that the issue of responsibility can be misused to create a more authoritarian approach—"the velvet hammer." These are fears that must be handled properly lest they become realities. According to The Managerial Challenge,

> "The psychology of self-determination may be perverted from a wholesome desire to be responsible for one's behavior to an unwholesome egocentricity that demands to be indulged. Thus, psychological theory, inherently not at fault, can be twisted into a justification for troublesome behavior."[21]

When the MBR system is effectively implemented, everyone wins. Both managers and employees increase their ability to influence working conditions and to become more productive. Eventually, all segments of the work force will find that it is much more powerful to influence rather than to control.

At the opposite pole, MBR is not a panacea either. Despite enthusiastic claims by many MBR graduates, MBR is not going to eliminate all organization problems. There will still be problems after the MBR system is implemented—and that is how it should be. However, individuals within the organization should be better able to identify problems and do something about them before a problem becomes a crisis.

Implications for Managers in the Future

THE NEED TO BE MORE FLEXIBLE

Future managers will need to become extremely flexible and adaptable to the changes and new challenges that the future will hold. Rather than a restricted approach of being an "expert," or a "motivator," the new manager will by necessity become multi-faceted in response to a wide range of employees:

> "... managing is not today, nor will it be tomorrow a unitary function, a universal formula to be followed, a duty to be performed according to a set of rules regardless of the situation. The effective manager will be skillful in adapting his managerial activities, his role, to the needs of the moment. He cannot only authorize, direct, and order as a means of securing action. The future manager must be, in truth, a person of many parts."[22]

THE NEED TO BE MORE CREATIVE AND RESOURCEFUL

Since the ability to reward positive performance may be severely restricted, because there will be fewer managerial positions available and the work force itself may be static, future managers will have to become creative in their approach in motivating employees to achieve and to grow.

THE NEED TO BE LESS AUTHORITARIAN

Because of greater awareness and increased levels of maturity on the part of employees, the old-style authoritarian boss will no longer be the model of management. Tomorrow's workers will either rebel against such treatment or will quit their jobs in response. Instead, greater emphasis on acting responsibly will enhance communication skills, goal-setting, and the ability to lead without force for the manager of the future.

> "Credibility will outweigh command as a way of securing cooperation from subordinates. This style of exercising power <u>with</u>, rather than <u>over</u>, people is not a <u>new</u> technique or an adjustment to the individual of the present day. Rather it is a managerial philosophy that respects the capacity of others to contribute to the enterprise and actively solicits their ideas."[23]

THE NEED TO BE MORE SYNERGISTIC

Managers of the future will no longer be able to be isolated in their approach to problems and goal-setting. By necessity, other departments and sub-contractors will have to be consulted and greater emphasis on team work will have to be established if even large organizations are to survive. This will particularly affect labor negotiations between management and labor unions. In many cases, all areas of the organization will need to act synergistically, or the resulting disintegration may be death to the structure itself.

THE NEED TO BE MORE OPEN TO INVOLVEMENT

In order to be ultimately successful, managers of the future will need to create greater opportunities for involvement on the part of all members of the organizational community. Involvement, one of the key factors at the Responsible Level, may by necessity, become an integral part of future management. Management consultants of Rohrer, Hibler and Replogle, Inc., suggest four steps to follow to promote such involvement:

> "The individual of the future may want to be involved in the policy and procedural decisions that affect him.

> Managements may react to these developments with fear, scorn, passivity, or puzzlement. But again, there are several positive steps that can be taken: First, selection must be improved so only those capable of participating in the process of managing will do so; second, the training and education programs of the organization must be modified so that, instead of concentrating as usual on skills training and management practices, they will emphasize philosophy and principles, thus concentrating on the reasons why than on merely how; third, the criteria for promotion must more explicitly define the qualities of performance inherent in being an effective participant in managing; fourth, management must be flexible, for adjusting to the need or demand of employees to influence policies, procedures, and plans requires the need of flexibility that expresses a stronger value system and a deeper commitment than does a more narrow-minded and absolutist position."[24]

The Challenge, the Alternatives, the Choice

As the theme of this book emphasizes, change can only come from within the individual and within the work unit. It cannot be created from an external technique to "fix" individuals nor can it be borrowed from another culture. It must be decidedly American in nature, and thus based upon individualism as a construct, if it is to produce permanent effects.

Courses, books, instructors, management trainers and consultants can only provide an awareness and emphasize the need. As Buddha stated, "It is **you** who must make the effort. The masters only point the way."[25] As executives and human development specialists, we have to trust that individuals themselves, given the information and insight into their own growth process, will be able to actualize their own potential. As Brouwer states, ". . . the most one can do is to help the manager understand himself in his own situation, and then trust him to find the best direction himself."[26] Changes that are self-directed and chosen are more likely to be lasting and productive.

As Americans, we will need to rekindle that spark of independence, drive and commitment to excellence that made this country what it is. The challenge to increase our wisdom is **now**. We can become the experiment in independence that only worked for a short period, or we can become the nation that will provide a blueprint for human dignity for all nations. Our problems are many—our opportunities unsurpassed.

> American management is the door through which that growth can take place. Responsibility is the key. We are the ones on the threshold. The choice is ours. . .

Footnotes

Chapter One

[1]Abraham H. Maslow, <u>The Farther Reaches of Human Nature</u>. (New York, 1976), pp. 57, 96.

[2]John W. Gardner, <u>No Easy Victories</u> (New York, 1968), p. 232.

[3]Soren Kierkegaard, <u>Either-Or</u>, trans. W. Lowrie (Princeton, 1968), Vol. 2, p. 13.

[4]Maslow, p. 13.

[5]Paul J. Brouwer, "The Power to See Ourselves," <u>Harvard Business Review</u>, XLII, No. 6, (November/December, 1964), 158-159.

[6]Nathaniel Branden, <u>Breaking Free</u> (New York, 1972), p. vi.

[7]Jane Loevinger and Ruth Wessler, <u>Measuring Ego Development</u> (San Francisco, 1970). William Gladstone, <u>Test Your Own Mental Health</u> (New York, 1978). Abraham H. Maslow, <u>The Farther Reaches of Human Nature</u> (New York, 1971). Harry Stack Sullivan, <u>The Interpersonal Theory of Psychiatry</u>, (New York, 1953). Gordon W. Allport, <u>Patterns and Growth in Personality</u>, (New York, 1961).

[8]Douglas McGregor, <u>The Human Side of Enterprise</u>, (New York, 1960).

[9]Robert R. Blake and Jane S. Mouton, <u>The New Managerial Grid</u>, (Houston, 1978).

[10]Carl G. Jung, <u>Psychological Reflections: A New Anthology</u> (Princeton, 1970), p. 182.

Chapter Two

[1]Georges Gurdjieff as quoted in P.D. Ouspensky, <u>In Search of the Miraculous</u> (New York, 1949), p. 52.

[2]R.D. Laing, <u>The Politics of Experience</u> (New York, 1967), p. 168.

[3]Nathaniel Branden, <u>The Psychology of Self-Esteem</u> (Los Angeles, 1980), p. 947.

[4]Buddha, <u>The Dhammapada</u>, edited by Thomas Byrom (New York, 1976), p. 11.

[5]William James, "The Energies of Men," <u>Essays on Faith and Morals</u> (Cleveland, 1962), p. 43.

[6]Edward Albee, <u>Behind the Scenes</u>, edited by Joseph F. McCrendle (New York, 1961), p. 204.

[7]Henry Miller, <u>The Air-Conditioned Nightmare</u> (New York, 1945), p. 145

[8]Anne Morrow Lindbergh, <u>The Steep Ascent</u> (New York, 1944), p. 103.

[9]Carl Nightingale, "on Winning," tape recording by Nightingale-Conant Corporation, Chicago: 1981.

[10]Henry James, <u>The Ambassador</u> (New York, 1903), p. 211.

[11]Stephen MacKenna, <u>Journal and Letters of Stephen MacKenna</u> (New York, 1922), P. 169.

[12]Branden, pp. 46-47.

[13]Gladstone, p. 65.

[14]<u>Ibid.</u>, p. 68.

[15]Thomas A. Harris, <u>I'm OK - You're OK</u> (New York, 1973).

Chapter Three

[1]Harris, p. 82.

[2]Kenneth Keyes, <u>Handbook to Higher Consciousness</u> (Berkeley, 1975), p. 16.

[3]Harry Browne, <u>How I Found Freedom in an Unfree World</u> (New York, 1973), p. 112.

[4]Alexander Pope, <u>The Great Quotations</u>, compiled by George Seldes, (New York, 1971), p. 947.

[5]Henry Ford, quoted in <u>Ibid</u>, p. 781.

[6]Branden, <u>Psychology</u>, p. 53.

[7]Alfred North Whitehead, <u>Dialogues of Alfred North Whitehead</u> as recorded by Lucien Price, (Boston, 1954), p. 123.

[8]Alan W. Watts, <u>Psychotherapy East and West</u>, (New York, 1961),p. 88.

[9]Rainer Maria Rilke, <u>Letters to a Young Poet</u>, (Paris, 1911), p. 115.

[10]Antoine de Saint-Exupery, "Airman's Odyssey," <u>The Crown Treasury</u>, ed. Edward F. Murphy, (New York, 1978), p. 408.

[11]Eric Gill, quoted in <u>Modern Christian Revolutionaries</u> by Donald Attwater, (New York, 1947), p. 178.

[12]Kahil Gibran, <u>Sand and Foam</u>, (New York, 1926), p. 12.

[13]George Groddeck, quoted in <u>The Unquiet Grows</u> by Cyril Connally, (New York, 1958), p. 203.

[14]Antonin G. Sertillanges, quoted in <u>The Great Quotations</u>, p. 592.

[15]Gladstone, p. 5.

[16]Ralph Waldo Emerson, <u>Journals of Ralph Waldo Emerson</u>, (Cambridge, Mass, 1960), p. 153.

[17]Whitehead, p. 213.

[18]Gladstone, p. 55.

[19]Branden, <u>Psychology</u>, p. 112.

[20]Gladstone, p. 16.

[21]Bulgarian Proverb, <u>The Crown Treasury</u>, p. 250.

[22]Helen Merrill Lynd, <u>On Shame and the Search of Identity</u>, (New York, 1958), p. 201.

[23]Gladstone, p. 5

[24]Laing, <u>Politics</u>, p. 204.

[25]Maslow, p. 155.

[26]Branden, Psychology, p. 49.

Chapter Four

[1]Branden, Psychology, p. 157.

[2]Maslow, p. 125.

[3]David Grayson, Adventures in Friendship (Los Angeles, 1910), p. 118.

[4]Jung, Psychological Reflections, p. 160.

[5]Carl Rogers, On Becoming a Person (Boston, 1961), p. 235.

[6]Branden, Psychology, p. 157.

[7]Ibid., p. 158.

[8]Maslow, p. 81.

[9]Gladstone, p. 40.

[10]Loevinger and Wessler, Vol. 1, p. 18.

[11]Maslow, pp. 80-81.

[12]Branden, Psychology, p. 38.

[13]Carlos Castaneda, Tales of Power (New York, 1974).

[14]George Bernard Shaw, quoted in The Intelligent Women's Guide to Socialism and Capitalism (New York, 1928), p. 241.

[15]Gardner, 122.

[16]Branden, Psychology, p. 186.

[17]Maslow, p. 83.

[18]Gladstone, p. 47.

[19]Ibid., 42.

[20]Loevinger and Wessler, Vol. 1 p. 67.

[21]Gladstone, p. 43.

[22]William James, Varieties of Religions (New York, 1963), p. 56.

[23]John Dewey, Human Nature and Conduct (New York, The Modern Library, 1922).

[24]Mark Rutherford, quoted in The Great Quotations, p. 716.

[25]Woodrow Wilson, Woodrow Wilson Selections for Today, ed. Arthur Bernon Tourtellot (New York, 1944), p. 38.

[26]Gladstone, pp. 44-45.

[27]W. Robertson Davies, Marchbanks Almanac (Montreal, 1968), p. 109.

[28]Gladstone, p. 46.

[29]Maslow, p. 267.

[30]Stephen Karpmann, "Fairy Tales and Script Drama Analysis," T.A. Bulletin, 7:26 (April, 1968), 39-43.

[31]Buddha, p. 26.

[32]Branden, Psychology, p. 68.

[33]Erich Fromm, Man For Himself (New York, 1947), p. 206.

[34]Branden, Psychology, p. 186.

[35]Eric Berne, Games People Play (New York, 1971).

[36]Maslow, p. 82.

[37]Branden, Psychology, p. 157.

[38]Gladstone, P. 50.

[39]Abraham H. Maslow, Religions, Values, and Peak-Experiences (New York, 1980), xii.

Chapter Five

[1]Eric Hoffer, The Great Quotations, compiled by George Seldes, (New York, 1971), p. 341.

[2]Meyer Friedman and Ray H. Rosenman, Type A Behavior and Your Heart (New York, 1974), p. 204.

[3]Buddha, p. 8.

[4]Friedman and Rosenman, p. 163.

[5]Ibid., p. 168.

[6]Ibid., p. 67.

[7]Fromm, Man For Himself, p. 227.

[8]Friedman and Rosenman, p. 4.

[9]Francois de Fenelon, quoted in The Great Quotations, 731.

[10]Gladstone, p. 34.

[11]Friedman and Rosenman, p. 72.

[12]Grayson, p. 70.

[13]Ralph Greison and Myron Branton, The American Male (New York, 1966), p. 246.

[14]Gladstone, p. 35.

[15]George A. Morgan, Prophetic Voices, ed. Ned O'Gorman (New York, 1969), p. 203.

[16]Friedman and Rosenman, pp. 221-222.

[17]Ibid., p. 79.

[18]John Oliver Hobbes, The Crown Treasury, compiled by Edward F. Murphy (New York, 1978), p. 118.

[19]Bhagwan Shree Rajneesh, When The Shoe Fits (Poona, India, 1976), p. 47.

[20]Smiley Blanton, Love Or Perish (New York, 1956), p. 113.

[21]Loe Tolstoy, quoted in The Great Quotations, p. 592.

[22]Friedman and Rosenman, p. 70.

[23]Ibid., p. 62.

[24]Ibid., p. 188.

[25]Katharine Butler Hathaway The Journals and Letters of the Little Locksmith (New York, 1946), p. 186.

[26]Gladstone, p. 38.

[27]Loevinger and Wessler, p. 18.

[28]Friedman and Rosenman, p. 197.

Chapter Six

[1]R.C. Benson, From a College Window (New York, 1934), p. 16.

[2]Winston Churchill, quoted in The Great Quotations, p. 955.

[3]Henry Miller, quoted in The Crown Treasury, p. 601.

[4]Maslow, Farther Reaches, p. 13.

[5]Ibid., p. 188.

[6]Jakob Wasserman, The Book of Marriage, ed. Count Hermann Keyserling (New York, 1932), p. 18.

[7]Sir Richard Livingston, quoted in The Great Quotations.

[8]A.J. Huxley, Evolution in Action (New York, 1953), pp. 162-163.

[9]Chinese proverb quoted in The Crown Treasury, p. 40.

[10]Denis Waitley, "The Psychology of Winning," tape series by Nightingale-Conant Corporation (Chicago, 1981).

[11]Maslow, Farther Reaches, pp. 64-65.

[12]Oscar Wilde, De Profundis (New York, 1964), p. 123.

[13]Bonaro Overstreet, Understanding Fear in Ourselves and Others (New York, 1951), p. 58.

[14]Rollo May, Man's Search For Himself (New York, 1953), p. 218.

[15]Maslow, Farther Reaches, p. 17.

[16]Ibid.

[17]Brouwser, p. 158.

[18]Jung, p. 116.

[19]Maslow, Farther Reaches, p. 83.

[20]Ibid., p. 87.

[21]Waitley, op cit.

[22]Henry David Thoreau, Journal (New York, 1962), p. 18.

[23]Branden, Psychology, p. 118.

[24]Maslow, Farther Reaches, p. 9.

[25]Friedman and Rosenman, pp. 71-72.

[26]George Bernard Shaw, "Androcles and the Lion," Selected Plays (Binghamton, N.Y. 1898), p. 53.

[27]W.H. Auden, A Certain World (St. Paul, Minnesota, 1970), p. 26.

[28]Rogers, p. 260.

[29]Castaneda, p. 29.

[30]John Jay Chapman, Memories and Milestones (New York, 1915), p. 23.

[31]Maslow, Farther Reaches, p. 44.

[32]Thaddeus Golas, The Lazy Man's Guide to Enlightenment (New York, 1972), p. 16.

[33]D.H. Lawrence, Selected Essays (New York, 1974), p. 119.

[34]Albert Einstein, Ideas and Opinions (New York, 1974), p. 191.

[35]Maslow, Farther Reaches, p. 59.

[36]Hathaway, p. 203.

[37]Rainer Maria Rilke, The Journal of My Other Self, trans. by John Linton (New York, 1930), p. 142.

[38]Emerson, p. 82.

[39]Golas, p. 153.

[40]Mark Twain, Mark Twain at Your Finger Tips, ed. Caroline T. Harnsberg (New York, 1967), p. 42.

[41]Hugh Prather, Notes To Myself (Moab, Utah, 1970).

[42]Fromm, p. 112.

[43]Maslow, Farther Reaches, p. 191.

[44]Rainer Maria Rilke, Letters of Rainer Maria Rilke: 1892-1910 (London, 1947), p. 64.

[45]Twain, p. 57.

[46]Gladstone, p. 18.

[47]Ford, p. 282.

[48]Pope, P. 580.

[49]Kemmons Wilson, quoted in The Great Quotations, p. 508.

[50]Henry Haskins, Meditations in Wall Street (New York, 1972), p. 111.

[51]Albert E. Gray, "The Common Denominator of Success," noted on a tape by Earl Nightingale, op cit.

[52]Kingman Brewster, Jr., quoted in The Great Quotations, p. 486.

[53]Nightingale, op cit.

[54]Branden, Psychology, p. 107.

[55]Waitley, op cit.

[56]Branden, Psychology, p. 131.

[57]Henry Ward Beecher, Eyes and Ears.

[58]Kathleen Norris, Hands Full of Living (Mattituah, N.Y. 1931), p. 108.

[59]George Bernard Shaw, Man and Superman (New York, 1903), p. 73

[60]Blanton, p. 171.

[61]Bertrand Russell, The Conquest of Happiness (New York, 1930), p. 113.

[62]Branden, Psychology, p. 131.

[63]German proverb quoted in The Crown Treasury, p. 209.

[64]Oliver Wendell Holmes, The Mind and Faith of Justice Holmes, ed. Max Lerner (Boston, 1947), p. 63.

[65]Haskins, p. 46.

[66]Albert Schweitzer, Out of My Life and Thought (New York, 1949), p. 6.

[67]Sigmund Freud, Civilization and Its Discontents (London, 1930), p. 201.

[68]Jung, p. 131.

[69]May, p. 126.

[70]Harry Stack Sullivan, Conceptions of Modern Psychiatry (New York, 1953), p. 72.

[71]Laing, p. 203.

[72]Maslow, Farther Reaches, p. 176.

[73]Buddha, p. 23.

[74]Waitley, op cit.

[75]Wilde, p. 72.

[76]Gibran, p. 18.

[77]Maslow, Farther Reaches, p. 35.

[78]Sigmund Freud, quoted in Life Against Death by Norman O. Brown (New York, 1949), p. 157.

[79]Maslow, Farther Reaches, p. 116.

[80]Waitley, op cit.

[81]Wayne Dyer, Your Erroneous Zones (New York, 1976), pp. 19-20.

[82]Gladstone, p. 31.

[83]Sarah Bernhardt, quoted in The Crown Treasury, p. 10.

[84]E.F. Benson, The Author's Kalendar 1915, completed by Anna C. Woodford (New York, 1915).

[85]James, p. 117.

[86]Maslow, Religions, p. x-xi.

[87]Branden, Psychology, p. 162.

[88]Overstreet, p. 83.

[89]Nicholaus Birdyar, quoted in Best Quotations, p. 206.

[90]Maslow, Farther Reaches, p. 184.

[91]Maslow, Religions, p. xii.

[92]Don Marquis, quoted in The Great Quotations, p. 193.

[93]Albert Camus, Resistence, Rebellion, and Death, trans. by J. O'Brian, (New York, 1960), p. 114.

[94]Ordway Tead, The Art of Leadership (New York, 1967), p. 145.

[95]Anais Nin, The Diaries of Anais Nin, Vol II (New York, 1966), p. 18.

[96]Bob Toben, Space, Time and Beyond (New York, 1975), p. 108.

[97]Waitley, op cit.

Chapter Seven

[1]Peter F. Drucker, "People Are Our Greatest Asset," Harvard Business Review 48:12, (January/February, 1978), p. 18.

[2]Booker T. Washington, Up From Slavery (Boston, 1901), p. 8.

[3]Dale McConkey, No-Nonsense Delegation (New York, 1974).

[4]"Completed Staff Action," Guide to Administrative Action (Washington, D.C., 1954), U.S. Air Force.

Chapter Eight

[1]Seneca (the Younger) quoted in The Great Quotations, p. 382.

[2]Rogers, p. 147.

[3]Webster's New World Dictionary of the American Language (New York, 1978), p. 214.

[4]David Campbell, If You Don't Know Where You're Going You'll Probably End Up Somewhere Else (New York, 1973).

[5]Rajneesh, p. 116.

Chapter Nine

[1]Marcus Aurelius quoted in The World's Best Thoughts on Life and Living, compiled by Eugene Raudsepp, (Los Angeles, 1981), p. 47.

[2]Lila Sewell, Ibid., p. 37, 48, 78.

[3]Thomas Mann, forward, Joseph and His Brothers, (New York, 1952), p. ix.

[4]Fromm, p. 73.

[5]Rogers, p. 183.

[6]Desire Joseph Cardinal Mercier quoted in The Life of Cardinal Mercier by John A. Gade (New York, 1934), p. 130.

[7]Virginia Wolfe, quoted in The Great Quotations, p. 532.

[9]Pearl Buck, To My Daughter With Love (New York, 1967), p. 5.

[9]John Dewey, Reconstruction in Philosophy (New York, 1963), p. 103.

[10]Brouwer, p. 158.

[11]Christopher Argyris, Personality and Organization (New York, 1957), p. 99.

[12]Kenneth Thomas, "Conflict and Conflict Management," The Handbook of Industrial and Organization Psychology, Vol. II, ed. Marvin Dunnette (Chicago, 1975).

[13]Argyris, p. 103.

[14]Paul Hersey and Kenneth H. Blanchard, Management of Organizational Behavior: Utilizing Human Resources (Englewood Cliffs, N.J., 1977).

[15]Johann Wolfgang Von Goethe, Wisdom and Experience (New York, 1933), p. 94.

[16]John Newman, Release Your Brakes (New York, 1976).

[17]Haskins, p. 82.

[18]Lillian Smith, The Journey.

[19]Maslow, Farther Reaches, p. 203.

[20]Shakespeare, Measure For Measure I.V. 214-217.

[21]John F. Kennedy, Message to Americans for Democratic Action, May 12, 1961.

[22]William Feather, quoted in The Great Quotations, p. 81.

[23]Joshiah Royce, William James and Other Essays on the Philosophy of Life (New York, 1911), p. 78.

[24]Friedman and Roseman, p. 206.

[25]Castaneda, p. 116.

[26]Arnold Bennett, quoted in The Great Quotations.

[27]Dewey, p. 81.

Chapter Ten

[1]Wyndam Lewis, America and Cosmic Man, (Port Washington, New York, 1969), p. 132.

[2]Richard Tanner Pascale and Anthony G. Athos, The Art of Japanese Management, (New York, 1981), p. 33

[3]Jerome Roscow, as quoted in People, Productivity and Profits, by Joel E. Ross, (Reston, Virginia, 1981), p. 101.

[4]Dewey, p. 127.

[5]The Staff of Rohrer, Hibler and Replogle, Inc., The Managerial Challenge: A Psychological Approach to the Changing World of Management, (New York, 1981), p. 67.

[6]Pascale and Athos, p. 29.

[7]Ibid., p. 34.

[8]Maslow, Farther Reaches, p. 91

[9]Jung, p. 101.

[10]Argyris, p. 95

[11]Browne, p. 257

[12]McGregor, p. 216.

[13]Daniel Yankelovich, "Work, Value, and the New Breed," an unpublished paper presented by Yankelovich, Skelly, and White, Inc., at Quality of Work Life Conference, (New York, 1980), p. 9.

[14]Ibid., p. 10.

[15]Maslow, Farther Reaches, p. 151.

[16]Yankelovich, p. 14.

[17]Ibid., p. 10.

[18]Barett Wendell, Barett Wendell and His Letters edited by M.A. DeWolfe Howe, (New York, 1942), p. 210.

[19]Einstein, p. 167.

[20]Pascale, p. 180.

[21]Rohrer, Hibler, and Replogle, p. 3.

[22]Ibid., p. 68.

[23]Ibid.

[24]Ibid., p. 51.

[25]Buddha, p. 14.

[26]Brouwer, p. 64.

Recommended Reading

Allport, Gordon W. Patterns and Growth in Personality. New York: Henry Holt & Co., 1961.

Argyris, Christopher. Personality and Organization. New York: Harper & Row, 1957.

_____. Intervention Theory and Method: A Behavioral Science View. Reading, Mass.: Addison - Wesley, 1970.

_____. Interpersonal Competence and Organizational Effectiveness. Homewood, Ill.: Irwin, 1962.

Augsburg, David. Caring Enough to Confront. New York: Regal Press, 1980.

Batten, J.D. Tough-Minded Management. New York: American Management Association, 1963.

Beier, Ernst G. and Evan G. Valens. People-Reading—How We Control Us and How We Control Them. New York: Stein and Day, 1975.

Berne, Eric. Games People Play. New York: Grove Press, 1964.

_____. Sex In Human Loving. New York: Simon and Schuster, 1971.

_____. The Structure and Dynamics of Organizations and Groups. Philadelphia: Lippincott, 1963.

_____. What Do You Say After You Say Hello? New York: Grove Press, 1972.

Blake, Robert R. and Jane S. Mouton, Managerial Grid. Houston: Gulf Publishing Co., 1964.

Branden, Nathaniel. Breaking Free. Los Angeles: Nash Publishing, 1970.

_____. The Disowned Self. Los Angeles: Nash Publishing, 1971.

_____. A Nathaniel Branden Anthology. Los Angeles: J.P. Tarcher, 1980.

_____. The Psychology of Romantic Love. Los Angeles: J.P. Tarcher, 1980.

_____. The Psychology of Self-Esteem. Los Angeles: Nash Publishing.

Bristol, Claude M. The Magic of Believing. New York: Prentice Hall, 1948.

Brouwer, Paul J. "The Power to See Ourselves." Harvard Business Review 42:6 (November - December, 1964): 158-164.

Browne, Harry. How I Found Freedom In An Unfree World. New York: Avon, 1973.

Buber, Martin. I and Thou. New York: Scriber, 1958.

Buddha. The Dhammapada, ed., Thomas Byrom. New York, Vintage Books, 1976.

Bucke, Richard M. Cosmic Consciousness. New York: Dutton, 1923.

Campbell, David. If You Don't Know Where You're Going You'll Probably End Up Somewhere Else. New York: Argus, 1973.

Castaneda, Carlos. Journey to Ixtlan. New York: Simon and Schuster, 1971.

_____. A Separate Reality. New York: Simon and Schuster, 1971.

_____. Tales Of Power. New York: Simon and Schuster, 1974.

_____. The Teachings of Don Juan. New York: Simon and Schuster, 1968.

Dass, Ram. Be Here Now. Albuquerque, N.M.: Lama Foundation, 1975.

_____. The Only Dance There Is. Garden City, N.J.: Anchor Press, 1973.

Drucker, Peter. Management: Tasks, Practices, Responsibilities. New York: Harper & Row, 1974.

Durst, G. Michael. Napkin Notes: On The Art of Living. Chicago: Center for the Art of Living, 1982.

Dyer, Wayne. Pulling Your Own Strings. New York: T.Y. Crowell Co., 1978.

_____. The Sky's the Limit. New York: Simon and Schuster, 1980.

_____. Your Erroneous Zones. New York: Funk and Wagnalls, 1976.

Erickson, Erik H. Identity and the Life Cycle. New York: International Universities Press, 1959.

_____. Insight and Responsibility. New York: Norton, 1964.

Feinberg, M. Effective Psychology for Managers. Englewood Cliffs, N.J.: Prentice Hall, 1965.

_____. et.al. The New Psychology for Managing People. Englewood Cliffs, N.J.: Prentice Hall, 1975.

Frank, Federick. The Book of Angelus Silesius. New York: Random, 1976.

Frankl, Victor E. Man's Search For Meaning. Boston: Beacon Press, 1962.

Frederick, Carl. est: Playing the Game the New Way. New York: Dell, 1976.

Freud, Sigmund. Beyond the Pleasure Principle. London: International Psychoanalytical Press, 1922.

Freudenberger, Herbert J. Burn Out: The High Cost of High Achievement. New York: Anchor Press, 1980.

Fromm, Erich. The Art of Loving. New York: Harper, 1956.

_____. Escape From Freedom. New York: Avon, 1971.

_____. Man For Himself. New York: Fawcett, 1947.

_____. The Sane Society. New York: Rinehart, 1955.

Gardner, John. Excellence: Can We Be Excellent and Equal, Too? New York: Wiley, 1961.

Gibran, Kahil. The Prophet. New York: Knopf, 1924.

_____. Sand and Foam. New York: Knopf, 1926.

Gladstone, William. Test Your Own Mental Health. New York: Arco, 1978.

Golas, Thaddeus. The Lazy Man's Guide to Enlightenment. New York: Bantam, 1972.

Greenwald, Jerry. Be The Person You Were Meant To Be. New York: Simon and Schuster, 1973.

Gurdjieff, Georges I. All And Everything. New York: Dutton, 1964.

_____. Meeting With Remarkable Men, New York: Dutton, 1969.

Harris, Thomas. I'm OK - You're OK. New York: Avon, 1973.

Heaton, D. Explorations In Maturity. New York: Appleton - Century - Crofts, 1965.

Heaton, Herbert. Productivity in Service Organizations: Organizing for People. New York: McGraw - Hill, 1977.

Hesse, Herman. Journey to the East. New York: Noonday Press, 1956.

_____. Siddhartha. New York: Holt Rhinehart, 1951.

_____. Steppenwolf. New York: Holt Rhinehart, 1970.

Hersey, Paul and Kenneth H. Blanchard. Management of Organizational Behavior: Utilizing Human Resources. Englewood Cliffs, N.J.: Prentice Hall, 1977.

Herzberg, Fredrick. Motivation To Work. New York: Wiley, 1959.

_____. Work and the Nature of Man. New York: Wiley 1966.

Huxley. Aldous. Island. New York: Holt Rhinehart, 1962.

Huxley. Laura. This Timeless Moment. New York: Holt Rhinehart, 1975.

James, Muriel and Dorothy Jongeward. Born to Win. Reading, Mass.: Addison - Wesley, 1971.

James, Muriel. The OK Boss. Reading, Mass.: Addison - Wesley, 1975.

James, William. The Varieties of Religious Experiences. New Hyde Park, N.Y.: University Books, 1963.

Janov, Arthur. The Primal Scream. New York: Putnam, 1970.

Johnson, David W. Reaching Out: Interpersonal Effectiveness and Self-Actualization. Englewood Cliffs, N.J.: Prentice Hall, 1972.

Jourard, Sidney M. Disclosing Man to Himself. Princeton, N.J.: Van Nostrand, 1968.

_____. The Transparent Self. New York: Van Nostrand Reinhold, 1971.

Jung, Carl G. Psychological Reflections: A New Anthology. Princeton, N.J.: Van Nostram, 1970.

_____. Contributions to Analytic Psychology. New York: Harcourt - Brace, 1928.

Kagen, J. and H.A. Moss. Birth to Maturity. New York: Wiley, 1962.

Karpmann, Stephen. "Fairy Tales and Script Drama Analysis," T.A. Bulletin. 7:26 (April, 1968) 39-43.

Keen, Sam. To a Dancing God. New York: Harper and Row, 1970.

Keyes, Ken. Handbook to Higher Consciousness. Berkeley, Cal.: Living Love Publishing, 1975.

_____. Taming Your Mind. Berkeley, Cal.: Living Love Publishing, 1975.

Keyes, Ken and Bruce Burkan. How to Make Your Life Work. Berkeley, Cal.: Living Love Publishing, 1974.

Krishnamurti, J. Commentaries on Living. New York: Harper and Row, 1967.

_____. Education and the Significance of Life. New York: Harper and Row, 1981.

_____. You Are the World. New York: Harper & Row, 1972.

Kubler-Ross, Elizabeth. On Death and Dying. New York: MacMillan, 1969.

Laing, R.D. The Divided Self. New York: Pantheon, 1969.

_____. Facts of Life. New York: Pantheon, 1967.

_____. Knots. New York: Random, 1972.

_____. The Politics of Experience. New York: Pantheon, 1982

_____. Testimony of Experience. New York: Pantheon, 1982.

Lakein, Alan. How to Get Control of Your Time and Your Life. New York: New American Library, 1974.

Lair, Jess. I Ain't Much Baby, But I'm All I've Got. New York: Fawcett - Crest, 1976.

Lao Tzu. Tao Te Ching: Way of Life, trans. F. Blackney, New York: Knopf, 1955.

Leonard, George. The Ultimate Athlete. New York: Viking Press, 1975.

Likert, Rensis. New Patterns in Management. New York: McGraw - Hill, 1961.

_____. The Human Organization. New York: McGraw - Hill, 1967.

Lilly, John C. The Center of the Cyclone. New York: McGraw - Hill, 1967.

_____. Simulations of God: The Science of Belief. New York: Simon and Schuster, 1975.

Loevinger, Jane and Ruth Wessler. Measuring Ego Development, 2 Vol. San Francisco: Jossey -- Bass, Inc., 1970.

Luft, Joseph. Of Human Interaction. New York: National Press Books, 1969.

MacKenzie, Alec R. The Time Trap. New York: Amacom, 1975.

MacKenzie, Alec R. and Ted W. Engstrom. Managing Your Time. New York: Zonderwan Publishing House, 1968.

McCormick, Paul and Leonard Campos. Introduce Yourself to Transactional Analysis. Berkeley Cal.: International T.A. Association, 1969.

McGregor, Douglas. Human Side of Enterprise. New York: McGraw - Hill, 1960.

_____. The Professional Manager. New York: McGraw - Hill, 1967.

Maltz, Maxwell. Creative Living For Today. New York: Pocket Books, 1972.

_____. Psycho-Cybernetics. New York: Pocket Books, 1969.

Marrow, A.J. Behind the Executive Mask. New York: American Management Association, 1972.

_____. Failure of Success: The Middle Class Crisis. New York: Milner, 1968.

_____. et.al. Management by Participation. New York: Harper & Row, 1967.

Maslow, Abraham H. The Farther Reaches of Human Nature. New York: Harper, 1976.

_____. Motivation and Personality. New York: Harper & Brothers, 1970.

_____. New Knowledge in Human Values. New York: Harper & Row, 1959.

_____. Religions, Values, and Peak Experiences. New York: Penquin Books, 1980.

May, Rollo. The Courage to Create. New York: Bantam, 1976.

_____. Love and Will. New York: Norton, 1969.

_____. Man's Search For Himself. New York: Norton, 1953

Mishlove, Jeffery. The Roots of Consciousness. New York: Random House, 1975.

Myers, Scott M. Every Employee a Manager. New York: McGraw - Hill, 1970.

Nierenberg, Gerald and Henry H. Calero. Meta-Talk. New York: Pocket Books, 1978.

Odiorne, George. Management By Objectives. New York: Pittman Publishing, 1967.

Olson, Ken, The Art of Hanging Loose in an Uptight World. New York: Fawcett - Crest, 1978.

Oncken, William Jr. and Donald L. Wass. "Management Time: Who's Got the Monkey?", Harvard Business Review. (November - December, 1974): 75:80.

Ornstein, Robert. The Nature of Human Consciousness. New York: Freeman, 1973.

Ouchi, William. Theory Z: How American Business Can Meet the Japanese Challenge. Reading Mass.: Addison - Wesley, 1981.

Ouspensky, P.D. The Fourth Way. New York: Random House, 1971.

_____. A New Model of the Universe. New York: Harcourt Brace, 1934.

_____. The Psychology of Man's Possible Evolution. New York: Harcourt - Brace, 1965.

_____. In Search of the Miraculous. New York: Harcourt - Brace, 1965.

Overstreet, Bonaro. Understanding Fear in Ourselves and Others. New York: Harper, 1951.

Pascale, Richard Tanner and Anthony G. Athos. The Art of Japanese Management. New York: Warner, 1981.

Pearce, Joseph C. The Crack in the Cosmic Egg. New York: Pocket Books, Inc., 1974.

Perls, Frederick S. Gestalt Therapy Verbatim. New York: Bantam, 1969.

_____. In and Out of the Garbage Pail. New York: Bantam, 1972.

Porat, Frieda and Karen Meyers. Changing Your Life Style. New York: Bantam, 1973.

Prather, Hugh. I Touch the Earth, The Earth Touches Me. Moab, Utah: Real People Press, 1972.

_____. Notes to Myself. Moab, Utah: Real People Press, 1970.

Rajneesh, Bhagwan Shree. When the Shoe Fits. Poona, India: Rajneesh Foundation, 1976.

Rogers, Carl. On Becoming a Person. Boston: Houghton - Mifflin, 1961.

Rogers, Carl and Barry Stevens. Person to Person: The Problem of Being Human. Moab, Utah: Real People Press, 1967.

Seabury, David. The Art of Selfishness. New York: Cornerstone Library, 1979.

Shostrom, Everett. Man, the Manipulator: The Inner Journey From Manipulation to Actualization. New York: Bantam, 1968.

Sloma, Richard S. No-Nonsense Management. New York: MacMillan, 1977.

Smith, Adam. Powers of the Mind. New York: Random, 1975.

Smith, Manuel J. When I Say No, I Feel Guilty. New York: Dial Press, 1975.

Steiner, Claude. Scripts People Live. New York: Bantam, 1975.

Sullivan, Harry Stack. The Interpersonal Theory of Psychiatry. New York: Norton, 1953.

Tannenbaum, R. Leadership and Organization. New York: McGraw - Hill, 1961

Toben, Bob. Space, Time and Beyond. New York: Dutton, 1975.

Toffler, Alvin. Future Shock. New York: Random House, 1970.

Watts, Alan. The Book: On The Taboo Against Knowing Who You Are. New York: Random House, 1972.

_____. Psychotherapy East and West. New York: Ballantine Books, 1975.

_____. This Is It. New York: Random House, 1972.

Wilde, Oscar. De Profundis. New York: Vintage Books, 1964.

Wylie, Ruth C. The Self Concept. Lincoln: University of Nebraska, 1961.

You are Invited to Attend the Management By Responsibility Seminar!

The dynamic MBR seminar, presented by Dr. G. Michael Durst, has been attended by thousands of managers and employees from the Fortune 500 companies and government agencies throughout the country. This three-day seminar is offered in various locations, and is also available for particular "in-company" presentations.

Recognizing that productivity and effectiveness are an outgrowth of employee satisfaction and are in direct proportion to the responsibility assumed, MBR teaches responsible leadership and provides a management style that is both accountable and effective.

Here's what individuals from progressive organizations had to say about attending the Management By Responsibility seminar:

Blue Cross/Blue Shield: "I did not get what I had expected from MBR. . .I got much, much more! Most 'management' courses stress the mechanics of management. . .This is the first, (and possibly only), course that helps us deal with ourselves. I didn't realize how important that is. I do now. I was fascinated and enlightened during the course. . .and it's still working! Very few days go by that I haven't recalled something from the course. My boss, my wife, and my co-workers thank you."

Mountain Bell: "Best training course I have ever attended, and in the past 35 years of my professional experience, there have been plenty."

Time, Inc.: "The experience I had at the MBR seminar has had so many profound effects on my life, that it is a constant source of amazement to me. Thank you for providing so many insights. Keep spreading the word. The world needs this wisdom."

Federal Reserve Bank of Chicago: "This course makes sense out of MBO. I highly recommend it for all managers at all levels. There is simply not enough to say about this course. . .You have to experience to fully appreciate the benefits."

U.S. Air Force: "Without question, the most beneficial three days I have ever spent."

Stouffer International: "Thank you for providing the experience that allows me to unfold myself into a person with potential I didn't dream possible before. . ."

Department of Health, Education and Welfare: "This course picks up where MBO, the Managerial Grid, and other management theory courses leave off. It meets a particularly important need for those on our staff with a wealth of theoretical/professional training and a distinct poverty in the area of a willingness to act positively at work and in solving problems NOW!"

Mead World, Inc.: "I had no idea that anything could influence my outlook as much as MBR."

Call or write Training Systems, Inc., to find out how you and members of your organization can participate in the MBR seminar:

Training Systems, Inc.
P.O. Box 788
Evanston, IL 60204
(312) 864-8664

Now MBR is available in a Video Cassette Format

The unique MBR program is now available in a video instructional format. It is a complete twenty-four hour program built around eleven video tapes.

Based on long experience, Training Systems, Inc., has designed this new MBR video as an interactive involvement process rather than a passive viewer process.

Thus the program combines the best of a "live" presentation with the ease and convenience of a video format.

The video seminar works!

The experiential nature of the MBR program is ideal for video. Just as in the live program, information and experiences are shared among participants to produce new awareness and insight. This comes through with great clarity and impact in the video process.

Also Dr. Durst's charismatic style and unique ability to express complex terms and theories in simple, straightforward language keep viewers riveted to the screen.

Benefits of the video format

- Video makes MBR readily available to more managers.
- Video makes MBR available throughout the organization.
- Video makes individualization easy.
- Video is cost effective.
- Video is flexible and convenient.
- Video allows a built-in review program.

Through the use of licensed facilitators* from your organization and the in-depth Participant Manual, managers can ask questions and do exercises to underscore the learning proces. The video portion is correlated to the Manual, so participants are actively challenged to expand their understanding of MBR. Group exercises further ensure that the MBR program is an active learning process, not just passive TV watching.

*Facilitators are specially-trained instructors from your organization who present the video program, answer questions, and lead discussions and exercises. They thereby ensure that MBR concepts are directly applied to your specific organizational needs.

TrainingSystems,Inc.

P.O. Box 788   Evanston, IL 60204   312.864.8664

Napkin Notes: On the Art of Living

Dr. G. Michael Durst's first book, **Napkin Notes: On the Art of Living** is now in its third printing and is available through Training Systems. Written as a personal application of MBR priniciples, it is both profound in its implications, as well as being interesting.

Although countless "self-help" books have been published, none of them have been able to translate psychological theory into a practical, day-to-day application as well as **Napkin Notes.** By integrating Eastern and Western philosophy with science and religion, it provides a concise, easy-to-read guide for living.

To order **Napkin Notes: On the Art of Living**, send $7.95 plus 50¢ for handling and shipping to:
The Center for The Art of Living
P.O. Box 788
Evanston, IL 60204